Culture and
Customs of
India

Culture and Customs of India

Carol E. Henderson

Culture and Customs of Asia
Hanchao Lu, Series Editor

GREENWOOD PRESS
Westport, Connecticut • London

Library of Congress Cataloging-in-Publication Data

Henderson, Carol E., 1954–
    Culture and customs of India / Carol E. Henderson.
        p.   cm.—(Culture and customs of Asia, ISSN 1097–0738)
    Includes bibliographical references and index.
    ISBN 0–313–30513–7 (alk. paper)
    1. India—Civilization.   2. India—Social life and customs.   I. Title.   II. Series.
    DS423.G33   2002
    954—dc21   2001055607

British Library Cataloguing in Publication Data is available.

Library of Congress Catalog Card Number: 2001055607
ISBN: 0–313–30513–7
ISSN: 1097–0738

First published in 2002

Greenwood Press, 88 Post Road West, Westport, CT 06881
An imprint of Greenwood Publishing Group, Inc.
www.greenwood.com

Printed in the United States of America

The paper used in this book complies with the
Permanent Paper Standard issued by the National
Information Standards Organization (Z39.48–1984).

10 9 8 7 6 5 4 3 2 1

for Morton Klass

Contents

Illustrations

Series Foreword

GEOGRAPHICALLY, Asia encompasses the vast area from Suez, the Bosporus, and the Ural Mountains eastward to the Bering Sea and from this line southward to the Indonesian archipelago, an expanse that covers about 30 percent of our earth. Conventionally, and especially insofar as culture and customs are concerned, Asia refers primarily to the region east of Iran and south of Russia. This area can be divided in turn into subregions commonly known as South, Southeast, and East Asia, which are the main focus of this series.

The United States has vast interests in this region. In the twentieth century the United States fought three major wars in Asia (namely, the Pacific War of 1941–45, the Korean War of 1950–53, and the Vietnam War of 1965–75), and each had profound impact on life and politics in America. Today, America's major trading partners are in Asia, and in the foreseeable future the weight of Asia in American life will inevitably increase, for in Asia lie our great allies as well as our toughest competitors in virtually all arenas of global interest. Domestically, the role of Asian immigrants is more visible than at any other time in our history. In spite of these connections with Asia, however, our knowledge about this crucial region is far from adequate. For various reasons, Asia remains for most of us a relatively unfamiliar, if not stereotypical or even mysterious, "Oriental" land.

There are compelling reasons for Americans to obtain some level of concrete knowledge about Asia. It is one of the world's richest reservoirs of culture and an ever-evolving museum of human heritage. Rhoads Murphey, a prominent Asianist, once pointed out that in the part of Asia east of Afghanistan and south of Russia alone lies half the world, "half of its people and far more than half of its historical experience, for these are the oldest living civilized traditions." Prior to the modern era, with limited interaction and mutual influence between the East and the West, Asian civilizations developed largely independent from the West. In modern times, however, Asia and the West have come not only into close contact but also into frequent conflict: The result has been one of the most solemn and stirring dramas in world history. Today, integration and compromise are the trend in coping with cultural differences. The West—with some notable exceptions—has started to see Asian traditions not as something to fear but as something to be understood, appreciated, and even cherished. After all, Asian traditions are an indispensable part of the human legacy, a matter of global "common wealth" that few of us can afford to ignore.

As a result of Asia's enormous economic development since World War II, we can no longer neglect the study of this vibrant region. Japan's "economic miracle" of postwar development is no longer unique, but in various degrees has been matched by the booming economy of many other Asian countries and regions. The rise of the four "mini dragons" (South Korea, Taiwan, Hong Kong, and Singapore) suggests that there may be a common Asian pattern of development. At the same time, each economy in Asia has followed its own particular trajectory. Clearly, China is the next giant on the scene. Sweeping changes in China in the last two decades have already dramatically altered the world's economic map. Furthermore, growth has also been dramatic in much of Southeast Asia. Today war-devastated Vietnam shows great enthusiasm for joining the "club" of nations engaged in the world economy. And in South Asia, India, the world's largest democracy, is rediscovering its role as a champion of market capitalism. The economic development of Asia presents a challenge to Americans but also provides them with unprecedented opportunities. It is largely against this background that more and more people in the United States, in particular among the younger generation, have started to pursue careers dealing with Asia.

This series is designed to meet the need for knowledge of Asia among students and the general public. Each book is written in an accessible and lively style by an expert (or experts) in the field of Asian studies. Each book focuses on the culture and customs of a country or region. However, readers should be aware that culture is fluid, not always respecting national boundaries. While every nation seeks its own path to success and struggles to maintain its own identity, in the cultural domain mutual influence and integration among Asian nations are ubiquitous.

Each volume starts with an introduction to the land and the people of a nation or region and includes a brief history and an overview of the economy. This is followed by chapters dealing with a variety of topics that piece together a cultural panorama, such as thought, religion, ethics, literature and art, architecture and housing, cuisine, traditional dress, gender, courtship and marriage, festivals and leisure activities, music and dance, and social customs and lifestyle. In this series, we have chosen not to elaborate on elite life, ideology, or detailed questions of political structure and struggle, but instead to explore the world of common people, their sorrow and joy, their pattern of thinking, and their way of life. It is the culture and customs of the majority of the people (rather than just the rich and powerful elite) that we seek to understand. Without such understanding, it will be difficult for all of us to live peacefully and fruitfully with each other in this increasingly interdependent world.

As the world shrinks, modern technologies have made all nations on earth "virtual" neighbors. The expression "global village" not only reveals the nature and the scope of the world in which we live but also, more importantly, highlights the serious need for mutual understanding of all peoples on our planet. If this series serves to help the reader obtain a better understanding of the "half of the world" that is Asia, the authors and I will be well rewarded.

Hanchao Lu
Georgia Institute of Technology

Acknowledgments

INDIA is such a vast nation that one is humbled at the prospect of writing about it. It is only through the kindness of friends and colleagues that I could even begin to undertake this project.

In India, Komal Kothari deserves first place for seeing to it that I always learned something new, whether it was the compositions of Rajasthani folk musicians or postmodern architecture. Kamal Singh and Pami Singh's kindness to me in New Delhi introduced me to diverse aspects of urban life, again, quite far from my studies and no less important because of this. Also of great importance to me, the families of Surani village who with utmost hospitality and grace reached across the barriers of culture and language to invite me to step into their lives. This was in the middle of a devastating drought—then in its third year—not exactly the best time to show off, as everyone would like their best face to the world. I came away profoundly impressed by their courage, strength, and commitment to finding better lives for their children.

In New York, Philip Oldenburg, associate director of the Southern Asian Institute at Columbia University, encouraged me to take on this project. My colleagues in the department of Sociology and Anthropology at Rutgers University, Newark provided a stimulating and supportive environment. David Magier, director of Area Studies for the Columbia University Libraries was a cheerful and knowledgeable presence who steered me in the right direction on more than one occasion. I am very grateful to both the American Institute of Indian Studies and to the U.S. Educational Foundation in India for their support for basic research, as both a junior and as a senior scholar. I am also grateful to Greenwood Press editors Barbara Rader, Jennifer Wood, Wendi Schnaufer, and Emma Bailey.

In particular, I wish to acknowledge Joan Erdman, Edward S. Haynes, Marina and Rafael Pastor, and Gayatri Chakravorty Spivak, who each in his or her own way reminded me that there is always much more—of great interest—out there. Maxine Weisgrau did more than yeoman duty in vetting my ideas on our numerous walks around town and generously sharing books, photos, and India news. Lastly, to my husband Scott Horton who got to share his life with the writing of this book, my deepest thanks for his support.

Guide to Pronunciation

INDIAN languages make many sound distinctions that are unfamiliar to English language speakers. Across India, there are regional differences in the pronunciation of certain consonants and vowels. In this work, standard conventions for transliteration from Indian languages to English have been used. Indian words that have conventionalized English spellings have been rendered in this form. In the text, the spellings "sh" and "ch" have been used, rather than the conventionalized form (i.e., "Shiva" will be seen rather than "Siva"), and forms used in the text have been rendered without diacritical marks. A glossary of useful and important terms is included at the end of the text with complete transliteration.

a	/a/	as in cut, uh-uh, what
ā	/ā/	as in father
ai	/ai/	as in had
au	/au/	as in rod
b	/b/	as in rubber
bh	/b/	as in boy
c	/c/	as in lurch
ch	/c/	as in cheese
ḍ	/d/	as in rudder
e	/e/	as in late
g	/g/	as in bag

gh	/g/	as in goes
i	/i/	as in it
ī	/ī/	as in eat
j	/j/	as in ridge
jh	/j/	as in jump
k	/k/	as in racket
kh	/k/	as in kitten
m	/m/	as in made
ṃ	/m/	vowel nasalation
ṇ	/n/	as in sing
o	/o/	as in motion
p	/p/	as in happy
ph	/p/	as in piano
q	/q/	as in linking
ṛ	/r/	as in cheery
s	/s/	as in set
sh	/s/	as in sheet
ṣh	/s/	as in rushing
t	/t/	as in litter
ṭ	/t/	as in butter
th	/t/	as in teach
ṭh	/t/	as in butter with aspiration
u	/u/	as in look
ū	/ū/	as in hoot
v	/v/	as in revolve
y	/y/	as in yard

Chronology

7000 B.C.E.–5500 B.C.E.	Early agriculture, small settlements
5000 B.C.E.–2650 B.C.E.	Harappa Regionalization era (Preurban Phase)
2600 B.C.E.–1900 B.C.E.	Harappa Integration era (Urban Phase)
1900 B.C.E.–800 B.C.E.	Harappa Localization era (Posturban Phase)
800 B.C.E.	Small states, urbanism
599 B.C.E.–527 B.C.E.	Mahavira, founder of Jainism
566 B.C.E.–483 B.C.E.	Buddha, founder of Buddhism
327 B.C.E.	Alexander the Great invades India
325 B.C.E.–185 B.C.E.	Maurya Empire
325 B.C.E.–297 B.C.E.	Chandragupta Maurya
272 B.C.E.–235 B.C.E.	Ashoka Maurya
250 B.C.E.–100 C.E.	Indo-Greek States, northwest India, and Mathura
100 B.C.E.–200 C.E.	Satavahana State, Deccan, and south India
1 C.E.–250 C.E.	Kushana Empire, northwestern India
78–150	Kanishka, Kushana emperor, unifies western India, Indus basin, Bactria

300–500	Gupta Empire
319–335	Chandra Gupta I
335–375	Samudra Gupta
375–415	Chandra Gupta II
544–1138	Chalukya states, Karnataka
550–910	Pallava State, Tamil Nadu
606–647	Harsha of Kanauj unifies Gangetic plain
712	Arab conquest of Sind
748–990	Rashtrakuta state, central India
985–1232	Chola Empire, south India
1000–1025	Muhammad of Ghazni raids western India
1012–1044	Rajendra I of Chola State unifies most of south India
1192	Prithviraj III of Ajmer defeated by Muhammad Ghori
1206–1526	Delhi Sultanate, founded by Qutbuddin Aibak
1206–1287	Slave Dynasty of Delhi Sultanate
1287–1320	Khalji Dynasty of Delhi Sultanate
1292–1306	Mongols attempt to invade India
1320–1414	Tughluq Dynasty of Delhi Sultanate
1343–1538	Bahmani Sultanate in Deccan
1342–1564	Vijayanagara State
1398	Timur (Tamerlane) sacks Delhi
1414–1450	Sayyid Dynasty of Delhi Sultanate
1451–1526	Lodi Dynasty of Delhi Sultanate
1498	Portuguese explorer Vasco da Gama arrives in Calicut, initiates direct sea trade with European countries

1526	Babur and Indian allies defeat Lodi Sultan at Panipat
1526–1707	Mughal Empire
1530–1540	Humayan succeeds Babur, is dethroned by rival (non-Mughal) Sher Shah
1540–1545	Reign of Sher Shah, emperor
1545–1555	Reign of Islam Shah, emperor
1555–1556	Humayan regains throne for Mughals
1556–1605	Reign of Akbar, emperor
1600	Queen Elizabeth I of England charters East India Company (EIC)
1605–1627	Reign of Jahangir Mughal, emperor
1613	British establish trading post at Surat
1615–1619	Mission of Sir Thomas Roe to court of Jahangir on behalf of English crown
1627–1658	Reign of Shah Jahan, emperor
1658–1707	Reign of Aurangzeb, emperor
1660–1680	Shivaji Bhonsla establishes Maharashtra State
1661	Portuguese give British Bombay Island
1707–1712	Reign of Bahadur Shah, emperor
1707–1723	Murshid Quli Khan, ruler of Bengal, Bihar, and Orissa
1719–1748	Reign of Muhammad Shah, emperor
1720–1740	Baji Rao I consolidates Maharashtra State
1739	Nadir Shah of Persia sacks Delhi
1748–1754	Reign of Ahmad Shah, emperor
1754–1759	Alamgir II proclaimed Mughal emperor
1756	Ahmad Shah Durrani of Afghanistan takes Delhi

1757	British general Robert Clive and Indian allies defeat Bengal ruler at battle of Plassey
1759–1803	Shah Alam II succeeds to Mughal throne
1761	Ahmad Shah Durrani defeats Indians at Panipat
1761	Shah Alam II defeated by British
1761–1773	Mahadev Rao Peshwa, ruler of Maharastra State
1765	Treaty of Allahabad makes East India Company the Diwan of Bengal, Bihar, and Orissa
1769–1770	Bengal famine
1773–1785	Warren Hastings heads EIC in India
1786–1793	Lord Cornwallis, Governor-General, campaigns against Tipu Sultan in southernmost India
1793	Bengal Permanent Settlement
1799–1839	Ranjit Singh establishes Punjab State
1829	Abolition of Sati
1838–1842	First Afghan War ends in disaster for British
1843	British annex Sind
1848–1849	British conquer Punjab
1850	Railroad comes to India
1851	Telegraph comes to India
1852–1853	Second Burma War, annexation of northeastern India
1854	Postal service established
1856	British annexation of Awadh follows host of annexation of former independent states
1857–1858	Rebellion against British rule; Azimgarh Proclamation
1858	East India Company dissolved

1858–1947	British rule over India, the Raj
1861–1865	U.S. Civil War causes surge in cotton markets, stimulates production in India
1868–1869	Orissa famine
1874	Bihar famine
1876–1878	Famines in northern and central India
1878–1880	Second Afghan War
1885	Indian National Congress established
1899–1901	Famine in northern and southern India
1906	Muslim League is founded
1912	Capital moved to New Delhi from Calcutta
1919	Amritsar massacre
1922	Chauri Chaura massacre
1930	Mahatma Gandhi's Salt March protests British tax on salt
1943	Bengal famine
1947	India independence; Kashmir accedes to India, fighting breaks out
1947–1964	Jawaharlal Nehru, Prime Minister
1948	Mahatma Gandhi assassinated
1949	Indian Constitution adopted; United Nations line of control in Kashmir
1950	Militant movements in northeastern India; Chinese occupy Tibet
1950–1954	Legal reforms abolish feudal land tenure
1962	Border war with China
1964–1966	Lal Bahadur Shastri, Prime Minister; Green Revolution begins as new seeds, fertilizers, and farm mechanization help increase crops
1965	Border wars with Pakistan

1966	Tashkent Accords brokered by USSR set India-Pakistan boundaries
1966–1967	Bihar famine
1966–1977	Indira Gandhi, Prime Minister
1967–1977	Militant Naxalite movement in Bihar and West Bengal
1971	East Pakistan war of Independence creates Bangladesh; 20-year Peace and Friendship treaty signed with Soviet Union
1974	Nuclear test at Pokharan
1975–1977	Mrs. Gandhi declares India is in a State of Emergency; civil rights suspended
1979	Soviet Union invades Afghanistan
1980	Militant Khalistan movement begins
1980–1984	Indira Gandhi, Prime Minister
1984	Operation Blue Star, Indian troops attack Golden Temple
1984	Industrial accident at Union Carbide plant in Bhopal
1984	Mrs. Gandhi assassinated
1984–1989	Rajiv Gandhi, Prime Minister
1986	Shah Bano case
1987–1990	Indian peacekeeping force attempts solution to Sri Lanka's Tamil-Sinhalese War
1988	Militant Kashmir movement begins
1991	Rajiv Gandhi assassinated
1991–1996	P.V. Narasimha Rao, Prime Minister; economic liberalization
1992	Babri Masjid destroyed, Ayodhya; rise of Hindu fundamentalist movement in politics

Map of India.

1

Land, People, and History

THE WORLD received a jolt on May 11, 1998 when India exploded a nuclear test at Pokharan. Three years later, India lofted into space its Geosynchronous Satellite Launch Vehicle from an island in the Bay of Bengal. A nuclear, space-age India does not match Western perceptions of the nation as a quaint land of elephants, silk-clad maharajahs—former hereditary rulers—and ragged slum dwellers. How could this be?

Indians retort—the West has ignored India's true nature for a very long time. Westerners had forgotten India's first nuclear blast on May 18, 1974. To Indian eyes, too many Westerners seem unaware that India is an important industrial power, leader of the South Asian political and economic region.

India is the world's largest democracy and home to the world's largest middle class. In the middle of the 1990s, economic reforms pushed India's gross national product (GNP) above 6 percent per year, over twice the rate in the United States at the same time.[1] The past decade of growth may help to reduce the number who live at poverty level, somewhat less than half of India's population of one billion.

During this time, the popular media focused on the entry of India's brightest young people in financial markets, computer software, manufacturing, and media networks in cosmopolitan centers such as Delhi, Mumbai (former Bombay), Calcutta, and Bangalore. The real story—with enormous implications for culture and customs in everyday culture—is economic growth's revivifying impact on everyday life: on small-town and village society across the length and breadth of the land.

This book presents a fresh portrait of Indian culture and customs at the beginning of the twenty-first century. This India is incredibly diverse and defies conventional stereotypes in many ways. This book draws on new research by archaeologists, anthropologists, historians, and other social scientists. It addresses the processes that make India what it is today and that are importantly affecting culture at the beginning of the twenty-first century. The voices presented in this book include a cross section of everyday folk such as villagers, small-town residents, urban immigrants, and people whose families have lived in cities for generations. Not only are the voices in this conversation diverse, they often disagree on what is to be said.

A PASSAGE TO INDIA: AN OVERVIEW

How does one start? India is a huge place with a vast population, subdivided into hundreds of different social groups, members of which speak over 100 different languages. Perhaps one must begin with a traditional Indian folktale, the four blind men and the elephant.

When the blind men finally met the elephant, which they had never before encountered, each man grabbed a part of the animal and then reported his impression to the others. The first, who felt the leg, reported that the elephant is like a log. The second got his hands on the tail, and said that the elephant is like a rope. The third reached up to the ear and exclaimed that no, the elephant is like a fan. The fourth, feeling the elephant's body said, "No, you are all wrong! The elephant is so huge that it is something without beginning or end!"

India can seem that way when first encountered, too. As will be seen, India's cultural diversity reflects intense pressures of environmental transformation, colonialism, technological change, democratization, and globalization. Historically, India was a cosmopolitan crossroads. Its location in the Indian Ocean made it a key link between two significant universes, the Afro-Mediterranean world, and that of Southeast and East Asia.[2] The overland silk route that linked Europe to China sent a spur southward, making India an important source of spices, silks, and gems.

India's natural resources supported the emergence of powerful states that benefitted from this trade, fought with one another, and on occasion expanded to include most of the South Asian subcontinent. The continuous existence of the state, in one form or another since the fourth century B.C.E. (before the common era), is an important factor profoundly affecting Indian culture. States distinctively organize themselves on a basis greater than kinship. They institute a civil service and monopolize the use of force. India's most successful states are those that organized bureaucratic institutions that bridged group differences and incorporated potential rivals into the power elite.

States contain a complex society made up of many different social groups. There are centers of commerce, administration, religious centers, shrines, and temples. The division of labor is complex. At different times in history in India, farmers, traders, artisans, livestock herders, merchants, and the military have played key cultural roles.

The most important events and processes that undergird what people regard today as traditional culture jelled by the late nineteenth century. By this time, a series of interlinked processes had transformed a cosmopolitan cultural landscape into one that was extremely rural, poor, and localized. India's forests were cut for their valuable hardwoods and to clear the land for plantation crops such as tea. The production of crops such as jute, turmeric (a spice), and cotton expanded into fragile environmental zones. The result was increased soil erosion and a squeeze on nonfarming groups along this economic frontier.

The colonial economy introduced new vulnerabilities. Craftsmen and women lost out to imported manufactured goods. Towns declined along with their gentry, artisans, and supporting cultural institutions. India's biggest famine stalked the land from 1899 to 1901. By the end of the nineteenth century India—the land of shining, golden wealth as viewed by sixteenth-century European explorers—was seen as a land of poverty. How true is this now?

A snapshot of India's population at the beginning of the twenty-first century finds that about 70 percent live in rural areas. A formidable number, over 200 million, live in cities. These attract industry and rural people who are seeking the higher wages, bright lights, and freedoms of the city. A slight minority of the population is wealthy. A larger segment of the population, around 150 or 200 million, has the resources to live what Indians term a "middle class" lifestyle, comparable in many ways to that of the West. A stratum below this lives with fair comfort and security, though not with a lavish quantity of material goods. Finally, somewhat less than half the nation's population is poor.

Politics are framed by the fact that India is a democracy. Every Indian schoolchild knows this was achieved through struggle against colonial masters, reinforced by a free press, and underscored by the asylum given to the Dalai Lama, spiritual leader of Tibet's Buddhists, after the fall of Tibet. In

Sojati Gate, Jodhpur. Courtesy of the author.

recent years, Indian voters regularly "throw the bums out" and vote in new governments. Social justice movements struggle against discrimination and demand accountability in civic life.

All governments since independence have fought to overcome poverty. Nongovernmental organizations (NGOs) are important partners in this. Rural development focuses on education, clean water, communications, public health, the environment, and women's issues. India has made strides: devastating famines are past history. Literacy rates are rising.

Indians are immensely proud of their nation's ancient cultural monuments, history, and literary heritage. It is difficult to talk about Indian culture and customs without reference to these, for they are explicit reference points in everyday life. As this book will show, Indians continuously reinterpret these cultural resources to provide new meanings for life.

This is the land where Buddhism was born, one of the world's great religions, and a seed bed for human rights. Mahatma Gandhi, leader of India's mass independence movement, found in ancient texts the basis for nonviolent protest, the most significant philosophical concept of the twentieth century. After independence in 1947, leaders of India turned to a village concept, the council of five, as a model for rural democracy. Tradition and modernity merge, sometimes seamlessly. In the countryside, the farmer behind his plodding ox team chatting on his cell phone epitomizes these contradictions.

Boat, Srinagar, Kashmir. Courtesy of Maxine Weisgrau.

GEOGRAPHY AND CLIMATE

India's diamond-shaped land mass is centered in the South Asian subcontinent, a geological formation that thrusts into the Indian Ocean below the great sweep of the Himalaya and Pamir mountain ranges. India spans 2,000 miles from Kashmir to tropical Cape Comorin. At its widest point, India is 1,800 miles from east to west. The territory of India includes Kashmir, parts of which are claimed by neighbors Pakistan and China.

India's Himalaya zone contains three of the world's tallest peaks: Kanchenjunga, on the Nepal border (28,203 feet), third highest in the world; Nanda Devi (25,645 feet); and Kamet (25,447 feet), on the Chinese border. The Himalayas drop to an extensive foothill zone, the Terai.

Three great river systems drain northern India: the Indus, the Ganges, and the Brahmaputra. India's share of the Indus River basin includes sections of the Punjab, the plain drained by five rivers: the Jhelum, Sutlej, Ravi, Beas, and Chenab. Canal irrigation helped to make Punjab the center of India's green revolution in agriculture: farmers' adoption of high-yielding varieties of crops; farm mechanization; and chemical fertilizers.

The Gangetic plain, the vast rich soil zone of the Ganges river basin, comprises northern India's agricultural heartland—its "midwest." Wheat is the main crop in its western reaches. Irrigated rice dominates in the east. Here, the Brahmaputra loops through the Himalayas before it drops into the Bay of Bengal. This region gets approximately 60 inches of rainfall per year.

In the west, the Thar Desert stretches to the Pakistan border. The saline and marshy Rann of Kutch juts into the Arabian Sea. The west is difficult country. Rainfall is too low for many crops. This western zone is important for pastoralism, the herding of cattle, camels, sheep, and goats.

Northern and southern India conventionally divide at the Narmada River. Here, the Deccan plateau rises to around 3,000 feet. Highland soil quality varies from rich to poor. The climate ranges from semihumid to arid. Small and large reservoirs support irrigated agriculture.

South India's east and west coasts are guarded by mountains. The Western Ghats rise to 8,000 feet along the coastal strip of India's southwestern coast. The Eastern Ghats are lower and overlook the rich deltas of the Godavari and Krishna rivers. The coastal plain comprises a 50–60 mile wide strip and forms an important agricultural zone. Eastern India wraps around Bangladesh to the border with Myanmar. This region is hilly and forested. It, like large highland tracts of central India, traditionally was exploited by shifting cultivators. This farming depends on being able to cut a patch of forest, burn the residue, grow crops using hand tools, then in a few years move to a new patch of forest.

India falls into a variety of climatic zones. Its highest mountains have a temperate climate with four seasons and a snowy winter. Elsewhere, the year subdivides into three seasons: the rainy season, a cool—or at least not unpleasantly warm—winter, and the hot dry season. This results from the monsoon system, an annual weather cycle that consists of marked rainy and dry seasons.

By May, the moisture-laden air masses over the ocean begin to move toward the land from a southwest direction toward a low-pressure zone centered over Asia. Monsoon weather ranges from fierce blasts of rainfall and heavy storms, to a few midsummer showers in desert areas. The primary agricultural season occurs during this period. Starting in late September, warming of the Indian Ocean causes the air masses to reverse their movement. The retreating monsoon is also exploited for agriculture.

The brief, cool winter begins. Temperatures are pleasant between November and January. Migratory birds such as Siberian cranes appear. This is the wedding season and time when many tourists and nonresident Indians (NRIs, Indians who are residents of other countries) visit.

By the end of January, the first hints of the hot season have arrived. Soon heat and dust will fall upon the plains. Daily temperatures soar over 100 degrees. Those who are lucky retreat to the mountains, such as famous old

Table 1-1
Major and Selected Minor Languages of India

Language Family	Languages	States
Austro-Asiatic	Munda, Santali	Orissa, Bihar, Madhya Pradesh, Jharkhand
Dravidian	Kannada	Karnataka
	Malayalam	Kerala
	Tamil	Tamil Nadu
	Telugu	Andhra Pradesh
Indo-European	Assamese	Assam
	Bengali	West Bengal
	Bihari	Bihar
	Gujarati	Gujarat
	Hindi, Urdu	Haryana, Uttar Pradesh, Madhya Pradesh, Himachal Pradesh, Uttaranchal
	Kashmiri	Jammu and Kashmir
	Marathi	Maharashtra
	Oriya	Orissa
	Punjabi	Punjab
	Rajasthani	Rajasthan
Malayo-Polynesian	Andamanese	Andaman Islands
Sino-Tibetan	Bhotia	Jammu and Kashmir
	Boro	Assam

Source: Joseph E. Schwartzberg, "Language Families and Branches, Languages and Dialects." Plate X.B.1 in Schwartzberg, ed., with the collaboration of Shiva G. Bajpai . . . [et al.], *A Historical Atlas of South Asia* (New York: Oxford University Press, 1992), p. 100.

hill stations—Simla, perhaps, British India's summer capital—or to their air-conditioned chambers. Those who are not so lucky pass the long afternoons in sleep and talk.

LINGUISTIC DIVERSITY

Five great language families have representatives in India (Table 1-1). Pockets of Austro-Asiatic languages point to cultural relationships with Southeast Asia. Dravidian languages predominate in south India, while Indo-

European languages predominate in the north. Malayo-Polynesian and Sino-Tibetan languages are found along the Indian Ocean and the Chinese border.

These language families subdivide into over 3,000 mother tongues, classified into at least 110 different languages.[3] Hindi, the dominant language of north India, subdivides into over ninety-seven dialects. Some dialects are less mutually comprehensible than others.

Until recently, standard language forms were restricted to elites and to those who were literate. Education in Hindi and standardized regional languages is eroding local languages. The post-Independence reorganization of the states on linguistic grounds has also promoted standard forms. Andhra Pradesh, the Telugu-speaking state, formed in 1953. In 1960, the former Bombay state was subdivided into Maharashtra (Marathi-speaking) and Gujarat (Gujarati-speaking). In 1966, Punjab divided into Punjab (dominated by Punjabi speakers) and Haryana (Hindi speakers).

Knowledge of the evolution of languages is sketchy. The oldest surviving texts on the subcontinent, associated with the Indus Valley civilization of 2600 to 1900 B.C.E., are written in an as-yet-unreadable script. The next oldest Indian texts are Ashoka's edicts, which he engraved on stone and set at his empire's boundaries in the third century B.C.E. Coins and carved inscriptions on caves are also sources for reconstructing early languages. Unfortunately, much ancient writing was on palm leaf, which survives only in dry climates. Paper came into use only in the sixteenth and seventeenth centuries C.E. (common era).

Linguistic reconstructions suggest that Dravidian family languages evolved their early modern forms in the tenth through twelfth centuries. These languages include Telugu, Tamil, Malayalam and Kannada. India's Indo-European family languages developed from one progenitor, proto-Indo-Aryan.[4] This gave rise to Sanskrit and to Prakrit. Early modern forms of the main north Indian languages emerged around the fifteenth century.

Hindustani was the *lingua franca* of northern Indian society in the late nineteenth century. Its vocabulary was heavily influenced by Urdu, which uses many Persian and Arabic loanwords. Today's Bengali and Hindi languages reflect efforts to separate these languages from Urdu influences. In the case of Hindi—which, along with English, is one of India's two official national languages—a government commission discarded Urdu elements. The commission emphasized a Hindi vocabulary derived from Sanskrit forms. The dialect spoken around Varanasi (formerly Banaras) was selected as the standard for pronunciation.

POPULATION AND SOCIAL GROUPINGS

India's population can be subdivided in many different ways. Looking first at India's genetic resources, archaeological and DNA evidence link India's modern population to two prehistoric movements. The first and most significant (in terms of genetic resources, over 80 percent) occurred about 50,000 B.P. (before present), as an outward movement from Ethiopia and Africa's Horn. Most of the rest of India's genetic variation stems from a second ancestral group of West Asian descent. Their genes entered the Indian population roughly 9,000 years ago.[5]

Gene frequencies shift gradually across the subcontinent. Individuals living in northwestern India look like their neighbors in west Asia more than they do Indians in the east. These, in turn, resemble their closest neighbors. Groups in south India and coastal zones reflect commonalities with Sri Lanka and southeast Asia. In any locality, the members of its different groups tend to share more genetic characteristics with one another than with individuals elsewhere in India.

Second, the dimension of social class provides important categories through which Indians characterize themselves. Elites, such as members of important industrialist and commercial families, are joined by new "dot.com" entrepreneurs. The middle class is largely urban, college-educated, and employed in managerial and professional jobs. Its Western orientation makes it a focus of debate over identity.

The large urban working class includes factory workers, construction workers, artisans in traditional handicrafts industries, and mid- to lower-level employees, such as municipal sanitation workers. Part-time employment as casual day laborers, as proprietors of tiny businesses, and in housecleaning, laundry, and other services characterizes another segment of the urban population. Family units in this category often juggle several jobs. Finally, there is the urban underclass of those who are unemployed or whose wages simply are not enough to make ends meet.

The rural social landscape includes elites, who more often than not are the well-heeled farmers sometimes called "bullock capitalists."[6] These families are patrons to others, as employers and sources of credit. Family interests often extend beyond farming to ownership of a small company. Members of these families go to college and find work as professionals, in government service, or in the military. They are big donors to religious sites and local festivals. Being a good patron builds social capital and support, especially if one has political ambitions.

Poorer farmers are less likely to have economic interests outside farming

Shoemaker demonstrates his craft. Courtesy of the author.

than their better-off neighbors. In 1980s south India, work migration to the Gulf helped many families in this category. Rural society also includes those whose farms are so small—or who are landless—that they work as agricultural laborers or find other jobs. Underemployment is a crucial reason many rural people go to cities or abroad.

Looking at cultural subdivisions, the most prominent are the vast number of groups whose membership rests on shared lifestyle, religion, and beliefs about descent from a shared ancestral group and its origin. In many respects, these groups resemble ethnic groups. In other ways, they are quite unlike ethnic groups. Unlike ethnicity in the United States, there are literally thousands of these groups. Each state has its own set of groups, and each state differs as to which are the most important, and which are of minor significance. Not only that, but even when groups in different states claim to be part of the same social category, a closer look usually shows that they may fulfil different political and cultural positions, and be quite distant from one another's customs, because of regional subcultures.

In these groups, membership is by birth and most marriages take place within the group. The community ranks these groups in a social hierarchy. The difference with ethnicity lies in the nature of the supporting institutions and ideologies that frame this hierarchy, known as the caste system.

Three qualities—membership by birth, marriage within the group, and social hierarchy—are the fundamentals of caste. Caste institutions are spread broadly among the population, among Hindu and non-Hindu alike. Non-Hindu groups (such as Muslims and Jains) tend to be sandwiched into local hierarchies at levels that seem appropriate, given their putative origin, life-style, and socioeconomic status. Caste has an elaborate theory of ritual purity and pollution, which is the basis for ranking groups from high (least ritually polluted) to low (most ritually polluted). This will be described in Chapter 2.

In India, caste or caste-like institutions appear to have originated with agrarian states.[7] Today's version of caste bears the stamp of the historical processes that created modern India. Economic problems in the nineteenth century hardened the divisions between subgroups and strengthened caste's "guild-like" dimensions as groups defended their economic interests. The spread of peasant farming to other groups encouraged them to adopt caste institutions, too.

India's constitution bans discrimination based on caste. Severe social discrimination faces groups ranked at the bottom of the hierarchy. This discrimination is intensified by its intersection with social class. While the groups that rank at the top of the hierarchy include members of all social classes (rich, middle, poor), people in the bottom-ranking groups are generally very poor. Almost none are middle class or upper class.

The government has set up equal opportunity programs to help groups classified as belonging to the Scheduled Castes and Scheduled Tribes (SC/STs). Members of the Scheduled Castes (about 17 percent of the population) belong to groups formerly described as untouchables. Gandhi renamed them *Harijans* (children of God), and today many call themselves *Dalits*, "the oppressed ones." Most are Hindus. In recent years a number have converted to Buddhism, Christianity, and Islam in efforts to escape from their stig-matized status. Almost one-quarter of India's population belongs to the SC/ST category—the majority of all Indians who are poor.

Members of the Scheduled Tribes, approximately 6 percent of the popu-lation, belong to groups that historically did not claim to be castes and whose non-Hindu beliefs often emphasized equality, not hierarchy. Today, most tribal groups have been absorbed into local caste institutions. India's great tribal belts are regions that in the nineteenth century were occupied by shifting cultivators and foragers. Some of these groups had occupied these areas for long periods of time. Others resisted and were pushed into marginal environmental zones, as the economic frontier extended peasant farming.

In general, middle- to high-ranking groups have the most social power and status. Hindus among these groups belong to one of the four great Hindu categories of *Brahman, Kshatriya, Vaishya,* and *Shudra.* The values and norms of these groups regarding ritual purity, marriage, and gender relationships (to name just three dimensions) dominate local subcultures. Important groups have varied from region to region and over time. Rajasthan's prominent landed classes were Rajputs, members of the Kshatriya category. After Independence in 1947 they faced strong competition from Jats, who are Shudras. In Kerala, Brahmans were the primary landlords. Hindu and Sikh Jats dominated in Punjab and Haryana. Although Rajputs and Brahmans are important in Uttar Pradesh, the state's largest subgrouping is the lower-ranking Chamars. Chhattisgarh, one of India's newest states, has its largest population of SC/STs, roughly 44 percent of the population there.

In the Bay of Bengal, the Andaman and the Nicobar Islands, home to a penal colony during British days, have a population dominated by mainlanders, with very few belonging to the islands' older tribal groups. In the mountain state of Sikkim, Lepchas, Bhutias, and persons of Nepalese origin are important in the population. Tribal peoples predominate in the northeastern states along the border with Myanmar. Syrian Christians and the Hindu matrilineal Nayars are important groups in Kerala. And this list merely scratches the surface of social diversity!

Anthropologists and historians find that political and economic success has given successful groups the means to assert high status. Although social status might seem fixed at any one point in time, the historical perspective shows that group mobility has been the rule. This becomes clearer when put into the context of the historical processes that have created Indian culture and customs.

HISTORY AND CULTURE IN INDIA

This chapter concludes with a sketch of the historical processes that have shaped Indian culture, and important milestones within this. One cannot understand Indian culture without knowing something of these processes. Indians complain—and rightly so—that Westerners' misunderstanding of Indian culture is profoundly related to their refusal to see that Indian culture is historically situated. Indian culture reflects many processes, and is not something that is eternal, ageless, and "timeless," to cite three overused terms.

Anthropologists now find that the emergence of states provided an important setting for cultural development. Colonialism profoundly altered environments, economies, social groups, and their relationships to one another. During the past fifty years, democratization and economic transformation have ignited an intense debate over the nature of Indian culture.

Humans have occupied India for a very long time. Stone tools have been found that date to the beginnings of the Paleolithic, or Stone, Age (ca. 2 million years B.C.E. [before the current era] to 750,000 B.C.E.).[8] The first residents were foragers, who collected wild plant foods, fished, and hunted. The Early Food Production Era, as archaeologists call this, developed with cultivation of domesticated plant species at Mehrgarh (today in Pakistan) between 7000 and 6000 B.C.E. Agriculture laid the groundwork for the production of surpluses that could support the emergence of states, standing armies, and social inequality.

This small-scale society transformed itself into a major state over the period of about a century between 2650 and 2550 B.C.E.[9] The Integration Era, approximately 2600 B.C.E. to 1900 B.C.E., is associated with South Asia's first great state, known to us today as Harappa or as the Indus Valley civilization.

Urban centers, towns, and villages developed, including two major centers, Mohenjo-daro and Harappa. These shared a distinctive grid-based settlement pattern, sewage systems, baths, and mud-brick architecture. Writing, standard weights and measures, and art styles associated with urban settings flourished. Harappan seals and writing have been found in Middle Eastern sites, suggesting long-distance trade. Local crafts flourished and developed alongside elite urban traditions.

The Harappans herded domesticated cattle, water buffalo, and sheep. Crops such as wheat, barley, millet, rice, and date palm promoted exploitation of different environmental settings. Yet, by 1900 B.C.E., urbanism was in retreat. Settlements became smaller and fewer, rammed earth structures replaced brick ones, and the distinctive urban art styles disappeared.

What triggered this decline? Archaeologists now focus on desertification in the southern regions of the Indus basin and western India, along with economic difficulties.[10] It became too dry to cultivate wheat and barley in most years, and too unpredictable to make farming viable. Important rivers vanished or found new routes because of tilting of the earth's tectonic plates. Economic and political overextension of the Harappan state may have worsened the situation.

Elite arts and writing disappeared. Localized crafts traditions continued their development and provide evidence for the small-scale agricultural society that now developed. This stateless society endured almost a millennium in some regions, from approximately 1900 B.C.E. to sometime between 800 B.C.E. and 300 B.C.E.[11]

Sometime between the seventh and third centuries B.C.E., two new technologies, the use of iron and horses, promoted reemergence of the state. The superior cutting edge of iron to bronze and stone made it feasible to plow deep black soils efficiently in regions such as the Gangetic plain. The horse, domesticated in Eurasia, extended the reach of armed groups. Ties to west Asia appear to have grown with the expansion of the Persian and Greek empires. Both overland and sea links spread.

Developments in the eastern Gangetic plain led to the establishment of India's first historic state—that is, with readable texts, Magadha.[12] Ruler Chandragupta Maurya (r. 325/327–297 B.C.E.) swiftly dominated his rivals. The Maurya empire absorbed the nearby hill chiefdoms, which had developed a form of democracy, and established outposts in the west where India's trade met that of Persia and Greece. The Maurya empire expanded into peninsular India.[13] The empire controlled three strategic assets that would be critical for all later aspirants to empire status: access to the western overland trade routes through which war horses entered India and Indian goods exited to the Mediterranean and Europe; the east and west coast ports that connected India to the Indian Ocean trade system; and some kind of system for funneling agricultural surpluses to the rulers.

Buddhism, a popular new religion, spread its monasteries and shrines along the silk route and throughout central India. India's new rulers emphasized their status through sacrifice by ritual specialists, practitioners of a belief system termed the Vedic religion. Ashoka Maurya, Chandragupta's grandson, embraced Buddhism. These rulers practiced another value associated with India's greatest states, religious tolerance. Rulers supported Vedic, Buddhist, and Jain religious centers.

Regional powers developed as the Maurya empire declined. Some focused on west Asian and Mediterranean ties. The Romans loved sheer Indian cottons, and traded with South Indian ports. Indo-Greek kingdoms grew along the upper watershed of the Indus Valley and north to Central Asia. Fertile plains with coastal access emerged as important states, such as Kalinga, in Orissa. The sea brought India's earliest Christians. It was at this time that, traditionally, Saint Thomas (ca. 150 C.E.) established the Syrian Christian community.

In the fourth century, Chandra Gupta I (r. 319–335) led Magadha's return to empire. The Gupta Empire resonates as India's classical period, its benchmark for art and literature. India was the center of a vast Indian Ocean trading network that reached from China to Africa's east coast. Powerful landed gentry and merchant groups controlled agricultural production and commerce.

South Indian rulers found that they could control inland access to trade goods through ports. Rulers monopolized the import of horses and enriched themselves through Indian Ocean trade. In central and south India, semi-autonomous regional assemblies unified under the umbrella of sacred kingship institutions.[14] Hinduism provided a unifying framework through which diverse merchant, noble, and artisan groups were integrated into large-scale polities.

New political centers emerged on the plain of the Ganges River, in the Indus basin, and in western India as Gupta power waned. The most powerful were characterized by peasant agricultural production dominated by a militarized gentry. The Gangetic plain lacks choke points through which groups could monopolize strategic resources. This made it difficult for rulers to curb rivals, who frequently were able to exploit political disorder to carve out smaller independent states for themselves.

A newly revealed religion, Islam, spread with trade networks in the eighth and ninth centuries. West coast settlements, intermarriage, and conversions created Indian Muslim groups. Non-Muslim guilds focused on interior trade as Muslims began to dominate south India's international markets. Economic growth fueled expansion of the Chola state in south India. Under rulers Rajaraja I (r. 985–1014) and Rajendra (r. 1012–1044), the Cholas unified most of this region. In Kerala, the ruler chartered Joseph Rabban's settlement of Travancore Jews—also traders.

In north India, defeat of the Hindu king Prithviraj (1159–1192) by Shihab ad-Din Muhammad Ghori led to establishment of a Muslim-ruled state on the Gangetic plain. Known as the Delhi sultanate, its West Asian ties were evident in the spread of architectural styles, Arabic script, calligraphy, and the use of paper for manuscripts. Islam gained a distinctive Indian flavor.

The Hindu-ruled state Vijayanagara (1342–1564) unified the Deccan plateau. This landscape was dotted with reservoirs and canals, which provided the basis for irrigated agriculture. Vijayanagara's tributary system ensured ample surpluses to support a strong military. Vijayanagara astutely played off its neighbors against one another. Shifting trade and alliances eventually, however, contributed to Vijayangar's 1565 defeat to the combined forces of its neighbors.

The early sixteenth century saw the opening of European markets to India. Production of spices such as pepper—a target of traders from Portugal, the Netherlands, France, Denmark, and the British Isles—grew as the Europeans pioneered sea routes around Africa. A huge export of textiles to European,

African, and East Asian markets followed the advent of more efficient sailing technology. Mongol control in China strengthened the importance of silk route centers in Central Asia. Their growth, in turn, reflected intensified contacts with India.

It is not surprising that the Mughals came out of this region to defeat the heirs of the Delhi Sultanate. At its height, the Mughal Empire reached from Bengal in the east to Afghanistan in the north and the Arabian Sea in the west.[15] New World crops supported agricultural expansion and population growth. Financial and credit networks spread. Textile designs appealed to European, African, and New World markets. Merchant groups and nobles invested in ships, such as Empress Nur Jahan's *Rahimi*, a 1,500-ton vessel.[16] European and New World gold and silver flooded into the country to pay for Indian goods. Architecture and the arts flourished.

Founder Zahir ad-Din Muhammad Babur (1483–1530), a Central Asian warlord, descended from both Genghis Khan and Timur (Tamerlane). Babur's control over Mongol cavalry tactics, his use of the then-new technology of field artillery, and his alliance with Punjabi, Sindhi, and Mewari rulers set the stage for his April 21, 1526 victory, which Indians count as the starting date for Mughal power.

Babur and his successors emphasized Central Asian concepts of governance, along with a healthy disregard for clan and religious differences. This was evident in the reign of Babur's grandson, Abu'l Fath Jalal ad-Din Muhammad Akbar (r. 1556–1605), sometimes called "Akbar the Great." Akbar established the civil service. This attracted capable men of diverse ethnic and religious groups, such as his famed Hindu advisor, Todar Mal. The civil service handled tax duty, separate from the military, which guarded and expanded the empire. Frequent transfers of civil servants and military commanders ensured loyalty to the ruler. This also helped to reduce the likelihood of a charismatic commander's gaining a local power base. Marriages sealed political alliances with former foes. Over time, the sons of these women—many of whom were Rajputs—vied to become emperor, some successfully.

Shihab ad-Din Muhammad Shah Jahan (r. 1627–1658), the "Emperor of the World," epitomized Mughal India's wealth, power, and artistic achievements. His great gift to the world was the Taj Mahal, a white marble domed structure that is the tomb of his beloved wife, Mumtaz Mahal (d. 1631). His Peacock Throne was legendary, studded with rubies, emeralds, diamonds, pearls, and other precious and semiprecious stones.

Increased political centralization under Shah Jahan's successor, Muhyi ad-Din Muhammad Aurangzeb (r. 1658–1707), upset key political supporters and erased the division of power. Aurangzeb embarked on a crusade to conquer south India. This effort consumed several decades and turned into his

Vietnam. The technological development of improvements in the rate and accuracy of firepower and the training of infantry in the new close-order drill, backed by artillery, made it possible for disciplined small forces to decimate larger armies. Foreign military advisors were important in this process. Ambitious local strong men, handling both tax and defense roles, now had the resources to create their own independent states.

In Maharashtra, the Maratha leader Shivaji Bhonsla (1627–1680) appealed to both Hindus and disgruntled Indian Muslims. Maharashtra established a stable administration within its borders, regularized agrarian relationships, and negotiated control over the important west coast ports.[17] On the Gangetic plain, Awadh rose as a successor state to Mughal power.[18] South India's Hyderabad expanded under the canny Nizam, whose career had begun in the Mughal Civil Service. The northwestern provinces became part of expanding west Asian empires, first Persian, then Afghan. Rajasthan's states seized their independence.

The most significant development was Bengal's emergence as a key political center.[19] Sugar cane, rice, and tobacco cultivation flourished. Bengal's inland waterways in the lower Ganges and Brahmaputra basin facilitated far-flung networks. Marwaris of Rajasthan and the British East India Company bankrolled agricultural growth. Compared to the war-torn west, eastern India offered the advantages of relative peace and security and a thriving society with its local markets, regional markets, and urban centers.[20]

Core Mughal zones in the west experienced devastating Persian and Afghan invasions. In 1739 the Persian emperor Nadir Shah took Delhi and ordered one of the great lootings of history. The prizes were the peacock throne and Akbar's "Great Mughal" diamond, whose 287.5 carats Nadir Shah renamed the Koh-i-nur, the "mountain of light." Invasions wiped out the political center's financial base and fractured its military leadership.

Political disorder created opportunities for ambitious men. In 1751, Robert Clive (1725–1774) of the East India Company captured Arcot, near Chennai (former Madras). At stake was trade dominance on India's southeast coast. Six years later, Clive and his Indian allies reached for the plum of Bengal. They defeated its ruler at the battle of Plassey on June 23, 1757. Four years later, the chief Mughal successor, Shah Alam II (r. 1759–1806), became a British hostage.

The great famine of 1769–1770 added to the disorder. Eighteenth-century reports state that ten million Bengalis starved to death, about one-third of the population. Huge tracts of agricultural land reverted to forest. The disarray gave Clive the opening to dictate the 1765 Treaty of Allahabad, which granted the East India Company the overlordship of Bengal, Bihar, and Orissa, making "John Company" in effect the supreme political ruler.

Real power and profits lay with the holder of land revenue collection rights, a percentage of agricultural product paid by cultivators. This provided the East India Company with fresh capital for investment and financed its military expansion, such as the hard-fought conquest of Mysore in the 1790s.

The East India Company swiftly moved to put its own stamp on revenue procedures. In 1793 the British established the Permanent Settlement in Bengal.[21] On the face of it this was an effort to set a "fair" rate—one that did not starve the peasants, yet handed over as much income as possible to the state. Supposedly a neutral economic policy, the settlement profoundly affected culture and became a negative economic force. It established a new group of hereditary landlords and created markets in land, spawning in its wake new classes of moneylenders, debt collectors, and renters.

The East India Company, being a profit-minded firm, organized matters for its benefit. The Industrial Revolution in Britain made it possible to produce cloth more cheaply than that produced by Indian handloom spinners and weavers. Trade protectionism made sure that Indians did not get the new technology. Exports shifted from finished textiles to raw cotton. This went to British mills, where it was woven into cloth and reexported to India. A lucrative trade of Indian opium developed. Grown in central India, the opium was exported to China. Opium profits paid for China tea—a swiftly growing export to the British Isles. Tea profits helped pay for factories to process Indian cotton. For India and Indians, profits that could have been used for development went to British traders who shipped this "Home."[22]

Indian industry began a long decline. Artisans became unemployed. Fine handwork traditions disappeared. The intermediate level of rural gentry, artisans, and artists who linked city and country declined, along with their small town centers. By the early decades of the nineteenth century, India was beginning to be described as a land of "self-sufficient village communities." Caste institutions focused on farm communities became important. In fact, this was a new social landscape created by war, economic collapse, and political change during the previous century.[23]

These new pressures created social conflicts.[24] Agricultural settlements cut into former forest and grazing zones, at the cost of groups living there. Commodities such as cotton and cane competed with food crops. The new markets in land created by revenue settlements opened up opportunities for investment, but made farmers vulnerable to its loss through debt sales in bad times. New technologies such as the railroad (introduced 1850), the telegraph (1851), and the postal service (1854) had a similar mixed impact.

By the middle of the nineteenth century, discontent united elites, angered over the erosion of traditional politics, commercial groups unhappy with the shift of trade into foreign hands, middle-class peasants, who found themselves falling into the debt, and the poor. In 1857, disgruntled military units and rulers led a great rebellion that flared across India. Fighters called on Indians to cast off the British yoke and recognized the titular Mughal emperor, Bahadur Shah II, as Emperor of a free India.[25]

Leaders such as the Rani of Jhansi—who led her troops into battle—were hobbled by lack of war supplies and money.[26] Coordination was difficult. The conflict was brutal and short, largely over by the middle of 1858.

Queen Victoria's proclamation, read November 1, 1858 by Governor-General Lord Canning (1812–1862), ousted the East India Company and instituted rule by the British government. The Raj (as the government became known) favored those who supported the British side in the conflict. The Raj solidified relationships with the loyal elites and revamped legal codes to establish a uniform rule of law. Ironically, considering the rebellion's focus, the British rulers now saw Indian culture as basically apolitical and ahistorical, governed by ancient traditions.

To what degree did Indians resist these new pressures or buy into these depictions of their culture? It is difficult to say. The last half of the nineteenth century spawned many new intellectual movements. The most significant political move was the founding of the Indian National Congress (INC), which fought for independence. There was a stream of talented youngsters to London, where they studied for the civil service examination, or prepared to become lawyers. Textile plants, ironworks, and steel foundries were built. Jute, tea, cotton, and sugarcane became important commodities after the Suez Canal opened in 1865. Indian financial elites emerged as investors in the new industry. The building of canals in Punjab stimulated intensive peasant farming in this region.

But the new economy also came at a price. Major famines hit as the impact of the economic changes swelled.[27] Now, there were few jobs outside of farming to absorb people looking for work in zones when crops failed. Further, the new crops such as cotton and tea depended on world market prices—and when these fell, Indian farmers' incomes dropped yet again. The government's revenue policies reduced farmers' incomes and in some areas limited their ability to store a surplus, in case of bad times.[28] Debt grew in many rural areas.

These economic changes powerfully affected rural culture. The loss of small-town subcultures, with their artisans and gentry, pushed villages to turn inward and become insular. Caste differences strengthened. Land became the focus of power-seeking groups.

Major famines hit Orissa and Bihar in 1865–1866, Rajasthan and Punjab in 1868–1869. First south India and then the north experienced famines from 1876 to 1878. India reeled from the worst famine in its history in

1898–1901. People called this "Chappaniya Kal" ('56 famine) from its date in the Hindu *vikram samvat* (*v.s.*) calendar, which is fifty-six or fifty-seven years ahead of the Western calendar. These famines caused millions of deaths, a disaster beyond relief or aid.

New social movements emerged. Plains peasants and mountain peoples protested limitations of their customary rights by government agencies such as the Imperial Forestry Department. Westernized elites called for religious and educational reform. At Muhammadan Anglo-Oriental College at Aligarh, founder Sayyid Ahmad Khan created a curriculum that blended Western and Islamic education.[29]

The Indian National Congress initially pressed for democratic reform, then called for independence along with voices such as those of Maharashtra's Bal Gangadhar Tilak (1856–1920), Punjab's Lala Lajpat Rai (1865–1928), and Bengali Bipin Chandra Pal (1858–1932). By the first decades of the twentieth century, India's discontents exploded into a mass movement for independence articulated by Mohandas Karamchand Gandhi (1869–1948) known to most people as Mahatma Gandhi. The Mahatma ("great soul") inspired generations of activists.

Gandhi's life is richly documented.[30] Born in Gujarat and educated in London, Gandhi spent his early legal career in South Africa where his encounter with racism galvanized him to campaign to improve the rights of Indians there. Gandhi was swept up in events after his return to India. He proposed a new tactic, *satyagraha*, nonviolent civil disobedience. The term stems from the Hindi root "*sat*," which means *truth*. Gandhi urged Indians to boycott foreign goods and to buy locally manufactured items. The *swadeshi* movement promoted Indian goods and popularized a boycott of foreign imported goods.

Columbia University–educated lawyer Dr. Bhimrao Ramji Ambedkar (1891–1956) led the anti-untouchability movement, which called for an end to legal and social discrimination against groups which ranked at the bottom of the caste system. Mass movements in the princely states called for democracy to replace traditional rulers. Indian industrialists quietly supported the INC. Not all was peaceful. Between 1920 and 1925, over 30,000 people were arrested at nonviolent protests in Punjab. In Amritsar, troops shot over 400 civilians gathered in a garden. At Chauri Chaura, Uttar Pradesh, a mob burned two dozen Indian policemen to death in 1922.

Gandhi fasted to encourage Indians to recall the values of nonviolence. In 1930, he led a march from Ahmedabad to Dandi, where he evaporated seawater to make salt. This action protested the British monopoly on the production and sale of salt. World War II intensified discontent, as Indians asked why were they sacrificing to free others from a foreign yoke. Many Indians vowed noncompliance. Scores of freedom fighters were arrested.

In Bengal, the war drove prices of food out of the reach of most families and created famine. When the crop failed in 1942, farmers lacked resources to feed their families. By early 1943, tens of thousands of starving refugees poured into Calcutta. There was almost no way to get food to rural areas, because Bengal's boats had been grounded by order of the government (to make these inaccessible to the Japanese, in case of invasion). The extra food stocks were a reserve for the Army. Up to three million men, women, and children starved to death or died from malnutrition-related sickness.

Bengali leader Subhas Chandra Bose (1897–1945) escaped from prison and went first to Hitler, then the Japanese. In Singapore he set up the Indian National Army (INA) with volunteers released from Japanese prisoner-of-war camps. The Japanese gave the INA almost no material support, but one unit raised the nationalist flag in India on April 6, 1944.[31] Bose's efforts ended with his death in an August 1945 plane crash. As the war ended, Indian sailors mutinied—and were seen as heroes by their compatriots.

Intensive negotiations followed. The outcome was British India's division into two new states: Pakistan, carved from Muslim majority regions in Bengal and the northwest—and India. Gandhi and Jawaharlal Nehru (1889–1964), soon to be India's first Prime Minister, led India.[32] On August 15, 1947, India claimed her independence.

Partition—as Indians term the division into India and Pakistan—flared into political violence as Muslims streamed to the new Pakistan and Hindus migrated to the new India. Over ten million people changed sides. Kashmir's ruler delayed his decision—India or Pakistan? In a swift maneuver, India claimed Kashmir. Gandhi himself barely lived to see the new nation take shape, for an assassin struck him down in January 1948.

The new nation was desperately poor and faced challenges to its borders from Pakistan and China. Agricultural policy aimed to quell rural discontent and support agricultural growth. Industrial policy sought to jumpstart industry through protectionism and government-directed investment. During most of the next fifty years, the Congress Party dominated in Indian politics.

India's Constitution, adopted in 1949, established an elected bicameral Parliament, divided into upper and lower houses. A strong prime minister and his cabinet led the government. A Supreme Court oversaw a hierarchy of lower courts. This same parliamentary model is followed in each individual state, with a legislative assembly and government headed by a chief minister.

Land reforms redistributed land from big landlords to poor villagers.[33]

Reform boosted many households out of despised low-status work into the higher-status category of farming. Institutionalized exchanges that formed important components of rural culture disappeared. In the 1950s, "Pilot Project India," established in Etawah District, Uttar Pradesh, by Nehru and Alfred Mayer, an American, was the first on-site agriculture development scheme attempted by the new government.[34] The project combined the Gandhian volunteer worker ideal with the American agricultural extension concept. The project built housing, established schools, introduced new technology, and tried to stimulate civic participation. It became a model for similar efforts.

India's population grew rapidly in the first decades after independence. This alarmed demographers, who feared that population growth would overwhelm India's resources. Development emphasized technology transfer, most successfully in Punjab where by the early 1960s farmers had adopted a package of high-yielding seed varieties of wheat and rice, fertilizer, and irrigation. The Green Revolution became a model for the nation.[35] Other initiatives, such as Operation Flood, attempted to increase the nation's milk supply, bring electricity into rural areas, establish health clinics, and provide clean water.

Politics in the 1960s began the transition from the freedom fighters to a new generation of leadership, such as Nehru's daughter Mrs. Indira Gandhi (1917–1984). Mrs. Gandhi (her husband, Feroze, was not related to the Mahatma) led the nation through the Bihar famine of 1966–1967, Bangladesh's 1971 war of independence from Pakistan, and into a pact of mutual aid and friendship with the Soviet Union.

Mrs. Gandhi, a bold leader, declared a state of National Emergency in 1975. During this time, civil rights and press freedoms were suspended and 100,000 political opponents were arrested. Villagers who lived through these events recall this as the time when Mrs. Gandhi's son Sanjay headed up a much-hated family planning program. Mrs. Gandhi's authoritarian style got results—but it eroded democracy.[36]

Centralized decision making lost legitimacy as people regarded the Government's existing hybrid of socialism and capitalism, "license Raj," as a setup for inefficiency and corruption.[37] Regional movements demanded political autonomy or even independence. In Punjab, a movement supported an independent Sikh state, Khalistan. Terrorist tactics by some supporters included bombings, killings, and airplane hijackings. Indians were appalled when in 1984 Mrs. Gandhi ordered the Army to attack the Golden Temple, where leaders of the movement were hiding. Reprisals came when her personal guards, Sikhs, killed her.

Kashmir, hostage to Indian and Pakistani politics, flared into rebellion in late 1988. Erosion of democratic institutions under a strong-man chief minister had reduced space for dissent within the system.[38] Kashmiri Muslims were reluctant to migrate to other states on account of anti-Muslim prejudice elsewhere in the country. This flared with the rise of Hindu nationalist parties. Identity politics became significant as Rajiv Gandhi, Mrs. Gandhi's son and political heir, tried to cater to religious interests.

The Bharatya Janata Party (BJP) called for Indian unity based on its vision of Hinduism. Many who joined belonged to the growing urban middle class of mid- to low-level professionals and small-scale entrepreneurs. They felt excluded from politics, damaged by corruption, and unfairly excluded from government equal opportunity programs. The BJP mobilized protests at a mosque in Ayodhya that Hindus believed was built over the birthplace of their god Ram. In 1992, Hindu militants destroyed the mosque.

Inspired by the success of the Uttar Pradesh's environmentalist Chipko movement to protect the forest, NGOs demanded resource conservation, women's rights, and government accountability. An important movement formed in western India against a huge hydroelectricity and irrigation project focused on the Narmada River basin. Conflicts flared where disadvantaged groups now stood up for themselves or where previously dominant groups resisted loss of their customary rights.

As the twenty-first century began, the BJP found itself now in power, with its own Atal Behari Vajpayee becoming Prime Minister. Indians were aware that they were entering a new century, one in which issues of culture and customs would be key questions in civic debate.

NOTES

1. The World Bank, *World Development Report 1997: The State in a Changing World* (Washington, DC: International Bank for Reconstruction and Development, The World Bank–Oxford University Press, 1997), Table 1, "Basic Indicators," p. 209. *The Economist Intelligence Unit, Country Report India—Nepal, 1996,* 3rd quarter, p. 4. *The Economist,* "India's Economy: Work in Progress," Feb. 22, 1997.

2. K.N. Chaudhuri, *Trade and Civilisation in the Indian Ocean: An Economic History from the Rise of Islam to 1750* (Cambridge: Cambridge University Press, 1985).

3. Joseph E. Schwartzberg, "Language Families and Branches, Languages and Dialects." Plate X.B.1 in Schwartzberg, ed., with the collaboration of Shiva G. Bajpai ... (et al.), *A Historical Atlas of South Asia* (New York: Oxford University Press, 1992), p. 100, also see p. 234.

4. Franklin C. Southworth, "Reconstructing Social Context from Language: Indo-Aryan and Dravidian Prehistory," pp. 258–277 in George Erdosy, ed., *The Indo-Aryans of Ancient South Asia* (Berlin: Walter de Gruyter, 1995).

5. Todd Disotell, "Human Evolution: The Southern Route to Asia," *Current Biology*, vol. 9 (24), Dec. 16–30, 1999, pp. R925–R928.

6. Lloyd R. Rudolph and Susanne Hoeber Rudolph, *In Pursuit of Lakshmi* (Chicago: University of Chicago Press, 1987).

7. Morton Klass, *Caste: The Emergence of the South Asian Social System* (New Delhi: Manohar, 1993).

8. Mark Kenoyer, *Ancient Cities of the Indus Civilization* (Oxford: Oxford University Press, 1998), Table 1.2, p. 24.

9. Gregory L. Possehl, "Revolution in the Urban Revolution: The Emergence of Indus Urbanization," *Annual Review of Anthropology*, vol. 19 (1990), pp. 261–282. Also see Kenoyer, pp. 39–45.

10. Kenoyer, pp. 173–174.

11. R.A.E. Coningham, "Dark Age or Continuum? An Archaeological Analysis of the Second Emergence of Urbanism in South Asia," pp. 54–72 in F.R. Allchin, ed., *The Archaeology of Early Historic South Asia: The Emergence of Cities and States* (Cambridge: Cambridge University Press, 1995).

12. George Erdosy, "City States of North India and Pakistan at the Time of the Buddha," pp. 99–122 in F.R. Allchin, ed., *The Archaeology of Early Historic South Asia*.

13. F.R. Allchin, "The Mauryan State and Empire," pp. 187–221 in Allchin, ed., *The Archaeology of Early Historic South Asia*.

14. Burton Stein, *Peasant State and Society in Medieval South India* (Delhi: Oxford University Press, 1980).

15. John F. Richards, *The Mughal Empire* (Cambridge: Cambridge University Press, 1993).

16. Ellison Banks Findly, *Nur Jahan: Empress of Mughal India* (New York: Oxford University Press, 1993), p. 150.

17. Stewart Gordon, *The Marathas 1600–1818* (Cambridge: Cambridge University Press, 1993), pp. 142–144.

18. Richard B. Barnett, *North India between Empires: Awadh, the Mughals and the British, 1720–1801* (Berkeley: University of California Press, 1980).

19. Richard M. Eaton, *The Rise of Islam and the Bengal Frontier 1204–1760* (Berkeley: University of California Press, 1993).

20. C.A. Bayly, *Rulers, Townsmen and Bazaars: North Indian Society in the Age of British Expansion, 1770–1870* (Cambridge: Cambridge University Press, 1983).

21. Ranajit Guha, *A Rule of Property for Bengal: An Essay on the Idea of Permanent Settlement*, 2nd ed. (Durham: Duke University Press, 1996).

22. Hameeda Hossain, *The Company Weavers of Bengal: The East India Company and the Organization of Textile Production in Bengal 1750–1813* (Delhi: Oxford University Press, 1988).

23. Bernard S. Cohn, "Structural Change in Indian Rural Society 1596–1885," pp. 343–421 in B.S. Cohn, *An Anthropologist among the Historians and Other Essays* (Delhi: Oxford University Press, 1990).

24. Eric Stokes, *The Peasant and the Raj: Studies in Agrarian Society and Peasant Rebellion in Colonial India* (Cambridge: Cambridge University Press, 1978).

25. Michael H. Fisher, ed., *The Politics of the British Annexation of India 1757–1857* (Delhi: Oxford University Press, 1993).

26. Joyce Lebra-Chapman, *The Rani of Jhansi: A Study of Heroism in India* (Honolulu: University of Hawaii Press, 1986).

27. Amartya Sen, *Poverty and Famine: An Essay on Entitlement and Deprivation* (Oxford: Clarendon Press, 1981).

28. Romesh Chunder Dutt, *The Economic History of British India* (London: Kegan Paul, 1902).

29. David Lelyveld, *Aligarh's First Generation: Muslim Solidarity in British India* (Delhi: Oxford University Press, 1996).

30. Judith Brown, *Gandhi: Prisoner of Hope* (New Haven: Yale University Press, 1990).

31. Leonard A. Gordon, *Brothers against the Raj: A Biography of Indian Nationals Sarat and Subhas Chandra Bose* (New York: Columbia University Press, 1990).

32. A.J. Akbar, *Nehru: The Making of India* (New York: Viking Press, 1988).

33. Ronald J. Herring, *Land to the Tiller: The Political Economy of Agrarian Reform in South Asia* (New Haven: Yale University Press, 1983).

34. Albert Mayer et al., *Pilot Project, India: The Story of Rural Development at Etawah, Uttar Pradesh* (Berkeley: University of California Press, 1958).

35. Francine R. Frankel, *India's Green Revolution: Economic Gains and Political Costs* (Princeton: Princeton University Press, 1971).

36. Paul R. Brass, *The Politics of India since Independence*, 2nd ed. (Cambridge: Cambridge University Press, 1994).

37. Philip Oldenburg, *India Briefing: A Transformative Fifty Years* (Armonk, NY: M.E. Sharpe, 1999).

38. Sumit Ganguly, *The Crisis in Kashmir: Portents of War, Hopes of Peace* (Cambridge: Cambridge University Press, 1997).

SUGGESTED READINGS

Allchin, F.R., ed. *The Archaeology of Early Historic South Asia: The Emergence of Cities and States* (Cambridge: Cambridge University Press, 1995).

Bayly, C.A. *Rulers, Townsmen, and Bazaars: North Indian Society in the Age of British Expansion* (Cambridge: Cambridge University Press, 1983).

Chaudhuri, K.N. *Trade and Civilisation in the Indian Ocean: An Economic History from the Rise of Islam to 1750* (Cambridge: Cambridge University Press, 1985).

Gandhi, Mohandas Karamchand. *An Autobiography, or The Story of My Experiments with Truth* (Boston: Beacon Press, 1993 [1927]).

Oldenburg, Philip, ed. *India Briefing: A Transformative Fifty Years* (Armonk, NY: M.E. Sharpe, 1999).

Richards, John F. *The Mughal Empire* (Cambridge: Cambridge University Press, 1993).

Rudolph, Lloyd I., and Susanne Hoeber Rudolph. *In Pursuit of Lakshmi: The Political Economy of the Indian State* (Chicago: University of Chicago Press, 1987).

Stein, Burton. *A History of India* (Oxford: Blackwell Publishers, 1998).

2

Religion

A NEW Hindu goddess appeared in Jodhpur, Rajasthan, during the India-Pakistan wars of the 1960s. So many devotees venerated Santoshi Ma, the "Mother of Satisfaction," that she took over a temple dedicated to another goddess. People said that Santoshi Ma manifested herself in a local *satimata* (protective goddess) who flew between heaven and the earth, caught the Pakistani bombs, and made sure that they landed outside city limits where they wouldn't hurt anyone.

In one story, Santoshi Ma was in life the wife of a high ranking military officer, yet after her death had become a goddess who protected the city. Her Westernized life was such that she seemed the last person to become a minor deity—let alone one reinterpreted as a manifestation of an all-India goddess.[1] But in 1975 a popular film catapulted Santoshi Ma to the national scene, and her cult grew in northern India.[2]

Religion in India moves with the times, as the story of Santoshi Ma suggests. Modernization and secularism have brought new pressures to bear on people and they seek new ways to understand the meaning of life. One of the great changes that occurred at the end of the twentieth century was the emergence of Hindu fundamentalism as a significant ground for political activism. A second has been new deities' rise and old ones' transformation to meet the religious aspirations of the middle class.

In India, individual religiosity varies as much as it does in any country, ranging from atheism to deep belief. People think about religion and their role in it. A person can get angry at a deity, try to manipulate it, ignore it, or replace it with one that is more satisfactory. In fact, religion is not especially associated with otherworldly types in ashrams, communities established as religious retreats. It is firmly rooted in everyday life, and it ranges across a huge variety of belief systems.

According to the 1991 Census, slightly more than 82 percent of the population is Hindu.[3] Muslims are estimated at 11.67 percent of the population, Christians at 2.2 percent, Sikhs at 1.99 percent, Jains at 0.41 percent, and others at 0.38 percent. With India's population now at one billion, this means substantial numbers in each category. Muslims, for instance, are well over 100 million, more than that in most Muslim countries. India's states vary as to the degree of religious diversity. Kerala, for example, is one of India's most diverse states. Its population is Hindu (57%), Muslim (23%) and Christian (19%). Jammu and Kashmir state is predominantly Muslim, but it also has a very large Buddhist population in its Ladakh region. Punjab is dominated by Sikhs.

Christians are a majority in Mizoram (85%), Meghalaya (64%), and Nagaland (87%). About a quarter of the population is Muslim in Assam (28%) and West Bengal (24%). The highest percentage of Buddhists live in the former mountain kingdom of Sikkim (27%) and in Arunachal Pradesh (13%). A small proportion of the population belongs to movements, which worship spirits in nature, such as Arunachal Pradesh's Donyi Polo, focused on worship of the sun and moon.

This chapter focuses on religious belief and practice. Non-Indians often think of religion first when they consider the culture and customs of India, but, as will be seen, religious belief systems reflect the diverse and changing universes within which people live. In the twentieth century, anthropologists and sociologists studied religious practices in rural and urban settings. They found huge differences between elite and nonelite traditions, and also among India's different regions in terms of conventional behavior associated with religion.

Thus, the behavior expected of a Brahman in Bengal was different than that for a Brahman in Rajasthan. It appeared that about the only generalization about religion that one *could* make—other than that it was so diverse as to defy classification—was that all the different belief systems in a region shared features with one another. This was often evident when residents often visited one another's shrines and festivals.

In recent years, Hindu fundamentalist attacks on non-Hindus have promoted awareness of their minority status. One response has been efforts to reduce overlap between non-Hindu and Hindu beliefs and practices. Some groups have found this new, militant Hinduism attractive. They have moved their belief systems in this direction. Other groups energetically separate themselves from this. Yet, while religion has often been seen as an important source of social differences, the members of India's different religions share many significant aspects of worldview, ideas of life, and the good things in it.

SEEKING THE SACRED

There is an enormous literature on religion in India. India's earliest readable texts are religious in nature. Throughout history, visitors such as the Buddhist pilgrim Fa Hsien (ca. 400 C.E.) commented on temples, rituals, and religious practices. Muhammad of Ghazni, infamous for looting the temple at Somnath, Gujarat, of several tons of gold, inadvertently created a different sort of treasure for later generations when he dispatched Abu Rayhan Biruni (ca. 973–1048) to report on culture.

British administrators attempted to classify India's religions. They created the label "Hindu" to cover its largest and most influential category of belief. The eighteenth century saw the first English translations of Sanskrit texts. In the nineteenth and twentieth centuries, researchers for the Ethnographic Survey of India documented religious rituals. In the late twentieth century, anthropologists amassed an enormous literature on religion and its place in social life.

The early British view of Indian religion was negative. James Mill's 1820 *History of British India* (1975) regarded Indians as superstitious, idol-worshipping heathens.[4] The British focused on activities that they considered barbaric, such as *sati* and *thugee*—the burning of a woman on her husband's funeral pyre and human sacrifice by members of a Kali cult. *Sati* was outlawed in 1829. A campaign against *thugee* was deemed successful soon thereafter. The British debated over whether Christian missionaries should be permitted to convert Indians. One camp argued that this would alienate Indian allies and create social conflict. Another camp argued that India needed Christian values to become modern.[5]

India's earliest Western-influenced intellectual community asked itself similar questions. Indians saw a mirror of their society in Western views that they did not like—and they responded. The Brahmo Samaj, the Arya Samaj, Sikh, Jain, Parsi, and Muslim reform movements emerged in the nineteenth century. Bengal's Ramakrishna Mission established educational centers. The religious teacher Vivekananda (1863–1902) drew inspiration from his reading of ancient texts and called for a purified, assertive Hinduism. In the twentieth century, Aurobindo Ghose (1872–1950) established an influential religious center in Pondicherry. A concept of selflessness linked to a search for inner awareness energized many who called for social change.

In the 1980s and 1990s, the Hindutva (Hindu fundamentalist) movement gained influence. A key tactic was the claim that Hindus had been disenfranchised in their own country. This was symbolized by the 1992 struggle over the Babri Masjid mosque in Ayodhya that some Hindus believed was built over the Hindu god Ram's birthplace, and by Parliament's passage of a bill in 1986 ostensibly to "protect" the religious rights of Muslim wives, which Hindutva leaders claimed gave Muslims special rights not enjoyed by Hindus.[6] Anti-Muslim rhetoric heightened consciousness of group differences. Targets also included Christians, charged with stealing people away from Hinduism.

What is significant in these conflicts is their political aspect. Their focus is on the legitimacy or illegitimacy of certain belief systems within India, and therefore the legitimacy of non-Hindus in India. Currently non-Hindus are urged to conform their practices to Hinduism, and Hindus are encouraged to conform to conservative Hindu upper-caste religious norms. Aspects of the movement confound many, who note—quite rightly—that Hinduism itself is such an enormous, diverse tradition as to defy characterization as a single "religion."

HINDUISM

Hinduism refers to a vast array of religious movements. These claim a special connection with texts such as the Vedas, the Dharma Shastras, and the Puranas, the earliest written forms of which date to the Gupta era. Although people may venerate these works as sacred, they do not always regard them as dogma. Unlike religions "of the book," there is no single authoritative text and no religious hierarchy. Movements, deities, shrines, and temples rise or fall on their own merits and according to how their believers support them. Patrons control their own temples and define what is considered proper.

In the time of Emperor Ashoka Maurya (272–235 B.C.E.), Vedic religion began to face challenges from Jainism and Buddhism, and from local belief systems associated with agrarian states. Vedic religion reminded believers of brave warrior ancestors. Our knowledge of this religion today emphasizes its elitist aspects. In this, Brahmans advanced caste's model of the four categories of humanity (Brahman, Kshatriya, Vaishya, and Shudra), and placed themselves on top as most ritually pure.

Buddhism and Jainism contradicted this perspective. They appealed to many with their three key ideas: nonviolence; teachings that all could attain salvation; and *karma*, the idea of gaining merit in one's life through appropriate thoughts and deeds. Little is known of folk religious movements beyond the fact that at this point they were developing appealing deities.

By the early Gupta empire (ca. 300–400 C.E.), the result of these move-ments produced a combination of elements called the *Sanatana Dharma* (the eternal righteous duty). Sanatana Dharma taught that the four ends of hu-manity were righteous duty (*dharma*), action, experience, and salvation. The concepts of purity and pollution, *dharma*, and karma legitimized the social hierarchy.

Purity and pollution are supernatural qualities that adhere to individuals, to activities, and to processes. Although most Indians share concepts of purity and pollution, Hinduism's model is easily the most elaborate. Purity is easily disturbed. The person who wants to live in a ritually pure fashion finds his or her day shaped by its requirements. One achieves ritual purity by avoiding polluting activities and substances such as body fluids, blood, saliva, feces, and menstrual fluids. Menstruating women should not cook or fetch water. Dead animals and corpses are highly polluting. Birth and death generate pollution. Nonvegetarian foods are polluting.

Body parts are associated with purity and impurity. The head is the purest part of the body. The feet are the most impure. The right hand is pure and carries food to the mouth. The left hand, used for bathroom purposes, is not. The distinction of purity between right and left appears in other phe-nomena. One circles the shrine or the sacred wedding fire by keeping one's right shoulder turned to it. Mourners circle the funeral pyre with their left shoulders turned to the corpse.

Occupations that deal with body wastes and dead things are inherently polluting. The purity of the body's different parts provides a metaphor for the relationships between Brahmans, Kshatriyas, Vaishyas, and Shudras. The *Rg Veda*, a book of Vedic hymns, described their origin.[7] At the sacrifice of the primordial being Purusha, his head became the top-ranked group, *Brah-mans* (priests). His arms became the second-ranked group, *Kshatriyas* (war-riors). Purusha's thighs became the third-ranked group, *Vaishyas* (merchants), and his feet, the most impure part of the body, became *Shudras*—whose job was to serve everyone else. All others were outside the system and below these four groups.

In this model of the caste system, purity and pollution generate the hier-archy and restrict social interaction. The most general rules stipulate that members marry only within their group and limit which groups may prepare and serve certain types of foods to others. Accepting cooked food from some-one means that this person is of equal or higher status to oneself. In this scheme, only Brahmans may cook for all other groups, because they are the most pure. High-ranking groups practice vegetarianism and avoid polluting occupations.

Those at the top of the system often claimed a sacred status and elaborated theories of ritual kingship.[8] In eighteenth- and nineteenth-century Puduk-kottai, a princely state south of the Kaveri river in Tamil Nadu, the ruler embodied sacred power.[9] The key performance associated with kingship was the great sacrifice and the king's bestowal of honors and status on others.

The sacredness of individuals (who can transmit smaller quantities of this to others) is restricted to those who are virtuous, to holy women and men, and to those whom a deity graces with his or her presence. Such individuals transcend the constraints of caste. Gandhi's standing as Mahatma, "great soul," articulates this status, which set him apart from others during his lifetime.

Upwardly mobile groups that seek to position themselves higher in the system often adopt the habits of higher ranking groups and ban work and customs that stigmatize them. This process is called Sanskritization and con-trasts with Westernization, which is oriented toward modernity.[10] Sanskri-tizing practices include vegetarianism, worshipping the deities of upper-caste groups, and restricting women's work outside the house.

In some South Indian villages, the Dalit's shadow polluted the Brahman. Often Dalits have not been allowed to draw water from the same well as their upper-caste neighbors or to enter Hindu temples patronized by mem-bers of higher-ranking groups. In recent years favorable court decisions have forced temples to open their gates. The Indian Constitution officially bans untouchability.

The law books such as the *Manusmriti* elaborated the duties of the different broad categories of caste. This cultural vision is evident in the *Mahabharata*, the great epic whose first written versions are known for around the time of the Gupta era. In place of blood sacrifices, the Brahmans taught an ethic based on purity, expressed through reverence for life. Vegetarianism became an important dimension of ritual purity. The core of worship became *dar-shan*, the mutual sight of the deity and the believer.

Hinduism gained prestige from its ancient descent and possession of sacred texts known only to specialists. Over time, Hinduism has proven durable, giving birth to and absorbing new movements, such as the great devotional movements of the middle ages. Today's godmen and gurus successfully use modern idioms to meet their followers' spiritual needs.

Hinduism's durability also reflects its intimate relationship with social structure. Seen from the top down, its ideology of hierarchy can be viewed as an ethos of social control, with everyone and everything in its allotted place. Seen from the inside, Hinduism wears the face of family and home. A home's most sacred spot is its hearth. Most ritual occurs amid daily life. The acts of bathing, dressing, and eating are connected to ritual purity. Ancestral and local earth spirits protect families and their land. A person may

Bhomiyaji shrine, Surani. Courtesy of the author.

go to a shrine or to a temple only when the family needs special help. Movement outside this local context may occur infrequently, such as when on pilgrimage.

Most religious practice centers on prayer and *puja*, worship. Yoga, a meditative practice based on breathing and body posture exercises, which looms in the West as quintessentially Indian, is most likely to appear outside everyday life. Tantrism, a category of experience-based activities that violate societal norms, such as eating meat, likewise is far from ordinary life. The goal is to transcend earthly desires.

In a Hindu temple, worshippers bring offerings to the deity. Bell ringing, invocations, and other rites call the deity's attention to the worship. The deity partakes of the offering and blesses the worshipper with its presence. The sanctified offerings are given back to the worshipper to eat and in this way share the blessing. Priests frequently mediate between the worshipper and the deity. Priests perform *puja* on behalf of others, and may be ritually possessed by the deity at certain times.

Religious functionaries include both those who inherited such a position and those in whom the talent has manifested itself through shamanistic possession. Some deities have only Brahman priests. Other deities' priests belong to different castes. Outside great temple complexes, priests are usually part-time. Laymen and women drawn to a religious vocation also assist in maintaining the shrine, making preparations for festivals, and helping to lead worship.

Typical practices include prayer, worship, fasting, hymn-singing sessions, and festivals. Sometimes deities possess their believers in a trance, or altered states of consciousness. This can occur providentially, or be called up by specific sequences of events: prayer, chanting, and music. Sometimes this is done to perform a divination—to seek the supernatural source of trouble in the community or to find and capture deities who have gone "bad."

The story of Santoshi Ma reflects three important characteristics of Hinduism. One is its elasticity: local phenomena nest together with pan-Indian phenomena. The second is Hinduism's subdivision into three strands of worship: devotion to two male gods, Vishnu or Shiva, and devotion to the Devi, the Goddess. The third characteristic of Hinduism is its continuous reinvention. Thus, in the story told at the beginning of this chapter, a local protective goddess turns out to "really" be Santoshi Ma, the sister of the pan-Indian elephant-headed deity, Ganesh-Shiva's son. Devotion to Santoshi Ma is newly popular, and overtakes others.

Hinduism's elasticity, its reach from pan-Indian myths, motifs, concepts, and characters to beloved local manifestations of the divine is one of its most striking qualities. Just about anything can be claimed within the orbit of Hinduism—and probably has. Local deities divide between household god and village gods, worshipped by everyone who is a resident. Important local divinities include manifestations of the Goddess, earth spirits, and spirits who guard the health of children. These rise or fall in significance according to how well they do their jobs. This flexibility allows new deities to appear and older ones to be reinterpreted or retired.

Local traditions often blur the boundaries between religions. Villagers often emphasize that all forms of divinity are legitimate, and must be respected. In Karimpur, a North Indian village near New Delhi, Hindu women venerated the shrine of a local Muslim saint.[11] Muslims in Hindu communities take care to remember the local spirits, to the dismay of purist theologians. New religious movements braid together diverse influences from Hinduism, Sikhism, and other religions such as the new *Radhasoami* movement popular among the urban middle classes.[12]

The second characteristic of Hindu tradition is its subdivision into three strands: worship of the god Vishnu in one of his many forms (Vaishnavism), worship of Shiva (Shaivism), and worship of the *Devi* (the Goddess). The three most important male deities are Brahma, the creator; Vishnu, the preserver; and Shiva, the destroyer. These gods are usually depicted with many arms holding different objects, and sometimes many faces. These characteristics symbolize their various qualities. Each deity has a principal wife and is associated with an animal, his mount. Each deity also has several names, including local versions of his name, and can appear in different forms.

Four-faced Brahma creates the world. He holds symbols of time, such as the pot bearing the water of creation. His mount is Hamsa, the Central Asian wild goose. Brahma has only one temple dedicated to him, at Ajmer in Rajasthan. His consort Saraswati, goddess of learning and of music, receives more attention than he. She helps students at examination time.

Vishnu preserves the universe and maintains the social order. The first great strand of Hinduism, Vaisnavism, emphasizes social harmony and ideals of salvation through the goodly life of home and community. Vishnu's consort is Lakshmi, goddess of wealth. Her shrines are tucked away in shops all over India. Vishnu rides the cosmic bird, Garuda. His symbols include a mace, representing time's power, and a lotus, symbol of the world.

Vishnu has returned to earth many times in various guises, called avatars, to save the world from destruction. He has taken ten forms: the great Fish, the Tortoise, the Boar, the Man-Lion, the Dwarf, and as Ram, Krishna, Buddha, Kalkin, and Parasurama. Some regional religious movements claim additional incarnations such as a fifteenth-century Rajasthani saint venerated at his tomb near Pokharan's nuclear test site.

Most popular is Vishnu's incarnation as Krishna. The "dark lord," as he is called, conventionally is colored blue. Krishna was born in order to destroy a powerful demon. Fearing the demon's powers, Krishna's royal parents hid him with cowherd foster parents in his holy forest. Krishna was a mischievous little boy, thief of butter.

Krishna grew into a handsome flute-playing youth, thief of hearts. The women cowherds loved Krishna and longed to be his. Once he hid their clothes as they bathed. Krishna's special love was Radha—yet all the other women also wanted him. In the *Ras lila*, the divine play, each thought she danced with him alone—but he danced with all simultaneously.

Devotional movements associated with Krishna appear throughout India and abroad. Devotees of the Pushti Marga ("grace path") venerate Krishna in the image of Sri Nathji at Nathdwara in Rajasthan. Krishna is worshipped in the image of Jagannatha at the Puri temple in Orissa.

The second great incarnation of Vishnu is Rama. Rama has recently gained great popularity. Rama also had a demon to kill, Ravana. Ravana stole Rama's wife, Sita, and took her to Sri Lanka. There Ravana, the demon, attempted to unwind Sita's sari, which miraculously lengthened. The monkey god Hanuman and his army of monkeys and bears helped Rama defeat Ravana and rescue Sita.

The second great strand of Hinduism, Shaivism, focuses on Shiva. Shiva, the Great God, unites excesses of being and of power. Shiva is both creator and destroyer, ascetic and renouncer. He is the supreme lover. Shiva's matted locks and his favored haunts, such as cremation grounds, woods, and forests, symbolize his separation from domestic order.

When Shiva performs his dance of creation he holds symbols of power: the drum, which beats the universe into existence; the trident; and the flame, which some day will destroy the universe. His home is sacred Mount Kailash in the Himalayas. Shiva's wife is Parvati. She also appears in other guises: Kali is the most dreadful, Durga powerful, yet maternal. Shiva's mount is the bull. As Bhairava, "the Terrible One," Shiva receives blood sacrifices. Shiva has two sons, Skanda and Ganesha, the elephant-headed. Ganesha removes obstacles. Travelers worship him before setting off on a journey.

Shiva worship most often focuses on his form in the *linga*, a tall narrow stone that represents the male principle. This upright stone stands on a flat, broad base, which represents the female principle. Both are part of Shiva. In fact, Shiva sometimes is depicted as half male, half female.

Shaivism inspires movements in which individuals seek unity with the divine through extremes of austerity or excess. The stock character of the yogi on the bed of nails most likely would be a Shiva devotee. Shaivite ascetics ascend mountaintops, live in caves, and stride nude through rush-hour traffic.

The third great strand of Hinduism is worship of *Devi*, the Goddess. The energy of the universe is female. "Goddess" can refer collectively to all goddesses and as well as to individual goddesses.[13] Some are independent. Others function mainly as wives. Ganga Mata is goddess of all the waters. Bhudevi is goddess of the earth. Sitala Mata is goddess of smallpox and related diseases. River goddesses are a highly localized form who protect their regions.[14] Many goddesses protect villages. Female ancestral goddesses protect families.

Durga may be the most widely worshipped goddess. She was created in order to slay the buffalo demon. Durga rides a lion and her many arms hold weapons and instruments of power. She receives blood sacrifices. She is a powerful mother goddess. During the fall festival of Navaratri, special rituals commemorate her victory.

Kali is the most terrifying goddess. She was born from Durga's brow in order to destroy two demons that threatened the earth. To kill the second demon—whose drops of blood sprang to life as new demons—she swallowed him and licked up his blood. Kali was so overcome with blood lust that the other gods feared for the universe. Shiva pretended to be a corpse on the battlefield. Kali's passion evaporated when she saw that her feet were on her husband. The "terrible mother" protects her worshippers from harm with a deadly might.

Finally, beyond Hinduism's elasticity and its division into three strands, the third aspect of Hinduism is its continual reinvention through *bhakti* (devotional) movements. These emphasize individual devotion and religious experience. These movements often come together around the teachings of a charismatic holy man or woman. Contemporary movements include that of the godman Sai Baba. His themes of contemporary material advancement (symbolized by gold watches, luxury automobiles, etc.) speak to a middle-class congregation, intertwined with the classic enthusiasms of *bhakti* movements: union with the deity and equality in its sight.[15]

ISLAM

Islam is India's second largest religion. The branches of Sunni, Sh'ia, and Ismaili Islam have all found homes in India. Islam's biggest issues stem from its minority status in a society dominated by Hinduism.[16] This is complicated by historical factors. At independence, many of British India's leading Muslim figures migrated to Pakistan. Muslim centers such as Hyderabad largely lost their elite subcultures. This "brain drain" left Indian Muslims collectively poorer and less well represented in civic life than formerly. Recently, the leading voices among Muslims have tended to come from religious professionals rather than from Westernized and more secularized intellectuals.

About 70 percent of Indian Muslims are rural, poor, and live in villages dominated by Hindu norms.[17] Urban Muslims are similarly poor. Overall, Muslims lag in education and employment opportunities. They are hardly a ripple in India's government bureaucracy—just 3 percent of appointees in the prestigious Indian Administrative Service (IAS).[18]

Kashmir is India's Muslim majority state, followed by Assam, West Bengal, Kerala, Uttar Pradesh, Bihar, and Karnataka (Table 2-1). States with substantial numbers include Maharashtra (approximately 7.6 million Muslims), Andhra Pradesh (5.9 million), and the border states of Gujarat (3.6 million) and Rajasthan (3.5 million).

States tend to divide between those with large urban concentrations of Muslims, but few rural Muslims, and rural Muslims, but few urban ones. In Rajasthan's Jaisalmer, known to tourists for its towering sand dunes and walled city, one out of four rural residents is a Muslim. Yet in the town of Jaisalmer itself less than 3 percent of city dwellers is of this faith. West Bengal Muslims also tend to be more rural than urban: in Murshidabad district, 62 percent of rural residents are Muslim, but only 28 percent of those in urban

Table 2-1
**States with the Highest Concentrations of Muslims
(above 10 percent of total population)**

		Population
State	Percent	(millions)
Jammu and Kashmir	70	5.4
Assam	28	6.4
West Bengal	24	16.1
Kerala	23	6.8
Uttar Pradesh	17	24.1
Bihar	15	12.8
Karnataka	12	5.2

Source: Mushirul Hasan, *Legacy of a Divided Nation: India's Muslims since Independence* (Boulder, CO: Westview Press, 1997), Table 1.1, pp. 2–3.

centers. Yet in many other parts of the country, such as Madhya Pradesh and Tamil Nadu, Muslims tend to be concentrated in urban centers.[19]

Most of India's Muslims descend from converts. Islam arrived with merchants, military adventurers, religious and political refugees, teachers, and missionaries starting in the eighth century. Military successes and establishment of political regimes headed by Muslims added West and Central Asian influences to India's cultural mix. Across India, converts assimilated Islam to their prior worldview. In eighteenth-century Bengal, for instance, Islam spread along with irrigated rice cultivation. As non-Hindu forest peoples cut the trees and built rice paddies, they came into contact with Islam, incorporated it into their religious beliefs, and eventually replaced tribal deities with Allah, the God of Islam.[20]

Formally, Islam is a religion "of the book": the holy Q'uran and the *Hadith*, proverbs and stories about the Muhammad. Using these sources, learned religious scholars define orthodoxy and heterodoxy, the rules of right and wrong. Muslims venerate Muhammad. The Prophet received Allah's words through the Archangel Gabriel and denounced idolatry. All Muslims must perform the five duties: the five daily prayers; the profession of faith; alms giving; the fast during Ramadan, the holy month; and the pilgrimage to Mecca. Muslims are equal within the community.

Meat should be *halal*, killed with a knife thrust as Allah's name is uttered. Boys are circumcised sometime between the ages of two and six. Good Muslims do not drink wine or eat pork. Muslims bury their dead so that they face the holy city of Mecca. There is no concept of a rebirth. Marriage is a legal contract, not the sacrament that it is for Hindus.

Three branches of Islam appear in India. Sunni Islam, the largest, regards the Qur'an as the supreme authority. Shi'a tradition is followed by around 10–15 percent of Muslims in India.[21] Religious authority is vested in a line of Imams (religious leaders) who descend from Ali, Muhammad's son-in-law. Shi'ism emphasizes the festival of Muharram, which commemorates the martyrdom of Imam Hussain and his companions in 680. The Ismaili tradition within Shi'ism accepts a different line of descent from the prophet. India's best-known Ismaili groups are both in western India. These are the Khojas, whose religious leader is the Aga Khan, and the Bohras, a business elite of Maharashtra and Gujarat.

Popular Islam is highly influenced by regional customs.[22] In Rajasthan, cultural continuities linked Muslim musicians with their Hindu neighbors and patrons. These Muslim groups resembled subcastes and were embedded within the local caste hierarchy. Women wore the vividly colored long, full skirts so typical of the region and recoiled at the thought of putting on the long black burqa, like an overcoat with an attached hood to hide the face, seen in cities.

Saints' cults are popular and reflect the strong influence of Sufism, Islam's mystical branch. This features union with the deity through techniques such as music, prayer, meditation, repetitive motions, and breathing techniques. Congregational singing is a favorite activity at such gatherings.

Islam's most important Indian shrine is the tomb of Mu'in al-din Chishti (d. 1233) in Ajmer, Rajasthan, who brought his Sufi beliefs to India. The tomb draws pilgrims of many religions. Chishti's spiritual descendants include two important saints, Farid al-din Chishti (d. 1265), buried at Pakpattan in Punjab, and Akhi Siraj al-Din (d. 1357), who established the order in Bengal.

Currently, trends in India stem from West Asian religious movements in Islam. Migration by Indians to the Persian Gulf for work has affected Indian Muslims' perspectives. Aid to Indian mosques, religious schools, and charities by Saudi Arabia and other Gulf states has exposed Indians to the Gulf states' religious norms. Despite the low regard in which many outsiders hold Muslims, the religion has attracted converts. In a celebrated incident in 1981, Dalits in a South Indian village converted from Hinduism to Islam.

CHRISTIANITY

Christianity is practiced by about 2.3 percent of India's population, about nineteen million in all. It is one of India's fastest-growing religions. Most growth is among Dalits and members of tribal groups. The new Christians join a tradition that includes communities that go back almost to the founding of Christianity, the Syrian Christians and, later, the Goanese Catholics.

Caste divisions among Christians recently have been challenged by Dalits. First, new converts emphasize a liberation theology message focused on social equality.[23] Second, Christians have been shocked by violence against them by some groups of Hindu militants. The 1999 burning of an Australian missionary and his two sons in their jeep, the rape of nuns, and the destruction of homes by Hindu militants shocked Christians into an awareness of common interests.

Most Christians live in south India, about 10.5 million total in Kerala, Tamil Nadu, Goa, and Andhra Pradesh. About four million Christians live in the northeastern states of Mizoram, Meghalaya, Nagaland, Manipur, and Assam. Kerala's population of about 5.6 million Christians divides among Orthodox (Syrian Christian), Roman Catholic, and Protestant believers. Nagaland's Christians are Baptists. Most of these converted not from Hinduism, but from other religions. Their missionaries are Indians, not foreigners.

Syrian Christians claim that their ancestors arrived from West Asia, where they were part of the Orthodox Church. They appeared in fourth-century trade networks on the southwestern coast. This group Westernized in the early twentieth century.

Catholicism arrived in coastal South India in 1542. Catholic authorities established a regular church hierarchy in Goa and Pondicherry, the Portuguese and French colonies. Protestantism took longer to gain a toehold. Opposition by the East Indian Company kept missionaries out until the early nineteenth century. The first, William Carey, began his mission in Danish territories in 1793. In 1813 the Company admitted missionaries. India's first Anglican Bishop was appointed the next year. English, Scottish, and even American groups established Anglican, Methodist, Presbyterian, and Baptist missions. Success was modest, though the 1870s saw a jump in converts, largely among Dalits.[24]

Today about 70 percent of Christians are Dalits. Most are poor. Dalit converts in Tamil Nadu, one study affirmed, were at the bottom of the hierarchy: poorer than non-Christian Dalits, who in turn were poorer than non-Dalit Hindus. This study argued that converts' primary motivations are desire for social acceptance and a positive self-image.[25] A major issue connected to conversion is the converts' loss of eligibility for benefits as members of the Scheduled Castes and Tribes (SC/STs).[26] In general, local Christians share many of their neighbors' beliefs in local spirits and the common world view.

SIKHISM

Sikhism is practiced today by about sixteen million people in India, twelve million of whom live in Punjab. About one million are in Haryana, another half million are in Delhi, and another three-quarters of a million are in Rajasthan and Uttar Pradesh. At independence, Punjab lost its western half to Pakistan. Sikhs range from conservatives, who wear the visible and distinctive turban, beard, and steel bangle, to those who cut their hair and dress in Western style.

Sikh religion emerged out of *bhakti* movements, which swept northern India in the fifteenth and sixteenth centuries. In this setting, Sikhism's founder, poet, and teacher Guru Nanak (1469–1539), taught that God, the "timeless being," is a formless entity. One knows God only through meditation on his true name and word. Guru Nanak criticized hierarchy, rituals, and idols. He taught that all were equal, symbolized through the believers' communal preparation and consumption of a meal.

A line of religious successors followed Guru Nanak's teachings. Followers collected Guru Nanak's poems, which became the Sikh holy book. In the late seventeenth century, Emperor Aurangzeb regarded the Ninth Guru, Tegh Bahadur (1664–1675), as a threat. He had the Ninth Guru arrested, tortured, and beheaded.

A generation later the Tenth Guru, Gobind Singh (1675–1708), transformed the Sikhs into the *khalsa*, the "army of the pure." In 1699, the Tenth Guru called for volunteers to give themselves up for a sacrifice. One man came forward and entered the Guru's tent. A moment later, the congregation heard a thud and saw a bloody sword raised. One by one, five men answered the call. Five times, the bloody sword was lifted high.

Now the Guru revealed the truth. The victim was a goat. Henceforth, the men would be the nucleus of the *khalsa*, today's community of believers. Members were known by its five signs: uncut hair; a comb; a sword or dagger that was carried at all times; a steel bangle; and shorts—so one could jump on a horse at a moment's notice. Members adopted Singh ("lion") as their surname. The Tenth Guru also announced that he would be the last human Guru. After his death, Guru resided in the holy book and in the *khalsa.*

Sikhs have disassociated themselves from Hindu influences.[27] The late-nineteenth-century Singh Sabha movement removed Hindu images and dismissed Brahman priests who officiated at temples. New rituals replaced old. Brides and grooms began to circle the holy book, instead of the sacred fire (a key ritual in Hindu weddings). Guru Nanak's birthday became a favorite festival. The Golden Temple in Amritsar replaced Hindu shrines as the focus of pilgrimage.

Hindu and Sikh subcultures shared many features as late as the 1970s. The sense of connection dissolved after the 1984 attack on the Golden Temple and Hindu mobs destroyed Sikh homes after Mrs. Gandhi's assassination. Hindu fundamentalism also prompted Sikhs to emphasize their faith. Sikh women stopped wearing saris, which had been adopted by many women to symbolize urban and modern values, and returned to the pants and tunic ensemble traditionally worn by Punjab's rural Sikh women. Congregations focused on inner spirituality, the community, and heroism in the face of oppression.

Today Sikhs are a modernized, middle-class community. Punjab's agricultural growth supported vigorous urban and rural communities. In the late nineteenth century, Sikhs migrated to British colonies and to the United States, mainly California's Central Valley. Remittances helped those back home to invest in Green Revolution technology.

BUDDHISM

Buddhists are less than 1 percent of the population, about 6.5 million in 1991. As recently as 1951 Buddhism seemed almost defunct in the land of its birth, with only 181,000 Buddhists counted in that year's census. Like Christianity, Buddhism has enjoyed growth, primarily from conversions of Dalits since the 1950s. The resettlement of the Tibetan spiritual leader, the Dalai Lama, and refugee Tibetans in India has raised Buddhism's profile in the land of its birth.

In 1956, B.R. Ambedkar led the conversion of half a million Dalits to Buddhism by receiving initiation from the hands of the senior Buddhist teacher in India.[28] Buddhism's appeal to Ambedkar reflected three factors: it is indigenous to India; it is a world religion; and its message is humanistic and egalitarian.

Buddhism was founded by Siddhartha Gautama (ca. 566–586 B.C.E.), who taught the "four noble truths": Existence was embedded in sorrow. This resulted from human desires. Humans could never fulfill all their desires. Hence, the way to end sorrow was to end desire. Buddhist teachings emphasized social equality, for every individual could seek to attain salvation.

Most of India's Buddhists live in Maharashtra—about five million in 1991. Most are neo-Buddhists, Dalit converts. There are 223,000 in Uttar Pradesh (where they are a negligible percentage of the population). Buddhists also live in the small states of Arunachal Pradesh, with 111,400 believers, and Sikkim, with 110,000 believers, as well as along the border with Tibet.

One small group of mountain people, the Bodhs of Himachal Pradesh illustrate aspects of local Buddhism in the Himalayas.[29] Bodh families kept a flag on a tall pole in the front yard to keep out the evil eye. They ate meat, including yak and cow, and observed ritual pollution after a birth or death. From spring blooms until the end of the harvest, people who died were not cremated (as during the rest of the year). Their bodies would be cut into pieces and left for the birds or thrown into the river. The family planted a white flag to honor the deceased on the one-year anniversary of death. The Bodhs worshipped a village deity, venerated nature spirits, and practiced exorcism to counter evil spirits.

A different picture of Indian Buddhists appears with Jatav shoemakers in Agra, who belong to the neo-Buddhist movement.[30] The Jatavs converted neighborhood Hindu temples into Buddhist ones and instituted new annual holidays such as Ambedkar's birthday, Buddha's birthday, Emperor Ashoka's victory day, and a commemoration of Dr. Ambedkar's death.

In the 1990s, Buddhists attempted to regain control of the Mahabodhi temple in Bodhgaya, Bihar, which marks the spot where the Buddha found enlightenment. Pressure by Buddhists led to their appointment to the previously Hindu-dominated management committee, expansion of facilities for Buddhist pilgrims, and use of the site to promote the teachings of the Buddha. A website managed by the temple committee outlines the temple's history and its activities and informs readers of upcoming events.

JAINISM

India has today approximately 3.4 million Jains, mostly in western India: Maharashtra (about one million), Rajasthan (600,000), and Gujarat (500,000). Industry, commerce, finance, publishing, law, and education are areas where Jains have found distinction. Jainism has profoundly influenced aspects of Indian thought, from religion to Gandhi's concept of *satyagraha*, nonviolent resistance.

Founder Vardhamana Mahavira (ca. 599–527 B.C.E.) taught that salvation lay in the soul's release from the material world. Liberation occurs when the individual abandons bodily desire. Every living entity has a life force, a soul. The ant's is equal to the king's. Thus was born the concept of nonviolence. Jainism took up the doctrine of transmigration, in which the soul was reborn in a completely different material entity. Everything, having a soul, is at some point in its struggle for liberation.

Mahavira is believed to be the last in a line of twenty-four Tirthankars, individuals who achieved liberation from earthly attachments and who also shared their knowledge of enlightenment with others. In addition to the

Tirthankars, who are most important, Jains venerate a variety of lesser figures of those who achieved liberation, great ascetics, and teachers. Jainism's "universal prayer" salutes these victors over earthly desires.

Jains divide into two groups, the Digambars, whose monks are "skyclad" (i.e., naked) and "Shvetambars," whose monks and nuns wear white garments. Jain nuns and monks wear undyed cotton garb, wooden sandals, and veil their mouths so that they do not accidentally inhale any living organisms. They carry small brooms to sweep any living beings out of their path. Shvetambar Jain laity divide into those who worship images and those who do not. There are also local cults whose members venerate saintly ascetics.

Jains do not consume animal products other than milk or *ghee* (clarified butter). Pious Jains do not eat root vegetables such as potatoes, because they may contain millions of living beings. The highest tribute to a Jain family's housekeeping or food habits is if a monk or nun drops by "grazing like a cow," people say, to share in the family's ordinary fare.

Jain rules of ritual purity and pollution are similar to those among high-ranking Hindus. Families venerate female lineage ancestors, perform fasts, and go to the temple on important occasions. In many ways their everyday religious practice resembles that of their Hindu neighbors. Yet, Jain worship differs in substantial respects from Hindu beliefs in at least three respects.

Jain offerings to Tirthankars are not returned to the worshipper as sanctified "leavings." The reason is that the Tirthankar is not there, "absent." Since liberated beings like this have transcended earthly ties, *darshan*, the mutual sight of worshipper and deity so central to Hinduism is irrelevant. Finally, Jain religious specialists who help worshippers in their rituals do not perform the actual worship ritual: they are not priests.

The Jain community's business wealth leads to a paradox. Surrounded by every luxury, the believer is enjoined to asceticism and discipline by monks for whom salvation is achieved through severe austerities. Most lay Jains do not take faith to this extreme, although they revere such examples. Business success means hefty donations to Jain educational, religious, and philanthropic organizations. Jains have richly endowed sacred sites, such as the temple complex of Ranakpur, in Rajasthan's Aravalli mountains.

OTHER RELIGIONS

India is home to many other religious traditions. Some are world religions, while others are local. Many of the local religions have been described as animistic. They hold that nature and inanimate phenomena have personalized supernatural aspects, such as are associated with spirits.

Zoroastrianism is practiced by about 54,000 Parsis in Mumbai and another 22,000 elsewhere in India.[31] The Parsis came to India from Iran as religious refugees. Parsis shot to prominence in the late nineteenth century as leaders in industrial development, commerce, banking, and real estate. Parsis rank among India's most Westernized and urbanized groups. The first Indian honored with a baronetcy by the British was a Parsi. Jamsetji Nusserwanji Tata (1839–1904) established the Tata group of companies, India's biggest. About half the community is of more modest means and employed for the most part in business, technical administration, and clerical work.

Zoroastrianism originated with Zarathustra, who traditionally taught in the second millennium B.C.E. The religion focuses on the struggle between good (truth, purity), represented by Ahura Mazda, and evil, represented by Angra Mainyu. Human choice can affect the outcome of this struggle. Parsi temples have an eternal flame that represents God. The fire temples are served by priests who say the prayers and ensure the fire is fed with sweet-smelling sandalwood. Religious practice is largely individual. Worship focuses on the recitation of prayers in the sacred tongue. One goes to the temple to recite prayers in the presence of the holy flames.

Parsis are known for the physical structure called the Towers of Silence. This is where the body of the deceased is laid after the initial rites of purification. The final ritual is to expose the deceased to vultures and kites, carrion-eating birds, which consume the body.

The biggest problem for Parsis is population decline. This reflects emigration, a low birth rate of members, and a high rate of intermarriage outside the faith. Recently, religious organizations have encouraged younger couples to have more children. A marriage bureau was set up to help potential partners identify one another.

India has long-established Jewish communities, which have different traditions of migration to India. Some groups adopted Indian characteristics and were absorbed into the local caste system. After World War II, emigration to Israel depleted the communities of the Cochin Jews of Travancore, the Bene Israel ("Sons of Israel") of Mumbai, and Baghdadi Jews.

The Bene Israel, who believe their forebears came to India in 100–200 C.E., were Marathi speakers who worked as rural oil pressers in coastal western India.[32] In the nineteenth century they moved to Mumbai and became clerks. Contact with other Jewish groups led to efforts to raise their status. In the 1970s, the Bene Israel, then some 10,000 strong, were preoccupied with the effort to claim equal status with the Baghdadi Jews. Although all initiated Jewish men qualify for admission to the men's prayer group, the Bene Israel complained that the Baghdadi Jews rarely asked them to read from the Torah, the Hebrew Bible.

India's smallest religions draw on distinctive visions of the universe. One religious movement, that of the Bishnois of western Rajasthan, has gained recent prominence because of its environmentalist ethic. Bisnoi religion blends aspects of Hinduism and Islam in its Twenty-Nine Principles, set out by the group's sixteenth-century founder. Bisnois famously protect trees and wildlife on their lands.

Today, all groups confront heavy acculturation to Hindu norms and worldview. Local movements within Hinduism face norms promoted by the mass media. Lower-caste movements confront elite standards and norms. The same is true for other religious traditions. Inside and outside Hinduism, new religious movements and new interpretations of the sacred continue to emerge.

NOTES

1. Komal Kothari, personal communication, Dec. 31, 1995.

2. Stanley N. Kurtz, *All the Mothers Are One: Hindu India and the Cultural Reshaping of Psychoanalysis* (New York: Columbia University Press, 1992).

3. Mushirul Hasan, *Legacy of a Divided Nation: India's Muslims since Independence* (Boulder, CO: Westview Press, 1997), Table 1.1, pp. 2–3.

4. James Mill, *History of British India*, 2nd ed. (Chicago: University of Chicago Press, 1975 [orig. 1820]).

5. Ainslie T. Embree, *Charles Grant and British Rule in India* (New York: Columbia University Press, 1962).

6. Peter van der Veer, *Religious Nationalism: Hindus and Muslims in India* (Berkeley: University of California Press, 1994).

7. Cited in Ainslie T. Embree, ed., *The Sources of Indian Tradition*, Vol. I (New York: Columbia University Press, 1988), pp. 17–19.

8. J.F. Richards, ed., *Kingship and Authority in South Asia* (Delhi: Oxford University Press, 1998).

9. Nicholas B. Dirks, *The Hollow Crown* (Ann Arbor: University of Michigan Press, 1993).

10. M.N. Srinivas, "The Dominant Caste in Rampura," *American Anthropologist* 61:1–16, 1959.

11. Susan S. Wadley, *Struggling with Destiny in Karimpur, 1925–1984* (Berkeley: University of California Press, 1994), pp. 246–248.

12. Mark Juergensmeyer, *Radhasoami Reality: The Logic of a Modern Faith* (Princeton: Princeton University Press, 1991).

13. John Stratton Hawley and Donna Marie Wulff, eds., *Devi: Goddesses of India.* (Berkeley: University of California Press, 1996).

14. Anne Feldhaus, *Water and Womanhood: Religious Meanings of Rivers in Maharashtra* (New York: Oxford University Press, 1995).

15. Lawrence A. Babb, *Redemptive Encounters: Three Modern Styles in the Hindu Tradition* (Berkeley: University of California Press, 1986). Morton Klass, *Singing*

with Sai Baba: The Politics of Revitalization in Trinidad (Boulder, CO: Westview Press, 1991).

16. Mushirul Hasan, *Legacy of a Divided Nation: India's Muslims since Independence* (Boulder, CO: Westview Press, 1997), Table 1.1, pp. 2–3.

17. Roger Jeffery and Patricia Jeffery, *Population, Gender and Politics: Demographic Change in Rural North India* (Cambridge: Cambridge University Press, 1997).

18. Hasan, op. cit., Table 8.6, p. 242. This figure is for 1981.

19. Ibid., Appendix A, "Distribution of Muslim Population in India," pp. 329–340.

20. Richard M. Eaton, *The Rise of Islam and the Bengal Frontier, 1204–1760* (Berkeley: University of California Press, 1993).

21. Hasan, op. cit., p. 4.

22. Pnina Werbner and Helene Basu, eds., *Embodying Charisma: Modernity, Locality and the Performance of Emotion in Sufi Cults* (London: Routledge, 1998).

23. James Massey, *Dalits in India: Religion as a Source of Bondage or Liberation with Special Reference to Christians* (New Delhi: Manohar, 1995).

24. Oliver Mendelsohn and Marika Vicziany, *The Untouchables: Subordination, Poverty and the State in Modern India* (Cambridge: Cambridge University Press, 1998), pp. 83–86.

25. Jose Kananaikil, *Scheduled Caste Converts and Social Disabilities: A Survey of Tamil Nadu* (New Delhi: Indian Social Institute, 1990).

26. Gauri Viswanathan, *Outside the Fold: Conversion, Modernity, and Belief* (Princeton: Princeton University Press, 1998).

27. T.N. Madan, "The Double-Edged Sword: Fundamentalism and the Sikh Religious Tradition," pp. 594–627 in Martin E. Marty and R. Scott Appleby, eds., *Fundamentalisms Observed* (Chicago: University of Chicago Press, 1991).

28. Eleanor Zelliott, *From Untouchable to Dalit: Essays on the Ambedkar Movement*, 2nd ed. (New Delhi: Manohar, 1996).

29. Rajendra Sarkar, "Bodh," pp. 112–120 in B.R. Sharma and A.R. Sankhyan, eds., *People of India: Himachal Pradesh*, Vol. XXIV (New Delhi: Manohar, 1996).

30. Owen Lynch, *The Politics of Untouchability* (New York: Columbia University Press, 1969).

31. T.M. Luhrmann, *The Good Parsi: The Fate of a Colonial Elite in a Postcolonial Society* (Cambridge: Harvard University Press, 1996).

32. Schifra Strizower, *The Bene Israel of Bombay: A Study of a Jewish Community* (New York: Schocken Books, 1971).

SUGGESTED READINGS

Babb, Lawrence A. *Absent Lord: Ascetics and Kings in a Jain Ritual Culture* (Berkeley: University of California Press, 1996).

Eck, Diana L. *Darsan: Seeing the Divine Image in India*, 2nd ed. (Chambersburg, PA: Anima Books, 1985).

Fuller, C.J. *The Camphor Flame: Popular Hinduism and Society in India* (Princeton: Princeton University Press, 1992).

Hasan, Mushirul. *Legacy of a Divided Nation: India's Muslims since Independence* (Boulder, CO: Westview Press, 1997).

Hawley, John Stratton and Donna Marie Wulff, eds. *Devi: Goddesses of India* (Berkeley: University of California Press, 1996).

Lopez, Donald S. *Religions of India in Practice* (Princeton: Princeton University Press, 1995).

Luhrmann, T.M. *The Good Parsi: The Fate of a Colonial Elite in a Postcolonial Society* (Cambridge: Harvard University Press, 1996).

Madan, T.N. (ed.). *Muslim Communities of South Asia: Culture, Society and Power* (New Delhi: Manohar, 1995).

Massey, James. *Dalits in India: Religion as a Source of Bondage or Liberation with Special Reference to Christians* (New Delhi: Manohar, 1995).

McDermott, Rachel Fell. *Singing to the Goddess: Poems to Kali and Uma from Bengal* (Oxford: Oxford University Press, 2001).

Oberoi, Harjot. *The Construction of Religious Boundaries: Culture, Identity and Diversity in the Sikh Tradition* (Delhi: Oxford University Press, 1997).

Srinivasan, Smriti. *The Mouths of People, the Voice of God: Buddhists and Muslims in a Frontier Community of Ladakh* (Delhi: Oxford University Press, 1998).

3

World View

A RECURRING THEME enjoyed by Indian moviegoers concerns the fate of two brothers. Separated at birth, one grows up to be a mafia kingpin, surrounded by molls and gangsters. The other brother rises through police ranks to become the chief. The plot's twists and turns—filled with mayhem, fight scenes, chases, romance, musical interludes, and a vast horde of characters ranging from beggars to high-society sophisticates—lead to the final confrontation between the brothers. At its heart, this is a story about family relationships, duty, and moral choices—all key elements that frame world view in India.

This chapter focuses on prized shared cultural values that contribute to Indians' sense that they are a distinct nation. These values, taken together, reveal a general orientation to life, the "conventional wisdom" about the nature of reality and of the place of humans in it. In this book the term "world view" refers to this shared system of values and ideas.

Unsurprisingly, this world view incorporates a vast range of ethnic groups, social classes, and religious belief systems. Some see themselves as promoting a more traditionalist perspective, while others see themselves as attuned to modernity—either by framing their religious experience as consistent with modernity, or by embracing a secularist perspective. World view includes the earliest lessons that a child learns, basic ideas about the nature of the universe, and humans' role in it.

Many efforts to write about Indian world view have simply presented the perspective of Hinduism, even though substantial numbers of Indians are members of different religious traditions and many Hindus disagree with elite ideologies. Recently, some members of the Hindu fundamentalist movement have attempted to disqualify others as not authentically Indian or told them to change their beliefs to conform to the fundamentalists' vision of who they should be.

Many Hindus and most non-Hindus belong to subordinated groups, whose perspectives contrast in important ways with those of elites. Being a member of a minority group means trying to keep one's distinctiveness, while coping with the pressures for conformity with the dominant ideology.[1] Region, social class, and religion all contribute distinctive components to world view. The diverse interplay among elements means that world view is not static. It has changed over time, and is changing still.

Growing Up Indian

The most important factor framing Indian world view is that of the family. Family is the great idiom of cultural life. It is the primary social institution within which individuals are born, learn, marry, work, play, and enact the main elements of world view.

Most Indians value the extended family, centered on the male line of descent, as the ideal structure. This unites paternal grandparents, paternal uncles and their wives and children, and unmarried paternal aunts under one roof. In addition, married daughters and their children, cousins, friends, and servants also may be in residence for longer or shorter periods of time.

This is the setting in which babies' earliest socialization experiences occur. The baby swiftly learns that members adjust their behavior according to the social situation. Mothers become formal in front of the baby's paternal grandmother and restrict their displays of affection when she is around. The positive side for a baby is a seemingly endless supply of adults and older children willing to entertain, hold, hug, and play with it. In fact, mothers encourage infants to develop close relationships with others, rather than developing an intense emotional relationship with her.[2] Over time, the mother's emotional distance pushes the child to renounce individual selfish desire for the more satisfying and certain pleasure of group membership. The child will identify with the larger family group for, as Indians say, "All the mothers are one."

In its simplest sense, this statement means that all the family's women mother the child and that it develops emotional attachments to all the family's women, instead of an exclusive and intense bond with one. In a somewhat broader sense, the mothers of the family are the living representatives of a much larger group venerated in family worship, its female ancestors, whom Hindus and some others venerate as a single undifferentiated group.

The statement "All the mothers are one" also is a link to an important philosophical concept: that the universe contains important spiritual or supernatural qualities, in which everything is ultimately linked to everything else. The relationship with "one" mother is also a relationship with "all" mothers.

As an infant grows into toddler stage, bargaining becomes important. "Do this," the mother says, "and I will feed you."[3] The child learns to obtain its goal through action, for the mother does not turn down the child outright. Children learn that they have rights as well as family obligations. They learn to stand up for their rights, within this group.

This course of socialization differs for boys and girls. Boys are more coddled than girls, at least initially. Girls learn from an early age that they have responsibilities. Boys learn subordination to adult men and older boys in the family, a sign of their attachment to family unity. A man's minority within the family lasts until his father's retirement or his mother turns over the household reins.

Small daughters often must help with younger siblings. Their play or school attendance will be interrupted to run an errand. The girl must develop an inner sense of self that can cross between the warmth of her natal home to the formality, restrictions, and duties of her life in her husband's family. The girl must learn a strong sense of discipline.

Early on, children also discover that they are members of specific social groups and that these groups have internal hierarchies. Older children outrank younger children. Boys outrank girls. Men outrank women. Seniors should be respected by all. Parents enforce these distinctions. Parents neither expect nor attempt to treat all their children alike. Children possess inherently different characteristics, based on birth order, sex, omens, dreams by the mother during her pregnancy, and the astrological conjunction of the stars at birth.

Group membership also means learning the values that differentiate groups from one another. These values may include negative stereotypes projected on groups by others. Groups are also ranked. Life looks very different at the bottom of the hierarchy than it does at the top. Groups at the bottom tend to be poor and this affects family life in significant ways. The poor have fewer children and their family units are about half the size of those that are better off. Husbands and wives are more easily pulled apart by stress and poverty than those who are better off. Sons move out. Children die. Poor families live in a cultural situation that idealizes large, extended families, but few poor families can actually sustain such units.[4]

The goal of childhood socialization is to create active individuals who are enmeshed in a web of family relationships and who are oriented within this to the obligations of duty, responsibility, and action.[5] The individual is poised to reach out to life, from within a strongly valued family life. These values are far from outsiders' stereotypes of Indians as passive, fatalistic, and otherworldly.

NATURE OF THE UNIVERSE

India's religions view the universe as one of intertwined supernatural and natural forces. This world view differs from Western Judeo-Christian philosophy, which divides the natural and supernatural into separate and opposed categories. In India, everything and everyone contain supernatural energy in one form or another. This world is filled with supernatural beings and forces. Deities, saints, ancestral spirits, ghosts, witches, and evil spirits inhabit the same universe as people. Malignant sorcery and curses cause harm. There is generalized bad luck. The Evil Eye exists. Parents dress small boys to look like little girls to escape its notice. They give children ugly names to suggest that the child is useless and undesirable, for the same reason.

It is dangerous to verbalize thoughts about the future, safer to say that fate is in God's hands. Words have magical power and consequences. Hence, one never says, "pretty baby," lest this draw the attention of the Evil Eye and harm results.[6]

Supernatural energy occurs in different forms. General qualities include auspiciousness and inauspiciousness, ritual purity and pollution, divine heat and cold, and the qualities of desire, inertia, and truth.[7] Auspiciousness and inauspiciousness, for instance, adhere to certain events (births, weddings), places (shrines, temples), times, and omens.

Inauspiciousness must be avoided: the wrong times and bad omens, such as the hooting of an owl or a lunar eclipse. Sunday and Monday, Wednesday, Thursday, and Friday are auspicious days. Tuesday is inauspicious: not a day to start a trip. Saturday, associated with Saturn, is very inauspicious.

These qualities also attach to the lunar cycle, which divide into a "bright half" (when the moon is waxing) and a "dark half" (when the moon is waning). The brightest day of the bright half, full moon, is extremely lucky. The sense of auspiciousness and inauspiciousness may be muted in everyday life, but it assumes special significance at a festival or a family event such as a wedding. Then religious specialists may be called to ensure that everything is correct.

Different supernatural characteristics balance one another in the ideal universe. When they do not, as in certain Hindu myths or in the principles of Ayurvedic (traditional Hindu) and Unani (traditional Islamic) medical systems, steps must be taken to restore the cosmic balance.[8]

Tamil villagers, for instance, believe that originally the fundamental elements of the universe were randomly mixed in the primordial being called Katavul.[9] Fire, earth, water, ether, and wind—the five elements—and phlegm, bile, and wind—the three humors—became distinct from the primordial undifferentiated universe when they began to move around. Their recombination created the three basic dispositions: desire, truth, and inertia. The combination of these makes the world as we know it today.

The essential nature of groups stems from combinations of the basic dispositions. The actions and qualities of one's ancestors and the quality of the soil upon which one is raised (which also has supernatural characteristics) affect the basic constitution of the individual. One's actions should be in accordance with this.

Thus, for instance, Rajputs, whose self-image is as warriors, consume "hot" foodstuffs such as meat and liquor. Others embrace a diet of "cold" foods—*ghee* (clarified butter), milk, vegetables and fruits—to reduce their susceptibility to physical passions that are incompatible with their basic nature. Women and men are inherently different. Women's sexuality is more robust than men's. Husbands must balance their wives' needs with their efforts to sustain a high degree of the life force believed to be present in semen.

The systemic quality of the universe is the basis for the concept of karma. One's actions result in magical consequences. Buddhism elaborated the idea that karma links present acts to one's status in future lives.

Concepts of purity and pollution, sketched in the previous chapter, are widely shared among India's diverse ethnic and religious groups. Shared ides of purity and pollution focus on life-crisis rites, such as birth rituals, which erase dangerous pollution and welcome the infant into the family. Funeral ritual transforms the deceased from a potentially dangerous ghost into a kindly ancestor. Running water purifies the body. Every morning, the pious individual should bathe and dress in freshly washed clothing before eating the first cooked meal of the day. Everyone washes and dons fresh, clean clothes before a religious ritual. Muslims avoid food that is not ritually pure.

There is evidence that some ideas about ritual purity and pollution are shifting. This transformation of world view is most noted among the urban middle classes. These have relaxed restrictions on dining at restaurants with unknown cooks, on sharing the table with members of different castes, and on bans on meat and alcohol consumption. Members of these groups also show an increasing tolerance for intercaste or interfaith marriages among young urban professionals.

Secularizing trends appear to be entering the countryside along with mass media and shifting power relationships. Weddings, formerly held in the bride's home, now may be celebrated at a town hall. Catering and religious services, instead of being performed by traditional specialists, may be contracted for from Westernized professionals, down to the video crew that records the event. Some groups have found the courts an ally in combatting overt discrimination based on caste—but in the realm of everyday life, purity and pollution continue to influence the interactions between those at the bottom and everyone else.

DUTY

As children grow, they learn about the supernatural and natural structure of the universe. They are constantly reminded that group membership, social position, and roles place obligations on the individual. There are duties to be performed. Hinduism articulates duty as righteous dharma, that which one must do in life. Through adherence to duty, humans sustain society against the chaos that is introduced through failure, supernatural forces, evil, and bad luck.

Concepts of duty are widely shared. Muslims emphasize obedience to God's will. Sikhs stress that the knowledge gained from meditation on the name of God leads to awareness of duty. Buddhism and Jainism enjoin individuals to the important duty of nonviolence.

Individuals are socialized to a strong sense of obligation to the family. The family is happiest if its members wholeheartedly embrace their duties, just as society is sustained when its different segments perform their ordained work. Tension appears when duties conflict with one another. A famous novel, *Samskara*, asked whose duty was it to remove the deceased Brahman who flouted his duties in life?[10] As the neighbors debated what was to be done, things got worse and worse. The film *Guide* (1965) followed the career of a slick tourist guide who—life in shambles after a failed love affair and jail stint—was mistaken for a holy man. Gradually the tourist guide took on this role and even assumed the ultimate duty, a fast unto death in order to end a drought.

The most famous statement of duty and its conflicts appears in the poetry of the *Bhagavad Gita*, which relates the most famous incident in India's great epic, the *Mahabharata*.[11] Many turn to the *Bhagavad Gita* for inspiration today. In this, the hero faces a conflict between his duty as kinsman to protect his cousins and his sacred duty to kill them as opponents on the field of battle, in order to prevent chaos from descending on the universe.

The hero's charioteer, none other than Krishna, embarks on a conversation with his master. Krishna explains that duty reflects not simply the mundane world, but cosmic relationships as well. Duty is revealed through devotion to and experience of the divine. On one level, the hero has his family duty, but on another, he faces his duty to the web of cosmic relationships.

ACTION

Life requires choices and positive action. A Bengali folktale tells of the evil snake who gave up violence.[12] All too soon the boys who lived nearby discovered that the snake was harmless and they teased it mercilessly. One day the holy man visited his new student. Bleeding, torn, and dusty, the snake questioned his teacher about nonviolence.

The holy man shook his head and said, "Just because I said you couldn't bite people didn't mean you couldn't hiss at them!"

Gandhi's philosophical formulation of nonviolent resistance powerfully affected the Indian world view. Yet Gandhi did not mean that "nonviolence" implied passivity and inaction.

"Non-violence is an extremely active force," Gandhi wrote. "It has no room for cowardice or even weakness. There is hope for a violent man to be some day non-violent, but there is none for a coward."[13]

Many Indian religions stress that action is necessary to salvation. For the Sikh, the act of thinking on God's name and his word discovers the right path. Islam teaches that human acts transform individual fate. Hinduism, Jainism, and Buddhism agree that renunciation of desire means a terrible struggle with oneself, for physical nature fights against it.

Women's struggles to become "good wives" also rest on moral activism and positive self-discipline.[14] The householder situates himself as the "man-in-the-world" who embraces its concerns through morally informed choices and acts.[15] The hero acts in a considered, disciplined fashion.

EXPERIENCE

In its learning, the child develops a self that can discriminate experience. Human bodies have senses, passions, and lusts. Experience can overwhelm the individual and distract from his or her duty. Indians divide this category into sensate or intellectual experience and the renunciation of experience. True experience and its opposite, renunciation, occur though disciplined action. Both are paths to self-realization. Many religious movements have taught that anyone can experience the divine, hence all are equal.

Most notoriously, tantric cults found eroticism to be the most intense human experience. Intense experience—which might also include violating many social taboos, such as drunkenness—can be used to lead the individual to an awareness that this, too, is illusion, and must be transcended. In a different—and far more popular—vein emotion is celebrated as an important aspect of life. Metaphors of emotion artistically depict the relationship between devotee and deity. The twelfth-century Sanskrit poem *Love Song of the Dark Lord* celebrates the love between Krishna and his love Radha. The language is deeply infused with emotional passion as Radha cries out and suffers from his absence.[16]

Sufi ritual chanting and movements provide intensive experience of divinity for Muslims. Intense emotional states are achieved through possession by a saint. For members of all religions, devotional singing and prayer meetings provide experiences that orient them to the divine.

The question for most people is how to organize experience in daily life. One should enjoy family life, yet not be a slave to its pleasures. Parents love their children—but with disciplined detachment. Too much of anything creates problems. In Rajasthani villages, men look down on the one who succumbs to opium addiction and can no longer fulfill his family duties.

Renunciation requires individuals to embrace an ascetic life, to give up sensation, desire, and ego. Great ascetics may literally starve themselves to death. Householders have duties to their parents and to their children that may not easily be set aside to take up the path of renunciation. Householders practice renunciation in smaller ways, such as by a fast. Nevertheless the guiding principle is balance in all these aspects of life.

The Indian world view incorporates a strong practical sense. Indians in all walks of life incorporate a sense of situation and context that guides behavior. In Bengal, a folktale tells of the holy man who practiced asceticism for twelve long years. He finally could walk on water and proudly showed this to a second holy man. This holy man replied that it had taken him twelve years to accomplish what anyone could do by paying the ferryman.[17]

The world view's emphasis on duty, action, and experience is consonant with modernity. Political change has shifted the balance of world view away from the Brahman-centered perspective that dominated at midcentury, to one that reflects newer groups' perspectives. The issue at hand is whose idioms, and which symbols.

NOTES

1. The Dalit literature approach highlights these issues. See Ranajit Guha and Gayatri Chakravorty Spivak, eds., *Selected Subaltern Studies* (New York: Oxford University Press, 1988) and particularly the key essay by Spivak, "Can the Subaltern Speak?" pp. 271–313 in Cary Nelson and Larry Grossberg, eds., *Marxism and the Interpretation of Culture* (Urbana: University of Illinois Press, 1988).

2. Stanley N. Kurtz, *All the Mothers Are One: Hindu India and the Cultural Reshaping of Psychoanalysis* (New York: Columbia University Press, 1992).

3. Alan R. Beals, *Gopalpur: A South Indian Village* (New York: Holt, Rinehart & Winston, 1962).

4. James M. Freeman, *Untouchable: An Indian Life History* (Stanford: Stanford University Press, 1979).

5. T.N. Madan, *Non-Renunciation: Themes and Interpretations of Hindu Culture* (Oxford: Oxford University Press, 1988).

6. Clarence Maloney, "Don't Say 'Pretty Baby' Lest You Zap It with Your Eye—The Evil Eye in South Asia," pp. 102–148 in C. Maloney, ed., *The Evil Eye* (New York: Columbia University Press, 1976).

7. McKim Marriott, ed., *India through Hindu Categories* (New Delhi: Sage Publications, 1990).

8. Ayurvedic medicine is the traditional Hindu medical system. Unani medicine is the traditional Islamic medical system. Indian medical alternatives include homeopathy and allopathy, Western medical systems.

9. E. Valentine Daniel, *Fluid Signs: Being a Person the Tamil Way* (Berkeley: University of California Press, 1984).

10. U.R. Anantha Murthy, *Samskara*, trans. by A.K. Ramanujan (New York. Oxford University Press, 1978).

11. Barbara Stoller Miller, *The Bhagavad-Gita: Krishna's Counsel in Time of War* (New York: Bantam Books, 1986).

12. Retold as "Nonviolence" in A.K. Ramanujan, ed., *Folktales from India* (New York: Pantheon Books, 1991), p. 233.

13. Cited in Stephen Hays, *Sources of Indian Tradition*, Vol. II (New York: Columbia University Press, 1988), p. 255.

14. Lindsay Harlan, *Religion and Rajput Women* (Berkeley: University of California Press, 1992).

15. T.N. Madan, *Non-Renunciation*, pp. 45–47.

16. Jayadeva, 12th century, *Love Song of the Dark Lord: Jayadeva's Gitagovinda*, trans. and ed. by Barbara Stoler Miller (New York: Columbia University Press, 1977), p. 89.

17. Retold as "Walking on Water" in A.K. Ramanujan, ed., *Folktales from India* (New York: Pantheon Books, 1991), p. 262.

SUGGESTED READINGS

Daniel, E. Valentine. *Fluid Signs: Being a Person the Tamil Way* (Berkeley: University of California Press, 1984).

Embree, Ainslie T. and Stephen Hay, eds. *Sources of Indian Tradition*, Volumes I and II, 2nd ed. (New York: Columbia University Press, 1988).

Kakar, Sudhir. *The Colors of Violence: Cultural Identities, Religion, and Conflict* (Chicago: University of Chicago Press, 1996).

Kurtz, Stanley N. *All the Mothers Are One: Hindu India and the Cultural Reshaping of Psychoanalysis* (New York: Columbia University Press, 1992).

Lynch, Owen, ed. *Divine Passions: The Social Construction of Emotion in India* (Berkeley: University of California Press, 1990).

Madan, T.N. *Non-Renunciation: Themes and Interpretations of Hindu Culture* (Delhi: Oxford University Press, 1987).

Trawick, Margaret. *Notes on Love in a Tamil Family* (Berkeley: University of California Press, 1990).

4

Art and Literature

THE QUESTION, "what do Indians mean when they say that something is 'beautiful,' or that it is 'good,' " has many answers. These answers can change, especially in art and literature.

In eleventh-century Bengal, for example, devotees produced an image of Kali that depicted her as a coal-black, blocky figure stiffly posed atop her husband Shiva. Kali's three large, flaming eyes glared at the worshipper and her tongue hung almost to her breastbone. A necklace of skulls garlanded her bare form. Jackals crowded around her feet to lap up the dripping blood of her victims. Eighteenth-century Westerners who viewed Kali images were horrified by this image, one that Indians of this era found aesthetically satisfying.

In the early twentieth century, a new Kali image appeared.[1] This Kali was "sweet." Her figure posed naturally and her skin lightened from black to pale blue or gray. This Kali showed only the tip of her tongue behind large, shapely lips. She gained the lustrous, beguiling eyes of a Hindi film goddess, and donned a middle-class housewife's bangles and sari. Calendar art now portrayed a girlish Kali, whose mischievous expression recalled that other icon of popular art, the child Krishna.

In this case, "satisfaction" refers to the aesthetic response, emotional engagement. The Kali image is aesthetic for its viewers, because it evokes culturally meaningful themes—characteristics that it shares with other art forms and with literature. In fact, the definition of aesthetics as something that evokes an emotional response coincides with ancient Indian aesthetic theory.

This highlights the different feelings that art is supposed to draw out of its audience.

Three key themes help to make sense of India's hugely diverse arts and literatures. One, since the state has been so important in Indian history, the arts often reflect its influence, either to celebrate the state—or to resist it. Two, audiences often find meaning in ancient art and literature, as these are reinterpreted today. Three, new influences and inspiration stem from global culture. In the example of Kali, shifts in her image reflect her nature as a powerful female deity worshipped by middle-class and middle-class aspirant groups. Images of modernity, so important to these groups, are clearly displayed in Kali's new exterior.

First, in many cases, styles reflect political or cultural initiatives. This is as true for the nonelite arts, often called folk art, as it is for elite arts. The difference is that almost nothing is known about the development of nonelite arts.[2] Almost all documentation prior to the twentieth century is of elites and their aesthetic tastes.

Throughout the twentieth century, elites to a large extent defined nonelite arts either as vulgar (too bloody, too erotic) or as non–political folk art. This view discarded or ignored art and literary productions that upset elite expectations. Important aspects of nonelite arts, such as their dimension of social commentary, were overlooked or romanticized. Understanding the cultural meaning of art and literature today now involves examining this wide context.

Second, many ancient works resonate with today's concerns. Rising literacy among the younger generation and inexpensive translations into regional languages bring the classics and folktales to a far wider audience than before. Third, the arts face the impact of global culture. Shifts in consumer tastes promote artists' incorporation of global styles—or their effort to distinguish themselves from this, by developing purer, more "authentic" styles.

AESTHETICS

India's art and literature are both familiar and alien to Western eyes. A number of Indian animal tales are known in the West as *Aesop's Fables.* The English language would be impoverished without words such as jungle, pariah, mogul, mugger, and, of course, the "nabobs" of "nattering nabobs of negativism"[3] from the phrase coined by U.S. Vice President Spiro Agnew in a 1970 speech in San Diego. This phrase popularly now refers to nitpicking, nagging political commentators, who usually consider themselves pundits— knowledgeable ones. This last word, of course, is also of Indian origin! Yet Indian aesthetics possess distinctive qualities.

India's art is famously neither religious nor sacred. Indians do not neatly divide the universe into mutually exclusive sacred and secular realms.[4] Hindu temples often include nonsacred images. These remind worshippers that life's secular purposes of duty, action, and experience are equal to the religious purpose of salvation.

The social setting in which Indians enjoy art also differs from the West. There, museums and galleries mount art to focus attention on every detail. Guards hover to prevent anyone from touching the image. The museum is a hushed, solemn place. Art is "for the ages." Massive resources help preserve images in a pristine state.[5]

Much Indian art has been produced in the context of religious use. In a Hindu temple, for instance, the same image that might be open to the gaze in an art museum is hidden underneath a mound of garlands, jewelry, outfits, silver and gold foil, ghee, and red paste. Some images lead elaborately choreographed lives. The deity awakens in the morning, bathes, dresses, breakfasts, receives guests, enjoys entertainments, and is put to bed at night. All day, the temple bustles with the comings and goings of worshippers. Worshippers hold or touch images during some points in ritual. Worshippers don't just look at an image—the image looks back.

Some images are used only once. Festival clay or straw images are worshipped and then sunk into a river or pond. The same fate awaits the huge painted scroll used by the Rajasthani epic singer when it gets old and has absorbed too much supernatural power. Women's art often uses fragile cowdung paste and rice powder, which are destined to fade and to be replaced.

One way to approach aesthetics is to ask, "What do people put on their walls and in their homes?" The poorest home or shop probably features at least one inexpensive, colorful print or calendar depicting images such as multiarmed gods and goddesses, saints, chubby babies, and iridescent bouquets of flowers. Wall and floor paintings adorn a home's threshold, courtyard, and interior. A small metal or brass figure may be displayed on a shelf, separate from family shrines.

Middle class homes often feature miniatures painted on cloth, a shelf of wooden, brass, or shiny cast aluminum figurines, and displays of women's crochet and embroidery needlework. Items may include works distinctive to members of the minority groups: masks, bronzes, painted works on cloth, carved wooden toys and objects, and terracotta animals. Wealthy people hang original modern, classical, and folk art on their walls.

Ancient art scholars synthesized art theory in the third and fourth century *Natya Shastra*. This stated that art's purpose is to provoke aesthetic feelings and sentiments. There are nine basic sentiments (1) erotic; (2) odious; (3) wondrous; (4) comic; (5) pathetic; (6) furious; (7) heroic; (8) terrible; and (9) quiescent.[6]

Artists combine these sentiments to achieve a distinct mood. For example, in the ninth century Chola state, sculptors developed the image of dancing Shiva, captured in the frenzy of the dance that creates the universe. Shiva raises one knee, and flings wide his four arms within a nimbus of flame. His foot is barely poised atop a demon—yet Shiva's eyes are serene and inwardly focused. A viewer grasps the stillness within frenzied action, a dualism that emphasizes Shiva's role as both destroyer and creator.

Figures lift their chests and torsos, ready to exhale. Surfaces are taut as if swelling from within.[7] Shiny paint, ghee, and foil emphasize surface form. Curves focus attention on movement, such as the three-bend pose of the female figure. She lifts her torso to one side and cocks her hip on the other. One knee bends in front of the other, while her raised and coiled arms extend these movements.

Artists often emphasize eyes, such as the almond-eyed beauties of Mughal and Rajput miniature painting, or a deity's huge saucer-shaped eyes. The finishing touch on an image destined for sacred use is that its eyes are "opened" to waken the deity.

Symbols of royalty include the lion, elephant, horse, bull, and fly whisk. Hindu iconography features creatures that are part human and part animal. Fertility and good luck symbols include the woman and tree motif, an embracing man and woman, and mango trees. Hand gestures convey meanings.[8] The uplifted hand, palm facing forward and fingers slightly bent toward the viewer, is the symbol of benediction. Westerners will also recognize the prayer gesture, which originated here.

Buddhists regard the Bodhi tree as a symbol of enlightenment, the wheel as a representation of the law. Jain iconography features holy men. Many Jain symbols resemble those of Hindu figures: the same folk images inspired both.[9] Elongated arms and legs symbolize Jain figures' supernatural nature. Holy men stand or sit in a lotus position. They never lie prone. Saucy female figures and fertility symbols enliven Jain art. And unlike Hindu art, Jain art possesses no violent images, no bloodthirsty demons.

Indo-Islamic traditions elaborate geometric, floral, and calligraphic motifs. Sculptors did not model the human form. Perhaps the most celebrated achievement of Indo-Islamic art was the development of wonderfully detailed miniature painting.

The artists who created—and who today create—aesthetic images worked on diverse projects for patrons who are members of different religions. Most artists usually worked—and still work—anonymously as members of specialized groups. These share an aesthetic ideal, which acts as a guideline. Patron wishes, tastes, and pocketbook also affect a finished product. Artists may refuse to produce images that violate their standards.

Interactive artist and storyteller, Rajasthan. Courtesy of the author.

Literary aesthetics focus on sound patterns, rhythm, rhyme, and the interplay of layered meanings conveyed by a word or a sequence of words. Literature traditionally divides into three genres: history, poetry, and stories of the old days. Poetry includes forms that have strict rules as to syllables, meter, rhyme, and content, plus free- and blank-verse forms. Some free- and blank-verse forms were developed over 1,000 years ago. Repetition, meter, internal rhyme, external rhyme, and alliteration heighten the impact of verbal arts.

In addition to professional storytellers, bards, and reciters, ordinary people tell stories in everyday settings. Jokes, proverbs, and riddles abound. Every village or neighborhood has at least one person who tells stories with style and verve. Everything is grist for this mill: politics, government officials, the foibles of tourists, Hindi films, and the latest news.

ART TO THE FOURTH CENTURY

Prehistoric art ranges from simple rock carvings (ca. 5500 B.C.E.) found near Bhopal to the sophisticated forms of Harappa (ca. 2600–1900 B.C.E.).[10] These sharply defined figures dance across the surface of seals and in bronze castings. One figure suggests a seated yogi—though until Harappan writing is deciphered, no one knows its meaning to the Harappans.

Ashokan pillars (ca. 272–232 B.C.E.) are towering shafts, topped by bell-shaped forms that support seated animals. The most famous pillar depicts four lions seated back-to-back. Other royal animals decorate the supporting platform beneath the lions. This motif was used for the seal of the Indian republic and on Indian money.

Originally, the Buddha was not shown in human form. At the Great Stupa of Sanchi an opened parasol and footsteps reveal his presence. West Asian influences appear in first century C.E. Indo-Greek art. At Mathura, on the Gangetic plain, a vigorous school developed this style. In the Indo-Greek kingdom called Gandhara in northwest India, Buddha wore flowing robes, like a toga, and dressed his hair in tight curls. Mathura's Buddha had a small curly head of hair, topped by his wisdom bump, a bun-like feature, and halo.

Sculptors indicated perspective through the convention that figures at the bottom of a panel were closest to the viewer, while those at the top were the farthest away. Narrative carvings were arranged chronologically or geographically so that viewers could read the story in a single panel.

During the Gupta period, Buddhist, Jain, and Hindu iconography coalesced.[11] Stylized angular figures, such as the image of Vishnu in his boar incarnation (ca. 401), gradually acquired curves. The Buddha began to look inward instead of directly at the viewer. His robes thinned to a sheer transparency and revealed his body shape, which now symbolized his inner state. Sculptors added a host of new Buddhist characters such as the female figures called Taras.

FIFTH TO TWELFTH CENTURY

A naturalistic style appeared at sixth-century Ajanta. This featured realistic paintings of secular scenes, such as kingly courts and everyday life. A new architectural movement, the free-standing temple, provided an important setting for stone sculpture. In tenth-century South India, sculptors of the Chola state produced bronze figures with long, rounded, loosely jointed legs and arms. This stylized, yet relaxed, modeling was accentuated by the images' finely detailed jewelry and adornments. An important Chola patron, Queen Sembayan Mahadevi (ca. 941–1006), supported art during her long widowhood.

Sculpted fertility figures are most exuberant at Khajuraho's Kandariya temple (ca. 954). This Shiva temple has drawn enormous speculation, because of its erotic images. Mother goddesses guard the base. Female figures flank four-armed deities to emphasize fertility and good luck. The erotic vignettes powerfully present the earthy power of the erotic rasa.

Jain temples feature nature images.[12] Mount Abu's eleventh century Vi-
mala temple ceilings are elaborate white marble rosettes, floral combinations,
and geometric figures, which represent the celestial sphere. Artists also produced illustrated Jain texts, letters, and magical mandalas. These highlight
boldly outlined figures on flat backgrounds.

THIRTEENTH TO EIGHTEENTH CENTURY

Mughal emperor Humayun recruited Persian artists for a workshop at his
court.[13] Humayun's successor, Emperor Akbar collected European, Chinese,
and Southeast Asian art. He encouraged his artists to develop a highly realistic
style of miniature painting. Its subject matter was vast: historical events, city
scenes, rural landscapes, portraits, animals, incidents from the lives of saints,
and even replicas of European works.

Rajasthan and the Punjab Hills also emerged as important centers of miniature painting. The Rajasthani courts at Mewar, Kishangarh, and Kota developed distinctive styles. Kota's Sheikh Taju, the late-eighteenth-century
master of animal portraits, used an almost modern style of swift, fluid brush
strokes such as in his famed painting *Tiger Hunt*.

European art influences were most intense in the colonies. In Goa, Indian
artists reinterpreted madonnas and saints, softening baroque sculpture to suit
local taste. British-dominated areas produced a hybrid style termed "Company Art." Subjects include British depictions of Indian painters at work and
Indian paintings of British artists at work! Patrons included Mary, Lady
Impey, wife of the first Chief Justice of Calcutta's Supreme Court. She com-
missioned many realistic nature studies by painter Shaikh Zayn al-Din. The
Nawab of Arcot, for his part, had Francis Swain Ward (1734–1794) paint
portraits for his collection.

Europe's Romantic Movement influenced painters in India to focus on
the picturesque, such as evocative landscapes and ruined monuments. In
addition to the professional artists who visited India, generations of amateur
artists filled sketchbooks. Emily Eden (1797–1869), sister to Lord Auckland,
Governor-General in the 1840s, was noted for her portraits and watercolor
sketches.

Pilgrims to the Kali temple in Calcutta snapped up souvenir paintings.
Called Kalighat paintings, these feature lively, brightly colored mythological
and secular subjects. One popular theme was caricatures of civil service employees with a fondness for bureaucratic red tape and hypocritical priests,
depicted performing various infamous acts.

NINETEENTH TO MID-TWENTIETH CENTURY

New patrons, art movements, and technologies make it possible to speak of the nineteenth century as the beginning of modern art in India.[14] Photography, introduced in the 1840s, eventually displaced portrait painters. Print technologies led to mass production. Modern art styles stimulated new aesthetics. Nationalism encouraged interest in folk and pre-Islamic art.

Early photography paralleled painted subjects, such as portraits, scenic views, archaeological monuments, architecture, and significant occasions. Raja Deen Dayal and Sons, the court photographer of the Nizam of Hyderabad in the 1870s, even opened a women-only studio. The firm gained the honor of hanging a plaque announcing, "By Appointment, Photographer to Her Imperial Majesty, Queen Victoria."

The European school of Academic Naturalism suggested new modes of representation. Painter Raja Ravi Varma (1848–1906) became the first Indian to achieve international fame. His naturalistic depictions of Hindu deities in oil on canvas were immediately popular.

Western art colleges were established at Chennai in 1850, Calcutta in 1854, and Mumbai in 1857. Artists trained here discovered that the general public had a powerful appetite for this art's images of deities and scenes from popular tales. Graduates working at the Calcutta Art Studio catered to this demand by mass-producing images of mythological themes.

Elite artists became engrossed in nationalism by the end of the nineteenth century. Archaeological discoveries at Ajanta and excavation of Gupta sites promoted knowledge of these periods. Agreement grew that Gupta art comprised India's classical art. Sadly for Indians, many Gupta era sculptures could be viewed only in European museums, prizes of empire.

Important figures during the late nineteenth and early twentieth centuries include the Tagore brothers, Abanindranath (1871–1951) and Rabindranath (1861–1942), who became India's most important figure in the arts. Abanindranath Tagore integrated global influences such as Art Nouveau and Japanese art with Indian art in an effort to create new aesthetic modes. His painting *Bharat Mata* (1905) depicted India as a young sari-clad woman. The image became iconic for the Nationalists. The Tagores' home hosted artists' gatherings, which soon became known as the Bichitra club. Later, art formed an important component at the school at Santiniketan. Soon, a Bengal School of art emerged, which blended modern and folk art motifs. Important artists of this movement include Amrita Sher-Gil (1913–1941) and Jamini Roy (1887–1972).

By midcentury, a group of artists in Mumbai propounded a muscular style influenced by French impressionism and German expressionism. In the late

1940s, these artists formed the Progressive Artists Group. This stimulated several international careers. Goanese Francis Newton Souza (b. 1924) became known for his irreverent paintings of Catholics and the upper classes. The group's most successful member, Maqbool Fida Husain (b. 1915), produced canvases in a similar vein as Pablo Picasso.

ART SINCE THE MID-TWENTIETH CENTURY

The nineteenth-century discovery of archaeological sites that predated the development of Indo-Islamic cultures energized artists' search for authenticity. In the twentieth century, the non-elite arts have played much the same role. Elites have defined which folk arts they pick up as influences and which they ignore. Thus, some are seen as national heritage treasures, and others are overlooked as vulgar, obscene, or inauthentic.

Elite artists, those who show in galleries that cater to upper-class audiences, now participate in a well-developed niche, comparable to that of artists in the West. Nonelite artists find that industrially produced items have replaced local arts in many cases, or that mass consumer tastes have displaced local aesthetics. Inability to make a livelihood has pushed many members of traditional artist groups into other occupations.

India's national and state governments have supported arts heritage conservation, with institutions such as the Crafts Museum in New Delhi, established in 1953. Efforts to support nonelite artists, such as through folk arts exhibits, have expanded the artists' repertoires through exposure to national and global tastes. Tourism has provided an important market through state-sponsored institutions and private dealers. Most recently, there have been efforts to construct "artists' villages" affiliated with museums, where the artists demonstrate and sell their work.

One vexing issue related to these efforts is the lack of connection between the artist and the art consumer. The result in most cases has been simplification of images and reduction of artists' repertoires to a few signature items. While some observers decry "airport art," it does support artists, who must eat.

Some art is produced by professional specialists, others by nonspecialists. Professionals include the painters who produce the small, painted scroll used by Bengali storytellers. Painters in Udaipur, Rajasthan, decorate house facades with bright images of elephants, warriors, and auspicious females. Nearby, potters make red or black fired clay plaques depicting deities. These images are supposed to be painted in bright colors and installed in shrines and temples. Collectors snap up these plaques before they are painted and display them in this nude state. Another beloved form is the terracotta horse image, such as at Tamil Nadu's Aiyannar shrines.

In Orissa, artists near Puri produce two genres of paintings, one for tourists, and the second aimed at pilgrims who wish to take home a painting to use in worship.[15] Artists evaluate these works in terms of factors such as the sure, steady hand that draws the line, the balance between foreground figures and background ornamentation, and attention to the details of each figure or scene. Whereas artists find the tourist-oriented paintings a good genre for experimentation, elite experts decry much of this as departing from traditional themes and values.

Women's art is most visible in the paintings that adorn walls and courtyard floors with auspicious white, ocher, and red geometric figures. These compositions celebrate life-cycle events, commemorate festivals, and punctuate life with good-luck wishes. In Rajasthan, the three basic designs are called "town," "market," and "well." Women center the largest motif in the courtyard floor and surround it with smaller motifs called footprints. In this way, the world outside enters the household.

In Tamil Nadu, women's designs cluster at the threshold. The design emerges from a single continuously drawn line that loops into a trellis-like pattern. Each loop has a tiny red seed at its center, symbol of life. Dots and wave-like figures, representing serpents, symbolize fertility and the supernatural power of the Goddess.

Brides in the Mithila region of Bihar decorate their marriage chamber with a large, colorful painted line drawing. Good-luck wishes, fertility symbols, and depictions of auspicious deities and couples highlight the painting. Maithili paintings are now also painted on paper and are popular with collectors.

LITERATURE TO THE FOURTH CENTURY

Ancient oral literatures appear to have made the jump to written form sometime between the era of Ashoka and the Gupta empire. The oldest readable texts are Ashoka's third century B.C.E. edicts. Knowledge of other texts relies on scholarly reconstructions and comparison with sources such as coins, archaeological sites, and art.

Written and oral traditions often have influenced one another, but differences remain. Oral arts are rooted in the moment and in the relationships of speakers and hearers. Oral texts create aesthetic patterns with set themes, motifs, rhythm, repetition, and poetry. Repetition numbs readers—but it delights listeners. Few written versions of oral texts, outside those produced by professional folklorists, include this material. And oral texts are fluid. Each performance is always a little bit different from any other performance.

An orally transmitted text may be reoriented when its tellers learn about written versions, especially those produced by elites. The hero of a local epic proves to be "really" a high Hindu deity. Many written texts have oral parallels. In practice, until the very recent past, written texts were produced and consumed by elites, whose perspective and aesthetic values dominated these works. The earliest examples of these would be the Sanskrit hymns and ritual manuals that express the Vedic perspective, and the third century B.C.E. edicts of Emperor Ashoka.

Two north Indian epics, the *Mahabharata* and the *Ramayana*, took their literary form around the fourth century C.E. Ilanko Atika's south Indian epic *Cilappatikaram* ("The Jeweled Anklet") represents an important independent tradition. Playwrights such as Kalidasa produced enduring works such as *Meghaduta* ("The Cloud Messenger") and *Shakuntala*, named for its heroine. A third favorite play was *Mrcchakatika* ("The Little Clay Cart"), attributed to King Shudraka. This is the story of a poor Brahman merchant who falls in love with a noble courtesan. Popular literature includes the animal tales of the *Panchatantra* and the Buddhist *Jataka* tales. These works' enduring appeal is seen in retellings, such as the 1980s television series of the two north Indian epics, comic book versions, and websites.

The *Mahabharata*, some 100,000 lines long, is regarded as India's greatest epic. This tells the story of the Pandava brothers and the war of succession between them and their cousins. The five Pandava brothers lost their throne in a crooked gambling game. Inexorably the war arrives and is fought at Kurukshetra. Right wins out, but at a terrible cost.

The *Ramayana* is a rousing epic of the god Ram. Key events hinge on the abduction of his wife, the virtuous Sita, by the demon Ravana. Popular episodes include the monkey army's aid to Ram in the invasion of Sri Lanka, where Ravana is holed up with his captive, and Ravana's failed effort to ravish Sita.

Cilappatikaram, in contrast, deals with ordinary people.[16] A wife is left by her husband for an irresistible courtesan. The husband's involvement leads to disaster: he is accused of stealing a gold anklet and executed by the king. Her heart enraged by this injustice, the wife rips off her right breast and hurls it at the city with a curse, causing the city to burn down. She becomes a goddess and ascends to heaven.

FIFTH TO TWELFTH CENTURY

A movement away from Sanskrit to vernacular languages emerged, stimulated by the development of *bhakti* traditions, whcih featured songs and poems celebrating the individual's longing for union with the deity. Bhakti movements emerged first in south India, then moved north. Tamil poets also created a rich vein of secular poetry. The ninth through twelfth centuries were significant for the development of the Tamil, Telugu, and Kannada languages. In Karnataka, tenth- through twelfth-century poets developed a form of free verse.

The most influential poem was the twelfth-century Jayadeva's *Gitagovinda* ("Love Song of the Dark Lord"), composed in Sanskrit. The poem rapidly spread throughout India.[17] Earthy, powerful language explores the artistic sentiment of eroticism, from longings through fulfillment. The poem expresses the believer's desire for union with the deity and desolation when he is absent.

THIRTEENTH TO EIGHTEENTH CENTURY

Development of regional languages intensified in the thirteenth through eighteenth centuries. Bhakti literatures continued to develop. The interaction with Islam—now also developing its distinctive cultural focus within India—intensified this process. A counterpart to the *bhakti* movements, which emphasized the common nature of all humans and religions, was the elaboration of institutions of sacred kingship in Hindu-ruled zones of south and eastern India. These emphasized hierarchy and relied upon ritual specialists who sustained Sanskrit traditions.

Many *bhakti* poets are recited today. These include Guru Nanak (1469–1539), founder of the Sikh religion; Sur Das (ca. 1485–1503); Meera Bai (ca. 1516–1546); Kabir (1440–1518); and Tulsi Das (1532–1623), whose works have been the most influential. Sur Das composed in *Braj Bhasha*, a form of Hindi associated with Mathura and devotion to Krishna.[18] Little is known of the historical Meera Bai beyond her status as a Rajput princess. Meera Bai abandoned her earthly husband to devote her life to adoration of Krishna, who she felt was her true husband. Her songs passed down in medieval Hindi, Rajasthani, and Gujarati.

Kabir (1440–1518) said that God was for everyone. He challenged the religious establishment and religious orthodoxy. In "The World Is Mad," Kabir criticized what he saw as mindless ritual, the Hindus bathing in the early morning and worshipping rocks, the Muslims men reading holy books, and the yogis, whom Kabir denounced as hypocrites. Kabir especially deplored religious violence.

Tulsidas retold the story of the Ramayana in his *Ramacharitamanasa.* Its plain, vivid language was hugely popular. Many of today's Ramayana performance traditions use this text.

Indo-Islamic genres also developed. One genre tells of a hero's adventures. Highest acclaim was reserved for the poetic Urdu-language form called a *ghazal.* Poets developed this to a high art, using a simple basic structure of a sequence of two-line rhyming couplets with internal meter and alliteration.[19] The *ghazal* genre expanded to encompass diverse themes ranging from love to social protest.

The first important Indo-Islamic poet was Khusrau, the pen name for Amir Dihlavi (1253–1325). All the Indo-Persian poets, including Mughal emperors, used pen names. The last emperor Bahadur Shah (1775–1862), composed under the pen name Zafar (Victory). The two most distinguished poets wrote virtually at the end of the Mughal period: Mir (Mir Taqi, ca. 1722–1810) and Ghalib (Mirza Asadullah Khan, 1797–1869), whose career as poet laureate to the last Mughal emperor was interrupted by the failed rebellion of 1857.

Literature also reflected the foreign presence. Indian views of the foreigners in their midst can be read in *The Private Diary of Ananda Ranga Pillai* by Pondicherry merchant A.R. Pillai (1709–1761). Abu Talib Khan (ca. 1752–1806) wrote about his trip to England in *The Travels of Mirza Abu Taleb Khan* (1810). The first Indian author in English, Dean Mahomet (1759–1851), penned his *Travels with the East India Company,* based on his army experiences between 1769 and 1784.

British interest in Indian literatures also grew, particularly after the announcement by Sir William Jones (1746–1794) that Sanskrit was related to European languages. The Asiatic Society of Bengal, which he founded, promoted interest in the comparative study of language, translations of texts and inscriptions, and investigation of archaeological sites.

NINETEENTH TO MID-TWENTIETH CENTURY

In the early nineteenth century, Rammohan Roy (1772–1833) established vernacular language presses and translated Sanskrit texts into Bengali and English. He founded the Hindu College (1816), which introduced English-language teaching and curriculum to Indian students. Roy's efforts stimulated the growth of Bengali as a written literary language, then considered inferior to Persian and Sanskrit. Roy sparked the important literary and cultural movement of the Bengal Renaissance, and is called the father of modern India.

At midcentury, new literary genres such as the novel began to take root. The masters of the *ghazal* poetic form, associated with Indo-Islamic courts, confronted difficulties after 1857 in the ensuing era of delegitimation of Islam within India. Print technology, Western-influenced colleges, and literary societies each promoted change, in their own ways.

Indian authors began to develop the novel. In Bengal, Bankimchandra

Chatterjee (1838–1894) published several historical romances such as his *Anandamath* ("The Abbey of Bliss" [1882]), about the 1779 Sannyasi rebellion in Bengal. Novelists working in Marathi, Tamil, Urdu, and Hindi produced works on themes ranging from military adventures to romances and detective stories. The most renowned nineteenth-century novel is the Urdu language *Umrao Jan Ada* (1899), by Mirza Muhammad Hadi Ruswa (1857–1931). This is the tale of a Lucknow courtesan caught up in the tumultuous months of 1857, and of her life in the revolt's aftermath. *Umrao Jan Ada* inspired many retellings, including film versions, in the late twentieth century.

The failed rebellion had the most telling impact on the poets who had been attached to the Indo-Islamic courts. The famous poet Ghalib (1797–1869) lost both friends and patronage. Libraries and important collections of poetry were destroyed.

This sense of a lost world is evident too in the works of Urdu poets such as Azad (1830–1910) and Hali (1837–1914). They established new patrons in institutions such as the Punjab Society. In 1874 the two announced a drive to modernize Urdu poetry. The poet was now to speak directly to the listener and to avoid obscure and cliquish references. Another response to this crisis of Urdu-language arts and the Indo-Islamic subculture arose as Sir Sayyid Ahmad Khan (1817–1898) created the Muhammadan Anglo-Oriental College at Aligarh in 1875.[20] Efforts to revitalize intellectual life included founding literary journals, and establishing poetry and writing prizes.

Modern Indian writing came sharply to Western attention when Rabindranath Tagore (1861–1941) received the 1913 Nobel Prize for literature. His most acclaimed work *Gitanjali*, "Song Offerings," published first in 1909 in Bengali and then in English in 1912, affirms life and trust.

Modern Hindi began its development in forms such as the novel, particularly the works of Premchand (1881–1936).[21] His style was social realism and his field was village life, seen in works such as *Godaan* ("The Gift of a Cow" [1936]). The generation of writers born as the nineteenth century turned to the twentieth century wrote of social concerns such as in the work of Mulk Raj Anand (b. 1905), particularly his *Untouchable* (1935), which tells of a day in the life of an outcaste sweeper. Another important novel is the Malayali language *Chemmeen* ("Shrimps" [1956]), by Thakazhi Sivasankara Pillai (1912–1999). Among these social realist works, the 1951 *Autobiography of an Unknown Indian*, by Nirad C. Chaudhuri (1897–1999), gained international recognition.

LITERATURE SINCE THE MID-TWENTIETH CENTURY

Multiple strands of development characterize Indian writing and oral literatures after independence. Prominent themes are partition and the encounter with the West. Poetry such as the *ghazal* has proven riveting to a growing audience. Oral literatures received the first sustained scholarly attention during this period and range across a wide number of genres: folktales, proverbs, epic masterworks, poetry, jokes, and stories.

Partition's impact appears in stories such as Saadat Hasan Manto's "Toba Tek Singh," which deals with the division of an insane asylum's inmates between Pakistan and India. Salman Rushdie's Booker Prize–winning novel *Midnight's Children* (1981) imagined the moment of India's birth. Rushdie counted as most influential of Indian fiction writers in the last two decades of the twentieth century. His magical realist style in this and later novels such as *The Satanic Verses* (1988) has had a tremendous influence on the most recent group of Indian writers.

Social realism continued as an important strand in works such as Kannada-language author U.R. Anantha Murthy's *Samskara*. Writing in a much more lyrical vein, R.K. Narayan's immensely popular tales of the fictional village of Malgudi span the century, from *Swami and Friends* (1925), to *Malgudi Days* (1982) and engage themes of oppression—with his signature light touch—to the discontents of Westernization. Anita Desai's urban, middle-class protagonists must cope with the disjunctures between India and the West. This theme also engages Vikram Seth in his *A Suitable Boy* (1993) and Arundhati Roy in her Booker Prize–winning *The God of Small Things* (1998).

Beyond these works that reach to international audiences are works of literature that are much less known, such as poetry by Dalit authors who write of oppression, and regional-language authors working out of folk traditions.[22] These, in turn, prove a bridge to India's oral literatures, which include still-vital genres and traditions.

Oral epics include the Tamil-language *Elder Brother Story*, Telugu *Epic of Palnadu*, Hindi *Alha*, and Rajasthani *The Epic of Pabuji*.[23] These are set in regional kingdoms and feature local rulers and deities. The epic *Pabuji* is named for its hero, who gallops to the rescue astride his courageous black mare, "Black Saffron."[24] Pabuji is the younger son of a second wife. In Rajasthani lore, younger sons become bandits, while the oldest son becomes the lord. Pabuji's friends belong to many different social groups—also true to many young men's experience. Pabuji's adventures closely parallel those recited for a popular form of deity in the region whose monuments dot village landscapes, the spirit of a man killed protecting the cattle from rustlers. Pabuji's fate is to die saving the cows.

Animal folktales are a popular genre.[25] Animals include the lion, king of beasts. Brave but somewhat dimwitted, the lion's downfall lies in his self-importance and pride. His traditional enemy is the intelligent, industrious elephant. The hare is the underdog trickster who manipulates the powerful.

The low status, poor documentation, and relative invisibility of most of those who sustain contemporary oral literatures, combined with their move into new occupations and adoption of new values, are leading to immense cultural loss. Studies of oral arts show major trends to be simplification of texts, loss of repertoire, and modification of texts according to new standards observed from mass and popular sources.

NOTES

1. Rachel Fell McDermott, "Bengali Songs to Kali," pp. 55–76 in Donald S. Lopez, Jr., ed., *Religions of India in Practice* (Princeton: Princeton University Press, 1995).

2. Joanna Williams, "Criticizing and Evaluating the Visual Arts in India: A Preliminary Example," *Journal of Asian Studies* 47(1):3–28, 1988.

3. "Mugger" is from the Hindi "crocodile," which lies in wait for its victim.

4. Stella Kramrisch, *The Art of India through the Ages* (London: Phaedon, 1954), p. 10. Vidya Dehejia, "All Indian Art Is Religious," *Education about Asia* 1(1):5–9, 1996.

5. Western museums argued that they have more resources to devote to this than museums in the country of origin, hence refusals to repatriate selected items.

6. Vidya Dehejia, *Indian Art* (London: Phaidon, 1997).

7. Stella Kramrisch, *The Art of India: Indian Sculpture, Painting, and Architecture*, 3rd ed., (London: Phaidon Press, 1965).

8. The classic description is Ananda Coomaraswamy, *The Mirror of Gesture* (New Delhi: Munshiram Monoharlal, 1970 [orig. 1917]).

9. Pratapaditya Pal, *Peaceful Liberators: Jain Art from India* (New York: Thames & Hudson, 1994).

10. Roy C. Craven, *Indian Art: A Concise History* (New York: Thames & Hudson, 1997). Vidya Dehejia, *Indian Art* (London: Phaidon, 1997).

11. Joanna G. Williams, *The Art of Gupta India: Empire and Province* (Princeton: Princeton University Press, 1982).

12. Pal, *Peaceful Liberators.*

13. Stuart Cary Welch, *India: Art and Culture 1300–1900* (New York: Metropolitan Museum of Art, 1997).

14. Partha Mitter, *Art and Nationalism in Colonial India* (Cambridge: Cambridge University Press, 1997).

15. Helle Bundgaard, *Indian Art Worlds in Contention: Local, Regional and National Discourses on Orissan Patta Paintings* (Surrey, England: Curzon Press, 1999).

16. Ilankovatikal, [*Cilappatikaram*], *The Cilappatikaram of Ilanko Atikal: An Epic*

of South India, trans. by R. Parthasarathy (New York: Columbia University Press, 1992).

17. Jayadeva, son of Bhojadeva, *Love Song of the Dark Lord: Jayadeva's Gitagovinda*, ed. and trans. by Barbara Stoler Miller (New York: Columbia University Press, 1977).

18. John Stratton Hawley, *Sur Das: Poet, Singer, Saint* (Seattle: University of Washington Press, 1984).

19. Frances W. Pritchett, *Nets of Awareness: Urdu Poetry and Its Critics* (Berkeley: University of California Press, 1994).

20. David Lelyveld, *Aligarh's First Generation* (Princeton: Princeton University Press, 1978).

21. David Rubin, *The World of Premchand: Selected Stories* (Bloomington: Indiana University Press, 1969).

22. Mulk Raj and Eleanor Zelliot, eds., *An Anthology of Dalit Literature* (New Delhi: Gyan Publishing House, 1992).

23. Stuart H. Blackburn, Peter J. Claus, Joyce B. Flueckiger, and Susan S. Wadley, eds., *Oral Epics in India* (Berkeley: University of California Press, 1989).

24. John D. Smith, *The Epic of Pabuji: A Study, Transcription and Translation* (Cambridge: Cambridge University Press, 1991).

25. Brenda E.F. Beck, Peter J. Claus, Praphulladatta Goswami, and Jawaharlal Handoo, eds., *Folktales of India* (Chicago: University of Chicago Press, 1987).

SUGGESTED READINGS

Beck, Brenda E.F., Peter J. Claus, Praphulladatta Goswami, and Jawaharlal Handoo, eds. *Folktales of India* (Chicago: University of Chicago Press, 1987).

Behl, Aditya and David Nicholls, eds. *The Penguin New Writing in India* (London: Penguin Books, 1992).

Dehejia, Vidya. *Indian Art* (London: Phaedon, 1997).

Embree, Ainslie T., ed. *Sources of Indian Tradition*, Vol. I (New York: Columbia University Press, 1988).

Flueckiger, Joyce Burkhalter. *Gender and Genre in the Folklore of Middle India* (Ithaca: Cornell University Press, 1996).

Hawley, John Stratton with Mark Juergensmeyer. *Songs of the Saints of India* (New York: Oxford University Press, 1988).

Hay, Stephen, ed. *Sources of Indian Tradition*, Vol. II (New York: Columbia University Press, 1988).

Miller, Barbara Stoler, trans. *The Bhagavad-Gita: Krishna's Counsel in Time of War* (New York: Bantam Books, 1986).

Mitter, Partha. *Art and Nationalism in Colonial India, 1850–1922* (Cambridge: Cambridge University Press, 1994).

Pal, Pratapaditya. *The Peaceful Liberators: Jain Art from India* (New York: Thames & Hudson, 1998).

Pritchett, Frances W. *Nets of Awareness: Urdu Poetry and Its Critics* (Berkeley: University of California Press, 1994).

Raj, Anand Mulk and Eleanor Zelliot (eds.), *An Anthology of Dalit Literature* (New Delhi: Gyan Publishing House, 1992).

Rubin, David. *The World of Premchand: Selected Stories of Premchand* (Bloomington: Indiana University Press, 1969).

Welch, Stuart Cary. *India: Art and Culture 1300–1900* (New York: Metropolitan Museum of Art, 1997).

5

Landscape and Architecture

INDIA is famous for its architecture. The Taj Mahal ranks among world monuments. The stunning white marble tomb of Mughal emperor Shah Jahan's favorite wife, built by him between 1632 and 1654, is often called one of the "wonders of the world." To Westerners, the Taj Mahal may be the ultimate exotic structure: its pearl-colored dome, flanked by four slender towers, floats between the land and sky, its ever-changing moods reflected in the long pool that connects it to a distant viewer's gaze. Visitors hear that the most magical time to see the Taj Mahal is on full-moon nights, when it seems cut loose from earthly bonds.

Yet if the Taj Mahal exemplifies romantic stereotypes of India, at first glance India's vernacular architectures, which use inexpensive materials such as grass, mud brick, cow-dung paste, corrugated tin sheeting, and heavy plastic tarp, seem a far cry from such cosmopolitan perfectionism. City planners grapple with slums and squatter settlements that ring India's four largest cities, Calcutta, Chennai (former Madras), Delhi, and Mumbai. Urban growth and its associated traffic congestion, air pollution, inadequate water treatment plants, and antiquated power grids create severe environmental hazards to humans and also to historic sites.[1] New industrial and residential suburbs encroach on farm land and engulf villages. In the 1990s, this process has transformed hamlets into villages and villages into small towns, the fastest-growing urban sector.[2]

As long as people have lived on the South Asian subcontinent, they have modified the environment, used available materials to create structures for shelter and work, and expressed their cultural values through architecture

Taj Mahal with Indian tourists. Courtesy of the author.

and landscape. Landscape, the physical imprint of culture on the environment, is important in looking at architecture for it links individual structures to two important elements: settlement pattern and sacred geography. These map the relationship of supernatural elements to the material world. In this sense, the Taj Mahal and even urban structures by contemporary architects share concepts of physical space and the sacred that are found in everyday practice.

Important architectural forms originated here. West Asian styles inspired the synthesis that became Mughal architecture. The British period introduced new technologies, landscapes, structures, and architectural motifs. The best new architecture blends cosmopolitan trends such as Modernism with vernacular forms.

Recent discoveries in archaeology and art history have added new information about the transformation of landscape and architecture over time. One of the great unfolding stories is the recovery of the social context of sites. Another positive trend is Indians' growing interest in historical preservation.[3] Groups such as the private voluntary organization, the Indian National Trust for Art and for Cultural Heritage (INTACH), are working to save endangered sites for future generations.

Waterfront steps, Varanasi. Courtesy of the author.

SHELTER AND SETTLEMENT PATTERN

Immediate practical issues of shelter in India involve climate, materials, and technology. India's climate includes uncomfortable extreme heat, torrential rains, humidity, and, in mountain zones, snow and seasonal cold. Diverse topography, vegetation, soil types, and other material variables influence the land use pattern, what can be built, and the forms it takes. This often intertwines with sacred concepts.

India's earliest urban centers were sited next to rivers, such as Harappa, built along the Indus River. Maritime trade stimulated ports. Water is critical for agricultural landscapes. Irrigation transforms dry lands into agricultural landscapes, such as the Thar desert's step wells, which descend several stories to reach underground channels, the small reservoirs and irrigation works that dot South India, and through large-scale projects such as the Indira Gandhi canal in the Thar desert.

Architectural signs of water's ritual significance include low stone steps that bathers descend into the water for a ritually purifying bath, and memorial pavilions near reservoirs and ponds. A small battery of shrines at water's edge in cities testify to these as meeting places of the sacred and the mundane.

Mountain terraces create fields where rice, barley, and other crops can be grown. In the old days, hereditary rulers backed their forts against steep hillsides or perched them on inaccessible hilltops.

Villages subdivide their lands by use: compact settlements and dispersed residences, crop lands, watersheds, forest, and pastures. Rural people are keenly aware of vegetation, soil type, and what can be done with landfill, contouring, organic manure, grazing, and crop rotation strategies. Yet a village map is also a map of its social relationships and history. A government proposal to install a new tube well can set off intense lobbying efforts by members of different neighborhoods, who want it closest to their own homes!

Indian rulers have never been shy about town planning. Harappan towns are the first known examples in the world. Ancient texts discuss city planning. Many rulers set up their own new capitals. Hindu rulers often laid out urban centers according to principles of sacred geography. New towns followed European models in the nineteenth century. In the twentieth century, industrial parks and suburban belts expanded beyond core urban centers.

Cities subdivide into commercial, industrial, government, and residential neighborhoods. These usually include a dense urban core that is often the old city, which contains historic residences, fortifications, and religious sites. Members of a single occupational, caste, or religious group sometimes are the exclusive residents of an urban neighborhood. Jodhpur's Brahman streets stand out, for example, because residents paint their houses blue. Ahmedabad's old town contains traditional gated neighborhoods. Each has its own elected leadership committee, rules of conduct, annual festival, and community chest supported by member dues and fines levied on members who break the regulations.[4] In fact, probably every neighborhood, whether a new squatter settlement or a village that reaches back generations, has similar institutions that are separate from the formal municipal government.

Traditionally, Indians distinguish between two categories of structures: *kaccha* and *pakka*.[5] *Kaccha* structures are made of perishable substances, such as wattle-and-daub (cow-dung paste over a wood or grass frame), adobe, bamboo, cardboard, grass thatch, and plastic sheeting. *Pakka* structures are built of permanent substances, such as stone, brick, concrete, glass, steel, and corrugated iron. Poor people live in *kaccha* houses. The rich live in *pakka* houses.

Indian architecture provides solutions to the problem of heat. Thick walls insulate interiors from the blazing summer sun. Surfaces covered with a plaster made up of cow dung, straw, and water dry to a pale tan color that increases sun reflectivity. Whitewashing or a plaster made of crushed shells performs the same function. Deep narrow slits, high vents, vaulted ceilings, decorative pierced screens, and loose thatch allow air to circulate.

Verandas (an Indian word) protect interior rooms from the afternoon sun.

Potter's house. Courtesy of the author.

Tall, narrow doors connect rooms to one another, permitting air to circulate. Shutters open or close to keep out hot air or let in cool breezes. Indians developed a forerunner of air conditioning. Wooden frames stuffed with sweet grass are hung over windows and periodically dowsed with water to create a cooling breeze. Middle- and upper-class homes and offices are equipped with swamp coolers and air conditioners.

Interior courtyards are often shaded by overhangs or interior porches, creating comfortable spots on the hottest afternoons. Rooms are multifunctional. Light furnishings such as string cots, flat-woven cotton rugs, small knee-height tables, and low wooden chairs can be moved from room to room to escape the heat or—in winter's cool days—to find a sunny warm spot. People often sleep on the roof to catch the faintest breeze on hot summer nights.

Areas that receive torrential monsoon rains pose the problem of coping with seasonal floods and heat. Bamboo is the material of choice in Meghalaya, in the humid northeast. These homes are built with raised floors and thick thatched roofs. Far to the south in Kerala, wooden houses meet the demands of high humidity and heat with their steeply pitched gables, upturned eaves, and deep verandas. Easily replaceable materials are also practical in low-lying, flood-prone zones: bamboo screens, mats, and straw thatch. These can be

House in Srinagar, Kashmir. Courtesy of Maxine Weisgrau.

rolled up, stowed, portaged to higher ground, or abandoned to the rains. Thick thatch, tile, and galvanized tin roofs with overhanging eaves protect these houses from moisture. Houses are built with a raised floor. Those fortunate to have a site on high ground can use *pakka* materials.

India's desert zone developed a distinctive mud architecture, used for houses, walls, sitting platforms, storage bins, and livestock pens for livestock. Thatch, tile, stone slab, or corrugated iron roofs protect these structures from rain, which—however infrequent—can melt away walls and horizontal surfaces. Rajasthan's vernacular architecture sets several round mud huts, sheds, and mud walls around a central court. The structures nearest the outer door are the men's area, while the inner areas are the women's domain. People rebuild these; women plaster over floors and walls and decorate these with vivid designs. Home is always a bit of a work in progress.

Square or rectangular timber-framed multistoried structures conserve heat in areas with seasonal cold. In Kashmir, three- or four-story wooden-framed houses stand on thick stone foundations, with wood framed and stone or brick-enclosed upper stories. Srinagar is best known for its houseboat dwellings, long wide structures built over a broad base. The wood architecture here includes mosques. Square, instead of the more rectangular shape common elsewhere, roofs stack one above the other in a style that reminds visitors of Japanese pagodas. Originally, these roofs were sodded with grass. Today corrugated metal is common.

SACRED GEOGRAPHY

The Indian perspective that supernatural phenomena are immanent in the material world is most evident in sacred geography. Qualities of sacredness attach to space, whether domestic architecture or the subcontinent itself. In intimate settings, this is seen as people take off their footwear when they move from public to domestic, private space. A house's threshold usually holds a dusty pile of sandals and shoes. Footwear comes off at temples, mosques, and tombs. Inside a house, the kitchen is its purest space. In some families, menstruating women and members of low-ranking castes do not go in there. The shady courtyard niche with its big clay pots of drinking water also may be off-limits.

An enormous range of geographical features possess sacred properties. Some are inherent and some are acquired through association with a holy individual or deity. Events can transform bits of landscape from mundane to sacred. Sometimes there is little agreement over the meaning of a sacred space and different groups present competing claims. The most notorious late-twentieth-century dispute over sacred space is the Babri Masjid–Ram Janmbhoomi issue at Ayodhya. Fundamentalist Hindus destroyed the mosque and propose to build a temple here to commemorate the deity Ram. Efforts to transform a small fort at Neemrana, Rajasthan, into a hotel have met demands that the site instead be restored as a memorial to Prithviraj, the last Hindu ruler of Delhi. Ironically, the Neemrana fort—sold to a hotelier by descendants in 1984—is often cited as one of India's best examples of historical preservation.[6] In recent years, neo-Buddhists have sought to liberate Buddhist sites from Hindu practices, a process that also took place among Punjab's Sikhs early in the twentieth century. The Archaeological Survey of India, keeper of India's monuments, often finds itself caught between competing demands of preservationists and those who seek new uses for sites.[7]

Conflicts such as these obscure the important fact that different religious groups often peacefully share sacred space. In some cases, different groups of worshippers use the same temple at the same time, but focus on different deities.[8] Shifts in interest by worshippers can redefine religious sites, such as when a new deity takes over a temple. Saints' shrines welcome visitors of many faiths. The elasticity of religious practice spills over into built environments, which reflect shared understandings of sacred geography and aesthetics.

South Indian temple. Courtesy of Maxine Weisgrau.

The most famous sacred form is the mandala, shared among Buddhists, Hindus, and others. The mandala's basic principle is that less sacred elements converge to a sacred center. The mandala may be drawn as a series of concentric rings, or as a grid of squares in which the innermost nine represent the core. The cardinal points, north, south, east, and west, along with the division of urban space into eastern and western halves, have special symbolic meaning.

The logic of the mandala can be identified in Varanasi, Hinduism's most sacred city.[9] Here, hundreds of thousands of pilgrims annually bathe in the purifying waters of the Ganges River. The Ganges is both river and the goddess called Mother Ganga. She is venerated at her headwaters and where she flows into the Bay of Bengal. Her passage through Kashi, as Varanasi is called by the pious, represents a sacred crossing point between the realms of the sacred and the mundane. One who dies in Kashi achieves the soul's release from the endless cycle of rebirth.

The landscape of Kashi is a sacred mandala that includes four concentric rings. The outermost and least sacred circle is the zone of Kashi. This contains within itself the smaller circle of Varanasi, which, in turn, encapsulates the circle called Avimukta. The innermost sacred circle is Antargriha, location of Kashi's sacred core, the Vishvanatha Temple. Kashi also includes shrines and points that symbolically represent all of India's sacred spots, such as the seven holy cities: Ayodhya, Mathura, Hardwar, Varanasi, Kanchi, Ujjain, and Dvaraka. Shrines mark the cardinal directions, symbolically associated with cities: Puri, for east; Dvaraka, for west; Badrinath, for north; and Ramesvaram, for south.

The mandala also inspired the city plan for Vijayanagara, established in fourteenth-century south India.[10] The 1565 defeat of Vijayanagara's ruler triggered the city's abandonment, leaving a remarkably preserved medieval archaeological site. The city's holiest center is the Ramachandra temple. South of this lies the royal center, whose axis lines up with it. The royal center divides into western and eastern halves, west being private, east being public. Substantial fortifications, irrigation tanks, and canals surround the city and its hinterland.

Similar considerations prevailed in the planning of Jaipur, today Rajasthan's capital. Jaipur was laid out by Raja Jai Singh II in 1728 to replace his old capital. The city's layout sets important temples at each cardinal point. This conception of the city-as-sacred-space reflects the ruler's assertion of his Hindu identity as the Mughal empire crumbled.

The eighteenth-century astronomical observatory Jantar Mantar seems modern in its conception of curves and staircases from which to peer into the heavens and line up star sightings. In the nineteenth century, a successor required all buildings not constructed of the area's pink sandstone be plastered over with a pink paint, giving rise to Jaipur's nickname, the "Pink City."

Rivers map a naturally sacred landscape. In addition to the Ganges, the sacred Saraswati River flows underneath India. Myths of this vanished river—also a goddess—are so potent that teams of scientists have used satellite technology to search for the river behind the Vedic accounts. Some scientists believe they have located the Saraswati in an ancient Rajasthani streambed. River headwaters assume special religious significance, such as Yamunotri and Gangotri, headwaters, respectively, of the Yamuna and Ganges Rivers.

Forests and trees have guardian divinities. Villages include many sacred sites: not just built temples and shrines, but trees, roadside points, a patch marked by a rock. When a new bride joins her husband for the first time, his female relatives and their friends show her these sites, guide her first worship, and teach her the stories of each.

ARCHITECTURE AND LANDSCAPE TO THE FOURTH CENTURY

India's Harappan sites are concentrated along western watersheds. The most important is Dholavira. Distinctive architectural features include grid town plans and mud-brick architecture. Larger, walled settlements reappeared by the fifth century B.C.E., along with colonization of inland agricultural zones. Three important settlements excavated by archaeologists are Sisupalgarh in Orissa, Ujjain in central India, and Pataliaputra in Bihar. Scientists working at Pataliaputra have an invaluable guidebook, a third century B.C.E. account of Ashoka Maurya's capital by the Greek visitor Megasthenes, which allows comparison between this and archaeological remains.

At this time, Pataliaputra extended along the south bank of the Ganges River. A moat, dirt embankment, and timber stockade protected the city core. Here archaeologists found the charred remains of a rectangular hall with eighty polished sandstone pillars. This structure, whose function is still unclear, was destroyed by fire around 150 B.C.E.

The stupa, associated with Buddhism, appeared. A stupa is basically a dome-shaped mound built up on a round or square platform that contains relics of a holy figure. The structure includes the following elements: a high fence or railing, which encircles the platform and leaves a space between the two where pilgrims can circle the stupa. A gateway marks each cardinal point of the railing. On top of the stupa mound a square platform marked off by a second railing is topped by a tiered umbrella. This symbolizes the sacred tree that rises to heaven.

Stupas were built throughout north and south India. The most spectacular is the Great Stupa at Sanchi, near Bhopal. This second century C.E. structure is about 120 feet in diameter and 50 feet high. Its nine-foot railing towers over visitors. Three elaborately carved crossbars top each gateway and mirror the triple parasol at the stupa's peak. A second significant stupa stood at Amaravati in the south. Unfortunately, this was dismantled and its stones burned for lime. Today this structure is known almost entirely through carvings of it at other sites. Although Buddhism left India, the stupa left many descendants, such as Thai and Chinese pagodas.

Almost no free-standing architecture is known for this early period.[11] Brick structures at Sarnath, Sanchi, and Bairat are simple, usually a rectangle with a curved or U-shaped end, which contained a stupa. The same shape appears in early rock-cut architecture, structures carved into hillsides or excavated completely from them. Rock-cut architecture became the most significant architectural medium from the second century B.C.E. to around the eighth century C.E.

This architecture includes shrines containing stupas, congregational halls, and monasteries.[12] Sites cluster along trade routes in the Western Ghats and central India. Architecture progressed from simple forms, such as the third century B.C.E. Lomas Rishi cave in the Barabar Hills, to elaborate complexes, such as the eighth century C.E. site at Elura, with its thirty-three cave temples. Twelve are Buddhist, four are Jain, and seventeen are Hindu. The greatest of these is the Hindu Kailasanantha temple. Its life-sized elephants, ramps, doorways, and an almost 100-foot-tall temple spire are carved from a single hill.

A distinctive feature of rock-cut forms at Lomas Rishi and in many later structures is the *chaitya* arch, which frames doorways and windows. The chaitya arch contains two barrel-shaped arches, one inside the other, giving the effect of a portico shaded with a vaulted overhang. The form clearly imitates a thatched hut with a shaded porch. In stone, the entire carving is of course in low relief on the wall surface. The chamber inside contains a stupa. Columns around the hall's perimeter create a pathway for pilgrims. Overhead, curved vaulted stone ceilings mimic those made of wood.

Important sites include the third century B.C.E. Bodhgaya site in the Barabar Hills (model for the Malabar Caves featured in E.M. Forster's [1924] novel *A Passage to India*); the second century B.C.E. site at Karle; and the Ajanta complex. This includes temples, shrines, and monasteries, all carved between the second century B.C.E. and the seventh century C.E. Hindu motifs began to appear by the fourth century C.E., such as the carving of Vishnu in his boar avatar at Udaygiri, Madhya Pradesh (early fifth century) and the sixth century shrine at Elephanta, an island near Mumbai. This celebrates the Hindu god Shiva with three monumental faces of the deity.

FOURTH TO TWELFTH CENTURY

The remains of the earliest known free-standing stone temples date from around the fourth century C.E. Their essentials include: (1) a platform, which supports the entire structure; including (2) the entrance porch; (3) assembly hall; (4) the innermost chamber of the deity; and (5) the temple's highest spire. The temple's sacred geography is that of a mountain that links the earth and heaven. Worshippers enter from secular space and successively move into increasingly sacred space, culminating in the temple's darkened heart.

Sanchi's Temple No. 17 (ca. 415) is a cubical chamber with an attached columned front porch. As the temple developed, it added assembly halls, one in front of the other. Both the platform and spire rose in height and assembly halls gained towers, too. Sometimes a hall was added in this lineup that could be used for performances of sacred dance. Two distinctive styles emerged, one associated with south India ("Dravida" or "Vimana" temples), and one associated with north India ("Nagara" or "Prasada" temples).

The Dravida temples developed an angular, tiered spire. This style includes both simple, low, pointed forms and elongated pyramids with dozens of horizontal layers stacked on top of one another. Mamallapuram possesses five seventh-century rock-cut, free-standing temples called "chariots" that seem

Khajuraho Temple. Courtesy of Maxine Weisgrau.

to be models of the era's architectural styles. One features a barreled vault with chaitya arch. Another illustrates the early Dravida form. Near these, the eighth century Shore Temple is dominated by a pyramidal tower and substantial front porch.

Important sites include Kanchi's eighth-century Kailasanantha temple, and the clusters of ninth- through eleventh-century temples in the Kavery delta in Tamil Nadu. Kerala temples include both the stone Dravida style and wooden temples. These have multiple tiered roofs, one set atop the other. Floor plans are rectangular, square, or round.

In north India, the Nagara temple developed a vertical spire that curved near its peak and was topped by a flattened round capstone. Early Nagara temples were small cubes and rectangles. This form developed into large, elaborate, octagonal, diamond, and multisided floor plans. Architects clustered miniature versions of the spire about its central peak. Temples elongated and added mass and height.

Early temples are at the sixth century shrine at Gop and Rajasthan's eighth- and ninth-century temples at Osian, not far from Pokharan. These structures seem almost taller than they are long, steep narrow platforms that support a small square chamber and pillared porch. In eastern India, the twelfth-century Jagannatha temple at Puri represents the form's development at this time. Nearby at Konarak, the thirteenth-century Sun Temple—which nineteenth-century visitors called the Black Pagoda—has been acclaimed as an aesthetic masterpiece.

Khajuraho, in central north India, has many tenth- through twelfth-century temples. These are overshadowed by the Kandariya Mahadeo temple (ca. 1000), celebrated for its erotic sculpture. Temple trends can be charted in Jain structures at Mount Abu, at the eleventh-century Udayesvara temple in Udaipur, at nearby Chitor, and at the Jain complex at Ranakpur. The fifteenth century Jain Adinatha temple Ranakpur sits on a high platform. Its roof is a forest of spires surrounding the temple's peaks and domes. In the Deccan, such as at Aihole, Dravida and Nagara temple styles met and mingled.

TWELFTH THROUGH EIGHTEENTH CENTURY

Cultural links with western Asia after the twelfth century promoted new fusion styles of Indo-Islamic architecture.[13] Islam brought the mosque, which accommodates congregational worship. The Islamic custom of burying, rather than cremating, the dead also led to the development of the tomb as a significant structure. Two important features associated with these movements are the pointed arch, rather than the corbelled arches produced by Hindu artisans, and the true dome.[14]

Mosques generally incorporate a large rectangular courtyard, surrounded by walls or arcades. The longest and most elaborate wall faces Mecca, and has at least one prayer niche and a pulpit. Indian builders often adapted vernacular architectures of the regions in which they worked—thus Bengal's Chhota Sona Masjid has the down-curved Bengali roof, while Ahmedabad's contemporary Jami Masjid (1423) has an unmistakeable Gujarati gateway reminiscent of the region's carved woodwork.

Starting around the twelfth century, the Muslim rulers of successive dynasties established new capitals in and around Delhi.[15] Today's New Delhi occupies the region of its traditional seven cities, from Prithviraj's reign in the twelfth century to Mughal times. This much-contested site lies between the ridge of the Aravalli mountains and the Yamuna River.

The earliest Muslim rulers built on defensible sites on the ridge or beside the river. In the early fourteenth century, Muhammad ud-din Tughluq of the Delhi Sultanate moved his capital to the Deccan, but the unhappy ex-Delhiites revolted and returned home. Muhammad ud-din's heir, Firuz Shah, established his capital on the banks of the Yamuna river in the middle of the fourteenth century. This was destroyed by Tamerlane in 1398. In the sixteenth century, Sher Shah refurbished the Old Fort. Mughal emperor Shah

Jahan built his Red Fort in the middle of the seventeenth century, a structure that is used today for ceremonial purposes by the government of India and also is a popular tourist destination.

Delhi's Quwwat-ul-Islam mosque (ca. 1195) reuses pieces of disassembled Jain and Hindu temples. This complex includes the period's most original early Indo-Islamic structure, the Qutub Minar. This 238-foot-tall tower is a thick fluted column ringed by four successively higher balconies.

Tombs grew in size with succeeding generations, a process notable around Delhi. Ghias-ud-din Tughluq of the Delhi Sultanate (d. 1325) was buried in a small domed tomb protected by its own miniature fort. Firuz Shah (d. 1388) set his octagonal, domed tomb at Hauz-i-khas. Many tombs cluster in the Lodi Gardens, named for this dynasty of the Delhi Sultanate period. These octagonal or square structures support handsome, plain domes. Soon architects added subsidiary domes to the main structures' corners. The increased height of platforms, along with rising numbers of subsidiary domes and development of multisided structures, recalls temple developments also taking place at this time.

Lakeside and riverbank sites and the formal garden with its grid of water channels provided attractive settings for tombs. Emperor Sher Shah, who briefly wrested control from Mughal Humayun in the mid-sixteenth century, built his tomb on a small lake at Sasaram, in Bihar. After Mughal emperor Humayan's death in 1556, his wife, Hajji Begum, assembled a team of architects and builders to create a grand tomb in Delhi. She placed the tomb in a grid with a garden. This setting became a signature of Mughal architecture and is most perfectly realized in the Taj Mahal. Gardens were also popular elements in both private and public spaces. By the Mughal period, Hindu and Muslim nobles' gardens were laid out according to similar geometrical principles.[16]

In the Deccan, Daulatabad and sixteenth-century Golconda were fortress capitals. Bijapur developed a distinctive architecture of massed shapes, such as its Jami Masjid (1565) and the domed tomb of Sultan Muhammad Adil Shah (d. 1656), the Gol Gumbaz. This dome's seventy-five-foot span is an engineering triumph. Four towers at each corner buttress the structure, and interior arcades add stability.

In the 1570s, Akbar built a new capital twenty-five miles west of Agra. Fatehpur Sikri consists of a series of interlocking courtyards, almost like a Mongol royal tent city. The Emperor's and Queens' residences are at the heart of the complex, ringed by successively more public spaces. Two important structures are the audience chamber and Jama Masjid, with its imposing arched gate. Yet within several decades, Fatehpur Sikri was abandoned, its central structures empty, the victim of inadequate water and shifting political needs.

The Shalimar Gardens (ca. 1619) overlooking the lake in the Vale of Kashmir used water and stepped terraces to create a summer pleasure garden. The plan of Delhi's Red Fort, parallel to the Yamuna River, sites its axis along the cardinal points. The fort's most private spaces are in the northeast, while the western half of the complex is public. Successor Aurangzeb constructed his Pearl Mosque inside Delhi's Red Fort. This little structure is generally considered its architectural crown.

EIGHTEENTH TO MID-TWENTIETH CENTURY

Eighteenth-century architecture shows the growth of regional traditions, new palaces, forts, merchants' homes, and other structures. Calcutta began its growth as a trade and administrative center. Mumbai, then called Bombay, began its steady expansion. Elsewhere in India, many towns and intermediate-level trade centers began a long, slow decline, losing population and industry throughout most of the eighteenth and nineteenth centuries.

Rural landscapes shifted from diversified farmscapes to large blocks of land occupied by a single crop. Tea plantations replaced forest landscapes in eastern India. The cutting of Gujarat's teak forests for shipbuilding reduced forest cover. The situation is complex, for while some areas experienced declines in quantity and quality of resources, others blossomed from investment in irrigation and other technologies. The most energetic architectural infusions appear among groups whose wealth stemmed from their connection with the emerging new economy.

The earliest Europeans used Indian structures, but as trade flourished, the Europeans introduced architectural forms familiar to themselves, little bits of "Home."[17] This process began a century or more before the inception of East India Company rule, but these styles only became significant in the latter part of the eighteenth century.

Portuguese Goa's churches and monasteries, French Pondicherry's seventeenth century Baroque cathedral, the Eglise de Notre Dame de Conception, and Fort St. George's seventeenth-century St. Mary's Church—complete with spire, though missing the country churchyard—are instantly recognizable European forms. During the last half of the eighteenth century, the Nabobs built Palladian mansions ornamented with Corinthian columns, classical pediments, and Greco-Roman statuary. Neoclassical structures include the Governor-General's Residence (1803) and the Library of the Asiatic

Society (1833) in Calcutta. Chennai's Fort St. George also has a concentration of such structures, including St. Andrew's Kirk (1821).

Perhaps the most influential new style was neo-Gothic, with its flying buttresses and pointed arches. The style was popular for decades, especially for government buildings, schools, and universities. Notable structures include Chennai's "Old College," Calcutta's High Court buildings (1872), and Bombay's Municipal Building (1893). This style was so prolific in government buildings that these were lampooned as Public Works Department Gothic or simply PWD Gothic.

Groups that prospered translated their success into fine new structures. In Rajasthan's Shekhawati region, traders built big stone houses, which they plastered with colorful designs. Gujarat's urban merchants constructed multistoried, half-timbered structures bracketed with elaborately carved wooden beam ends, balconies, and porticoes. The Nawab of Arcot cheerfully referenced European architecture in his Chepauk Palace (1768). Successful merchants and princely rulers constructed neoclassical palaces modeled on European landmarks.

This process of cultural reinterpretation went both ways. The British embraced the bungalow, a small, one-story structure with a steeply pitched, thatched, four-sided roof.[18] Deep surrounding verandas and interior rooms that opened into one another provided ventilation. The bungalow's veranda functioned as a transitional space between the outside public realm and inner, private rooms. Soon the bungalow form incorporated new styles, such as the stone, flat-roofed Military Board Style favored by the PWD, Gothic, and Swiss models.[19] Government settlements included bungalows sized according to the rank of the official who occupied them. The Dak bungalow, originally an overnight shelter for mail runners, grew into regular systems of halts for travelers on official business. The bungalow eventually traveled west, to England and North America.

British concepts of town planning featured a grid or radial system of streets. Settlements subdivided into three zones: the military cantonment, the civil station, and the Indian town. Domestic structures were set in independent gardens, not constructed as contiguous blocks. Universities, post offices, clock towers, racetracks, museums, hospitals, cemeteries, and rail stations began to appear. Industrialization brought with it new structures. Two engineering triumphs, the double deck Attock Bridge and Calcutta's Howrah Bridge, became architectural landmarks. The British standard brick replaced Indian-scaled brick.

Hill stations flourished as retreats from summer heat and epidemic disease. Here, the British built their little Englands, complete with rose gardens. Shimla (Simla), summer capital from 1865 to 1939, was queen of the hill stations. In Kashmir, foreigners were not permitted to own land, so they elaborated the houseboat into a floating palace.

The British saw their town planning as superior to Indian urban landscapes: a triumph of rationalism, as symbolized by the grid layout. The allegedly convoluted streets of Indian towns supposedly displayed Indian inferiority. British astonishment at Harappa and Mohenjo-daro in the 1920s focused on these cities' grid patterns—supposedly an impossibility to the Indian mind!

Late-nineteenth-century structures included a hodgepodge of styles, such as the Italianate Calcutta Indian Museum, Mumbai's French Renaissance Victoria and Albert Museum, Simla's Baronial Viceroy's Lodge, and, most famous, Mumbai's Victoria Terminus. These decades saw a romanticization of Indian architectures with the addition of motifs drawn from Indian models. Indo-Saracenic architecture mixed Western and Eastern motifs: classical facades topped with Mughal pavilions, Indian columns, Moorish allusions, and even Gothic towers.

Some rulers hired British architects to build new palaces.[20] Today, many of these have been converted into hotels or museums. Structures include Hyderabad's Falaknuma Palace, Baroda's Lakshmi Vilas Palace, Gwalior's Jai Vilas Palace, and Jaipur's Ram Bagh Palace. An English architect designed much of the Mubarak Mahal, a structure built inside Jaipur's eighteenth-century City Palace. Bikaner's Lallgarh Palace, built at the turn of the nineteenth century, also was the product of collaboration between an English architect and Indian master builders.

The twentieth-century high point for Indo-Saracenic style came in the plans for New Delhi (1911–1918), designed by Edward Lutyens and Herbert Baker. The Viceroy's Palace (today called the Rashtrapati Bhavan, official residence of the President of India) and Secretariat Buildings combine allusions to classical architecture with Indian proportions and decorative elements. These long red sandstone buildings appear deceptively low across the horizon, anchoring as they do the long ceremonial path and triumphal arch that stretch toward the Yamuna River.

In the final years of the Raj, other styles also appeared. Jodhpur's Umaid Bhavan Palace and Indore's Manik Bagh Palace are notable Art Deco structures. This style signals their rulers' cosmopolitan values (polo-playing Maharajahs were fixtures in international society), yet distances them from the Raj, with its Indo-Saracenic motifs. Art Deco inspired cinemas and decorative motifs on the facades of middle-class housing. It anticipated another architectural movement, which dominated in the first decades after independence: Modernism.

LANDSCAPE AND ARCHITECTURE AFTER INDEPENDENCE

Modernism swept through the new buildings constructed to meet the new needs of an independent India. There were many needs: for schools, government buildings, housing for the poor, urban renewal, even new capital cities—for India's new states. Collaboration with internationally renowned architects created distinctive design innovations that blended modernist and Indian style.

The best-known architect recruited to this effort was one of the founders of modernism in architecture, the Swiss Le Corbusier.[21] The showpiece of his Indian work is Chandigarh, built as the capital of Punjab and Haryana states. Le Corbusier used sweeping curves of concrete to create a sense of light. Forms reflected Indian models, such as the arched arcade on the High Court building, which recalls those on Indian structures. Outside Chandigarh, Le Corbusier's most influential structures include Sarabhai House and the Millowner's Association Building, both in Ahmedabad. In New Delhi, Le Corbusier designed the Interstate Bus Terminal and the Permanent Exhibition Hall of Pragati Maidan.

Gandhi had called on Indians to use only construction materials that could be found within a five-mile radius and to work from indigenous designs. His home consisted of four simple rooms constructed of timber, reed, bamboo, and mud, topped with a tile roof. Early rural housing experiments used local technologies, such as the mud brick construction at Gorakhpur, U.P., that was part of the Etawah experiment.[22]

By the 1970s, the growing environmental movement's "think global, act local" ethos inspired a new focus on appropriate technology, in housing for the poor, and communities founded by elites, such as Sri Aurobindo Ghose's Auroville.[23] These new designs reflect cultural history, vernacular building forms, energy efficiency, and environmentally clean techniques that utilize swiftly disappearing master carpenter and stone carver skills. New buildings are often inspired by rural forms and aesthetics. The vernacular has exploded into elite consciousness in a big way.

Important buildings include the Indian Institute of Management in Bangalore and Jaipur's Kala Kendra Museum, inspired by the mud architecture of Rajasthan. Hotels have found that designs that draw from rural architecture are popular with tourists seeking an authentic Indian experience. Another movement has been the restoration of old palaces and forts as hotels. In this case sometimes the structure in question, unknown to the tourists, reflects late-nineteenth-century European-inspired architectural fads!

Traditional Kerala forms inspire new homes, porches, porticoes, screens, and structures clustered so as to create private courts. An important house that uses vernacular styles and construction was designed by architects Vasant Kamal and Revathi Kamath, south of New Delhi. Its dome and parasol roof recall Delhi's grand structures of the past, while its shady, rambling brick veranda framed in wood timbers beckons a visitor to sit, rest, and enjoy the garden view.

What about the vernacular architectures and landscapes that have inspired these efforts? Most elite versions of vernacular architecture are selective. Elites reject middle-class tastes as vulgar and recoil from the use of plastic sheeting, bits of heavy canvas, flattened tin cans, corrugated tin, and cardboard.

The status symbol for anyone who aspires to become middle class is a *pakka* house, one that most likely eclectically borrows European motifs. Architecture critics decry this as Punjabi Baroque or Marwari Gothic.[24] Those who can afford it use concrete, stone, and brick to build homes with chunky exteriors, iron grills, and colorful trim. Colors range from vivid pink through electric green and blue—not the taupes, grays, browns, rusts, and white preferred by the elites.

The *kaccha* homes of the poor use local materials, and they often combine wattle-and-daub and straw thatch with diverse manufactured elements. Urban squatter settlements comprised of such structures pose a particular concern. Urban experts estimate that in cities such as Mumbai, up to 68 percent of the population lives in substandard housing.[25] This includes *kaccha* structures as well as *pakka* blocks of antiquated, poorly maintained apartments.

India's slums are largely suburban. This reflects the development of concentric rings of settlement around centers of government and commerce: a dense commercial and municipal core, its attached residential districts, often with plots of land and housing graded to the government employees' status, and finally, planned blocks for middle- and working-class families. Unused lands and those on the periphery of settlements beckon squatters. Sometimes these settlements spring up as temporary housing for construction workers working on a nearby site, and sometimes squatters' groups take over the land in a planned movement. They thereupon negotiate with the authorities for municipal services, in exchange for their votes.

The problems in slums shade into those faced by all urban residents: water and power may be available for only a few hours each day. Maintenance of roads and public spaces is poor, and sewage treatment and water purification facilities are inadequate. Slums, however, are the worst in terms of public health.

Within the universe of urban slums, certain patterns can be detected.[26] Neighbors tend to be members of the same or similar caste, religious, and occupational groups. As in other neighborhoods, the residents set up committees to negotiate with authorities and obtain scarce resources. If successful, an illegal settlement may be able to regularize itself. In other cases, squatter settlements have been bulldozed by developers anxious to cash in on rising property values. Villagers once an hour's ride from city centers now find themselves engulfed by urbanization. Sometimes villagers find that rising property values enable them to replace *kaccha* homes with spacious new stone or concrete homes, while investing in the real-estate boom. In other cases, those who lack standing in the community find themselves pushed out in favor of tenants who can pay higher rents.

Urban renewal, once focused mainly on slum clearance, has also begun to tackle other neighborhoods. In Jaipur, architectural preservationists achieved a victory when city authorities demolished the temporary wooden booths erected by merchants, which obscured elegant facades on the city's main thoroughfare.

NOTES

1. Alexander Stille, "The Ganges' Next Life," *The New Yorker*, Jan. 19, 1998, pp. 58–67.

2. Alain R.A. Jacquemin, *Urban Development and New Towns in the Third World: Lessons from the New Bombay Experience* (Aldershot, England: Ashgate Publishing Ltd., 1999).

3. Rohit Parihar, "Withering Glory," *India Today International*, Nov. 15, 1999, pp. 44–45.

4. V.S. Pramar, *Haveli: Wooden Houses and Mansions of Gujerat* (Ahmedabad: Mapin Publishing, 1989).

5. Ilay Cooper and Barry Dawson, *Traditional Buildings of India* (London: Thames & Hudson, 1998).

6. Rohit Parihar and S. Kalidas, "Laying Siege," *India Today International*, Oct. 30, 2000, pp. 44–45.

7. *India Today International*, Nov. 20, 2000, p. 40.

8. I owe this insight to Michael E. Meister, personal communication. See his and M.A. Dhaky's *Encyclopedia of Indian Temple Architecture* (New Delhi and Philadelphia: American Institute of Indian Studies Press, 1998).

9. Diana L. Eck, *Banaras, City of Light* (Princeton: Princeton University Press, 1982).

10. John M. Fritz and George Michell, *City of Victory: Vijayanagara, the Medieval Hindu Capital of Southern India* (New York: Aperture, 1991). Carla M. Sinopoli and Kathleen D. Morrison, "Dimension of Imperial Control: The Vijayanagara Capital," *American Anthropologist* 97(1):83–96, 1995.

11. Roy C. Craven, *Indian Art: A Concise History* (New York: Thames & Hudson, 1997).

12. Vidya Dehejia, *Early Buddhist Rock Temples* (Ithaca: Cornell University Press, 1972).

13. Satish Grover, *Islamic Architecture in India* (New Delhi: Galgotia Publishing Company, 1996).

14. Corbelled techniques overlap successive rows of blocks to bridge a gap, while the true arch uses the keystone principle.

15. Robert Eric Frykenberg, ed., *Delhi through the Ages: Essays in Urban History, Culture, and Society* (Delhi: Oxford University Press, 1986).

16. D. Fairchild Ruggles, "What's Religion Got to Do with It? A Skeptical Look at Symbolism in Mughal and Rajput Gardens," *Dak: The Newsletter of the American Institute of Indian Studies*, no. 4, Autumn 2000, pp. 1ff.

17. Jan Morris and Simon Winchester, *Stones of Empire: The Buildings of the Raj* (Oxford: Oxford University Press, 1983).

18. Anthony D. King, *The Bungalow: Production of a Global Culture* (New York: Oxford University Press, 1995).

19. Janet Pott, *Old Bungalows in Bangalore, South India* (London: Pott, 1977).

20. Sylvie Raulet, *Maharajah's Palaces: European Style in Imperial India* (New York: Vendome Press, 1997).

21. Adolf Max Vogt, *Le Corbusier, the Noble Savage*, trans. by Radka Donnell (Cambridge: MIT Press, 1998). Vikram Bhatt and Peter Scriver, *After the Masters: Contemporary Indian Architecture* (Ahmedabad, India: Mapin Publishing, 1990).

22. Described in Albert Mayer et al., *Pilot Project, India: The Story of Rural Development at Etawah, Uttar Pradesh* (Berkeley: University of California Press, 1958).

23. Herbert J.M. Yrma, *India Modern: Traditional Forms and Contemporary Design* (London: Phaidon Press, 1994).

24. Gautam Bhatia, *Punjabi Baroque and Other Memories of Architecture* (New Delhi: Penguin Books, 1994).

25. These and the following figures are from Alain R. Jacquemin, *Urban Development and New Towns in the Third World*, op. cit., pp. 89–90.

26. Paul D. Wiebe, *Social Life in an Indian Slum* (Durham, NC: Carolina Academic Press, 1975).

SUGGESTED READINGS

Allchin, F.R. *The Archaeology of Early Historic South Asia* (Cambridge: Cambridge University Press, 1995).

Bhatia, Gautam. *Punjabi Baroque and Other Memories of Architecture* (New Delhi: Penguin Books, 1994).

Bhatt, Vikram and Peter Scriver. *After the Masters: Contemporary Indian Architecture* (Ahmedabad, India: Mapin Publishing, 1990).

Cooper, Ilay and Barry Dawson. *Traditional Buildings of India* (London: Thames & Hudson, 1998).

Dehejia, Vidya. *Indian Art* (London: Phaidon, 1997).

Forster, E.M. *A Passage to India* (San Diego: Harcourt Brace Jovanovich, 1984).

Grover, Satish. *Islamic Architecture in India* (New Delhi: Galgotia Publishing Company, 1996).

Harle, J.C. *The Art and Architecture of the Indian Subcontinent* (Harmondsworth, Middlesex: Penguin, 1986).

Meister, Michael and M.A. Dhaky. *Encyclopedia of Indian Temple Architecture* (Philadelphia: American Institute of Indian Studies Press, 1998).

Morris, Jan and Simon Winchester. *Stones of Empire: The Buildings of the Raj* (Oxford: Oxford University Press, 1983).

Pramar, V.S. *Haveli: Wooden Houses and Mansions of Gujerat* (Ahmedabad: Mapin Publishing, 1989).

Yrma, Herbert J.M. *India Modern: Traditional Forms and Contemporary Design* (London: Phaidon Press, 1994).

6

Food and Dress

A PHOTOGRAPH of Mahatma Gandhi on the Salt March famously views him, staff in hand and *khadi* (homespun and handwoven) loincloth wrapped around his waist, striding toward his goal. Gandhi—who had once worn lawyerly tweeds—consciously selected this homespun garb to symbolize India's oppression under the British. His march to the sea to make salt protested the British tax on this humble—yet absolutely crucial—food item. Food and dress are the stuff of everyday life and, as Gandhi showed, possessed immense cultural significance, which he transformed into symbols of resistance to colonial rule. *Khadi* became the most important nationalist symbol. *Khadi* evoked memories of India's great past before the British mills drove weavers out of business and onto impoverished farms. The salt tax in its turn reminded Indians of the long arm of imperialism that reached to even the most humble necessity.

Food and dress link India to history, culture, and identity. In ancient times, fine clouds of muslin gauze wreathed proud Roman matrons. Indian spices were so rare in Western Europe that sailors risked their lives on uncharted seas to find routes to the subcontinent. The first English ship to reach India brought bales of wool broadcloth—decidedly not a success! But Indian fabrics—chintz, calico, muslin—found a ready home in the West.

The black soils of India's coastal plains produced the cotton woven into gossamer designs. Rural hinterlands connected with urban trade centers through chains of brokers, who bought, bulked, and put out raw materials, yarn, and cloth for processing. This protoindustrialization, the economic historian's term, was so thorough that producers specialized in goods made for European, Southeast Asian, and African tastes.

Trade brought New World plants, most prominently the *capsicum* chili, without which Indian cuisine would be unrecognizable. Silkworms and tea from China laid the basis for significant new industries. Another import was ice. The Mughals dispatched couriers to deliver precious Himalayan ice for their cooling sherbets. In 1833, the New England vessel *Tuscany* landed at Calcutta with 180 tons of ice. Thus began an encounter memorialized in Henry David Thoreau's idea that the waters of Walden Pond mingled with the Ganges.

Dress and food link people to cosmological theories of inner substance and its transformations, to concepts of ritual purity and pollution, to modernity and to tradition. Women's fasting and adoption of new food traditions—vegetarianism, for instance—blend together personal and group status goals.

Shifts in dress signal status changes. For some, defining and wearing traditional dress symbolizes their commitment to a group or region. Some protest restrictions that prevented members of some groups from wearing ornaments or other symbols claimed by higher-caste groups—gold, for instance. For others, new materials and designs signal commitments to modernity. Fashion is also a stimulant.

Overall, the great story of dress in the twentieth century has been the revival of handloom arts. The great stories of food in the twentieth century are the adoption of Green Revolution technology, movements to improve indigenous farming, and creation of a national distribution system that aims to ensure that every Indian will have access to an adequate—if basic—diet.

This chapter sketches the history of important adoptions to the diet. Second, the chapter examines food cosmology, the theories of food and diet that underlie cuisine and food-related etiquette in most regions of the country. The third section of the chapter takes a look at regional cuisines, and ends with a description of a meal.

Next, the chapter traces the development of textile arts and dress. Dress cosmology comprises the next section of the chapter, symbolism and form. This is followed by a description of basic materials and technologies, with an emphasis on regional differences.

EATING HISTORY

To sit down to the ordinary fare eaten by rich and poor alike in a small village is to touch many continents and historical moments. In Surani, the staple big round, dark-green bread is made from pearl millet, which migrated to India from Africa. Jujube (*Zizyphus nummularia*), small round, tart, berry-like fruit, was harvested from the wild bushes that grow outside the village. The red chilies that spike the sauce were domesticated in the Americas and arrived in India sometime in the sixteenth or seventeenth century. Tea came to India from China.

Many foods have been brought to India and naturalized into Indian food traditions.[1] Africa contributed sorghum, finger millet, and pearl millet. Rice's zone of domestication included India's far northeast. Rices from here and Southeast Asian stocks gave farmers the genetic resources to breed a dazzling number of varieties. Southeast Asia gave the coconut, banana, sago palm, and yam. Central Asia contributed the walnut and *basmati*, queen of rice. Pistachio—essential to rich dishes—came from the Mediterranean.

New World plants also include the pineapple, papaya, passion fruit, potato, maize, custard apple, sapodilla, peanut, sunflower, tapioca, and cashew nuts. The Hindi name for cashew, *kaju*, is straight from the Brazilian Tepi Indian *acaju*. The Tupi *nana* became *ananas*, pineapple. Tobacco proved a success and is the basis for production of Western-style cigarettes and the indigenous hand-rolled and unfiltered cigarette.

The first plant domestications in South Asia occurred at Mehrgarh, today in Pakistan. The early cereal staple was barley, joined by mung beans and lentil species. Eggplant, turmeric, and two crops grown as oil seeds, sesame and mustard, were also part of the diet. India's earliest peoples enjoyed hunting, judging by cave paintings of deer, bison, wild cattle, rhinoceros, and even giraffes and the ostrich.

The Harappan staple was barley, augmented with finger millet and wild millets, pulses, chickpeas, oil seeds, melons, pomegranates, dates, and jujube. Ancient sorghum has been identified. The Harappans bred cattle, buffalo, sheep, and goats—all of which they ate, along with wild game and fish from the Indus river and its tributaries.

The second phase of state building and urbanization involved the rainy environments of the eastern Gangetic plain. Soon rice became important. Ancient texts prized dairy products such as yoghurt, butter, and *ghee*. Other foods included honey, sugar cane, linseed, safflower, grapes, cucumbers, and dates.

One of the most mysterious of these ancient foods was the sacred drink *soma*, used in sacrifice. Evidently ingestion of *soma* produced altered states of consciousness. There have been many efforts to identify the plant base for *soma*, with one strong contender being *Amanita muscarita*, the fly agaric mushroom.[2] Ancient Indians knew of other stimulants, including marijuana (*Cannabis sativa*), beer, and distilled liquors.

The centerpiece of Vedic ritual was animal sacrifice. Animals included the horse, bull, buffalo, sheep, goat, and chicken. After the sacrifice, the victim was cooked and eaten. This pattern holds today, when a chicken, goat or—rarely—buffalo is sacrificed to a meat-eating deity. Ancient texts include recipes for meatballs, minced meat, meat pilaf, and even a barbecue sauce that uses tart tamarind and spicy pomegranate juice. The important first food ceremony held for a baby stipulated that rams' meat imparted strength.

One of the most-debated questions of Indian food history is the origin of vegetarianism and the ban on eating the meat of zebu cattle, India's humped cattle. One anthropologist argued that ecological problems that arose as human population density grew created a cultural environment receptive to the idea of vegetarianism.[3] Ecological factors made it more economical to use cattle for dairy and traction purposes, rather than slaughtering them for meat. Religious traditions such as Jainism, Buddhism, and Hinduism highlighted vegetarianism in their value systems. Vegetarianism became associated with the highest ritual status. As it became transformed into Hinduism, Vedic religion began to replace animals with coconuts and other plants. Blood sacrifice remained a powerful mediation of supernatural energy: just not in the elite, now-vegetarian Brahman context. The sacred cow emerged as a shared cultural symbol with emphasis on the special ritual purity of zebu cow milk and products.

Nevertheless, vegetarianism never did take hold among all sections of the population. About 70–75 percent of India's population is nonvegetarian.[4] The big vegetarian belts are in north India, particularly Gujarat and Rajasthan (70 and 60 percent of the population, respectively). Only 6 percent of the population is vegetarian in Kerala, Orissa, and West Bengal, where fishing provides significant dietary protein.

By the tenth century, intensified contacts with West Asia encouraged new culinary traditions. A visitor (ca. 1340) reported that a feast hosted by the Tughluq ruler included kebabs, meat pilaf, and pastries stuffed with vegetables or meat. The early sixteenth-century Mughal emperor Babur approved of Indian fruits such as mangos, which he called "really good."[5] Babur missed his Central Asian melons, cherries, peaches, and apricots. He and his heirs promoted these crops, and established an ice delivery system so that their chefs could make frozen dishes.

The Mughal period coincided with the arrival of New World crops. The use of New World plants in Mughal cooking, such as *dum aloo* (potatoes cooked in a rich sauce), suggests that some were prepared as exotica for elites. The potato and tomato appear to have become common in the diet later, in the nineteenth century.

Peanuts arrived in the middle of the nineteenth century, becoming popular in cooked dishes and as a street snack. This is usually served in a paper cone by a street vendor who roasts the nuts on the spot. British influence famously brought tea drinking, the national pastime in the late afternoon. Naturalized Western foodways in middle- and upper-class homes include the toast rack and the evening's scotch and soda. In the 1970s, Soviet agricultural advisors introduced Russian varieties of sunflower (also a New World plant). By the end of the twentieth century, urban snacks included Chinese food, pizza, sodas, chips, and burgers (vegetarian, buffalo, or mutton). In the 1980s, economic liberalization produced agreements to manufacture popular Western brands of carbonated beverages.

FOOD COSMOLOGY

Cosmology links food, medical perspectives, and concepts of purity and pollution. Foods have supernatural characteristics, including ritual purity. This reflects food's intrinsic aspects, plus who prepares it, how it is prepared, and how it is served and eaten. Food especially represents ritual purity and group membership. Jain temple complexes include a dining hall that serves vegetarian food. Sikhs follow religious services with a communal meal. Muslims should follow their religion's food prohibitions on pork and alcohol. During the Ramadan period, none may eat between dawn and sundown.

The big divide is between vegetarian and nonvegetarian dietary habits. In a strict Brahman household, for instance, meal etiquette is an exquisite dance among purity-producing and pollution-producing events.

As a general rule, Indian culture shares with much of the Middle East and Mediterranean the classification of foods as "hot" and "cold." Both "hot" and "cold" refer to supernatural qualities of food. The theory in India starts with the concept of the five basic substances (earth, water, fire, air [mind], and sky [ether]). These combine to make three special qualities: earth plus water makes *kapha*; fire is *pitta*; and air and sky make *vatha*.

The property of *kapha* is courage that verges on foolhardiness—since it is not linked to knowledge. Fire exemplifies excitement, energy, and passion. *Pitta* is intelligence, disciplined knowledge, and its pleasures. Courage and excitement are associated with heat. Foods with courage include pork, beef, fish that lack scales, and intoxicants. Foods with excitement make a person restless and eager for action. These foods are bitter, salty, and pungent. Food that is cold promotes spirituality: dairy products, honey, mutton, chicken, eggs, and wine.

Everything—including people—contains varying amounts of these three qualities. People can affect their inner nature or attain a desired state by what they eat. One can balance too much heat with cold foods, and vice versa. In the winter, hot foods help people to stay healthy. In the summer, cold foods are best. Members of certain groups, such as some Brahmans, do not eat garlic—because it has too much excitement. Rajputs, on the other hand, eagerly eat meat and drink alcohol. This maintains them in a proper state for vigorous action, as their nature requires.

Preparing, cooking, and serving etiquette transform food's ritual purity. Modernization has undercut many aspects of this model and replaced it with simplified versions and modern hygienic practices—but at special events, ritual purity practices may prevail. The kitchen must be ritually pure, in terms of both its location relative to other parts of the house and its internal state.[6] The kitchen must be completely washed before food preparation begins. Some foods must have preliminary preparation completed before they can enter the kitchen.

In a very strict purity situation, the cook prepares by taking a bath and putting on fresh clothes. Among one group of Brahmans, this also meant putting on special cloth, "vegetarian" silk made from the cocoon of a moth allowed to escape naturally from the cocoon (most silks unwind the cocoon while the moth is still inside, killing it). This dress is almost never seen today for cooking: the silk is now considered precious finery.

Food divides into two categories. Boiled foods rank on top. *Pakka* dishes are food that has been cooked in fat or *ghee* (clarified butter). Boiled foods include rice, *dal* (a thick soup or stew made of beans and lentils), *pullao* (rice pilaf), and *khichri*, a combination of rice and beans or lentils cooked together. Boiled foods easily absorb ritual pollution and are therefore usually eaten at home. *Pakka* food is much less liable to ritual pollution and is often prepared for trips and as something to be taken to work for lunch.

The most ritually pure food is the food that is left over after a deity tastes this in the temple. This includes milk, wheat, or rice-based sweets. Some temples are known for their special dishes served as sanctified leavings.

Food eaten by individuals would not be shared on one plate, except as a sign of intimacy. Leftovers have come into contact with the eater's saliva and hence are sources of pollution. Thus, in a formal situation of purity maintenance, only someone who is not eating touches the serving dishes or spoons. Cooks do not taste the food while they are preparing a meal—for the same reason.

Fasts are common. A fast consists of a limitation on a particular food, class of food, or set of foods and associated rules regarding food and dining. There is much diversity. Sometimes only boiled food is eaten, or only fruit. Sometimes a person eats only after sunset or before moonrise. Sometimes a certain number of guests must be fed.

Usually the context is domestic. Most of those who fast are women, and the purpose is to protect the family. Fasts also assert political protest. Gandhi's fasting rebuked the British in an idiom all Indians understood. Today's protestors also fast to draw attention to injustice and to achieve change.

REGIONAL CUISINES

Every region of India has its special *garam masala* (hot spice blend), a heady combination of scent and taste. A visit to any kitchen will be redolent with regional identity, religious grouping, subcaste, and personal family history, such as the decree of a protective mother goddess that bans certain foods. The most-noted general divisions in culinary traditions are between the north and south; between wheat and rice zones; and between regions that lack fish and those where it is available.

Recent politics have increased an emphasis by some groups on banning slaughter of zebu cattle for beef. This is enacted on a state-by-state basis. Usually, the beef that is offered on the menu is actually water buffalo. Mutton is usually goat, rather than sheep. People feel that goat meat rather than lamb is more compatible with strong spicing.

Ordinary fare is seasonal. Diet focuses on the staple, plus whatever vegetable is available. Northern Indians call this plain fare *dal-roti*, lentils with bread. Urban markets with middle-class consumers attract off-season fruits from distant agricultural zones, but even big markets have seasons. A favorite one is the mango season. India has hundreds of varieties of mangoes, and all have their fans.

Starting in India's humid northeast, West Bengal cuisine highlights rice, fish, and milk-based sweets. Numerous dishes feature fish. Spiced dishes gain a regional flavor from *Panch phoran*, a mix that includes fennel, cumin, black mustard seed, and fenugreek. Mustard oil imparts a smoky flavor. Calcutta's Anglo-Indians, descended from British fathers and Indian mothers, combined their forebears' cooking to create dishes such as mango fool and Country Captain, chicken simmered in ginger, garlic, and onion sauce.

Bengali sweets are famous. Cooks start with a base of *chhana*, curdled milk that has been boiled down and then set to drain off excess fluid, and finally flavored and sweetened. Beloved sweets include *rosgullahs*, which are boiled in syrup, and *ras malai*, sweet *chhana* floated in a milk, sugar, and almond cream.

In the northwest, wheat is the staple, made into the flat breads *nan, chappati*, and *paratha*. Noodles are fried or cooked in dessert dishes. In Delhi and Punjab, favorite foods include *tandoori* chicken, grilled in a special clay oven with a mix of spices and red food coloring. Other dishes include *sam* (savory turnovers), *kebab*, and *korma* (minced meat). Vegetable dishes in

Making Bajra Roti (bread), Tilwarra. Courtesy of the author.

cauliflower with potatoes, spinach with cheese, and *raita*, a salad of yogurt with vegetables.

Punjabi cooks adopted American maize (corn), which can be made into a bread (*roti*) that is popularly served with mustard greens.[7] Relishes include sour lime pickle, mango pickle, a mix of mint and chili pepper, and tamarind chutney.

Sometimes the best food around is at roadside fast-food stalls frequented by truckers. Here, the chef whips up flat bread, *tandoori* chicken or kebabs, *dal*, and a vegetable in spicy hot sauce. The price is modest, the food hot and very, very fresh.

In the far north, Kashmiri cooking features ingredients such as saffron, mushrooms, and lotus root. Around Srinagar, farmers build rafts of dirt and compost in the lake and use these floating gardens to produce mint, cucumbers, and melons. A simple favorite dish is collard greens sauteed in mustard oil.[8] Kashmiris fire up a samovar (a heated urn for making tea), and use it to keep tea warm all day. *Kahva* is tea with cardamom and almonds, sweetened with a little sugar.

In the west, Rajasthani cooking features millet, dairy products, and lentils. ᵗlet bread is so substantial that it needs only a little onion or bit of vegetable ᵗered with turmeric and a lot of ground red chili, garlic, and salt. People

Making noodles, Surani. Courtesy of the author.

enjoy millet bread broken apart and mashed up with a cooked vegetable, with a little brown sugar and *ghee*, or perhaps with just buttermilk. Festive foods of the state's Rajputs include wild boar and marinated barbecued meat. Highly spiced meat stews feature in nonvegetarian dishes.

Chickpea flour appears in both Rajasthani and Gujarati dishes. These include *kadhi*, a bright-yellow sauce of chickpea flour and yoghurt. Other chickpea-based foods include fried *masala*-spiced noodles; *papad*, the large, paper-thin rounds that crinkle when toasted; and *pakoras*, vegetables fast-fried in a batter coating.

South India's staple is rice. Pounded, soaked, and fermented rice batters make steamed cakes, noodles, and pancakes. The west coast's Kholombo powder combines coriander, cumin, curry leaf, cloves, peppercorns, coconut flakes, and split chickpea and black lentils. The east coast's Sambhar powder includes dry roasted black mustard, cumin, dried red chilies, black peppercorn, coriander, and the astringent and pungent asafoetida sauteed with a little oil and lentils. "Madras Curry Powder," manufactured here, is strictly for foreigners.

Kerala regional dishes include Syrian Christians' Easter lamb stew with coconut and cardamom, squid with curry, and eggplant with coconut milk. Seafood features in many dishes. Rice noodles and pancakes are favorites.

Goanese cuisine extends the west coast's spice traditions to Portuguese-inspired favorites such as roast suckling pig and beef pot roast. Vindaloo, Goa's most famous dish, is naturalized from the Portuguese *Vindalho*, vinegar (*vinho*), and garlic (*alhos*).

On the east coast, Tamil Nadu cuisine features *dosas*, crisp pancakes made from a batter of fermented rice and dal. These huge rounds can be two feet from tip to tip. A *dosa* is often stuffed with a potato or onion filling. The batter can also be made into *uttapam*, which vaguely resembles pizza. *Idli*, steamed rice cakes, also please. In addition to spicy fish and seafood, *idli* may be eaten along with *rasam*, a tangy thin lentil soup.

What accompanies a meal? Water of course, drunk at the meal's conclusion. Cool water is always available and kept in its own special spot inside or next to the kitchen. Many families store their drinking water in a big clay jar that cools by evaporation. Next to it will be a dipper and perhaps a small brass or steel pot with a handy curled lip. This makes it easy to pour a thin stream of water into one's mouth without touching the *lota* with one's lips.

Spice tea is a favorite on cold winter days. Black tea, water, milk, sugar, cinnamon, cloves, and a pinch of black pepper boil together until a milk skin forms, then the tea is strained into glasses. Cooling summer drinks include salt-spiked lemonade and lime soda, served sweet or salty. Buttermilk, salty or sweetened with sugar and a fruit flavor, also refreshes.

Among middle-class families, a festive evening may begin with whiskey or a beer. Each region has its distinctive intoxicating beverages. A number of states ban the sale of alcohol, so many of these beverages are illegally produced.[9] Traditional intoxicating beverages include the coast's toddy, made from the fermented sap of the palmetto palm. *Arrack* is distilled palm toddy. *Daru* is one name for the liquor distilled from the flowers of the Mahua tree, *Madhuca indica*. In Rajasthan, country liquor often starts from a base of fermented bark of *ber* or babul trees.[10] Distillers add anise or saffron, and sometimes double-, triple-, or even quadruple-distill the liquor. Government distilleries produce savory saffron-flavored liqueur using traditional techniques.

Other intoxicants, such as opium and marijuana, are often consumed in a weak infusion with water. In Rajasthan, important events such as a betrothal may be sealed with the two fathers-in-law imbibing together. The government's efforts to end the trade and to mitigate addiction problems confront embedded social customs such as this. Nevertheless, rural Indians and dwellers in urban squatter settlements may turn to illegal producers because of availability and price. There are risks to consumption, and not merely from the police and tax service, whose agents spend much time tracking down producers and traffickers in illegal intoxicants. Sadly, each year bad illicit liquor kills or blinds some of its users.

AT MEALTIME

Indians prefer to eat three meals a day: breakfast—even if this is just a cup of tea thick with milk and sugar; lunch, which may be a roti with *dal* or a vegetable; and a substantial dinner. Dinner is late in the evening, so the afternoon tea break refreshes.

Every diner has his or her own place setting: a round brass or steel tray, which may have separate small cups for different vegetable dishes; a banana leaf plate; or a Western-style plate. In Kashmir, four diners share a big plate. Each eats from a separate quadrant and avoids those of the neighbors on either side. Manners mean eating with the right hand and passing dishes with the left hand.

Some families serve senior members first, or serve on an individual basis, depending on work schedules. This member sits on a mat and eats quickly, as the cook serves rotis fresh from the fire on his plate and ladles food onto his plate. Middle-class families gather around the dining table. Everyone washes his or her hands before and after the meal, often adding a quick rinse of the mouth at this time. If they are seated outdoors, a servant or family member may go around the table with a jug and towel, offering to pour water for each guest, so that he or she can rinse off right there.

After dinner, guests may be offered a mixture of anise (a seed tasting like licorice), cardamom, and a little crushed rock sugar as a digestive. In urban areas, adults sometimes take the children out for a treat of *kulfi* (Indian ice cream) or Western ice cream. The adults may stop at a vendor to pick up a treat that is a blend of betel nut, sugar, and spice over a smear of lime inside a folded betel leaf. Different sellers may have different blends, and every enthusiast has her or his favorite.

DRESS

"Pink is the navy blue of India," the late fashion authority and *Vogue* magazine editor Diana Vreeland famously commented. Middle-class Indian youth show that they are trendy by following Western fashions. Middle-class wives prefer the wrapped, draped garment, the sari, often in an easy-care polyester. Their husbands' dress of choice is usually Western business garb. Farmers and other rural folk often prefer less Westernized fashions. Synthetic fabrics have a big following here, too, as women appreciate their durability, resistance to fading, and especially, that they are "wash and wear."

Three trends have shaped contemporary dress: technological change, the independence movement, changing social identities. Even today's traditional dress reflects sequences of historical change, selection of certain styles and not others.[11]

Technological developments profoundly affected textiles. In the nineteenth century, imported mill-made cloth replaced most produced on handlooms. A few Indian entrepreneurs were given permission to build factories such as Nagpur's Empress Mill and the Dharamsi Mill near Bombay initiated by Jamsetji N. Tata (1839–1904). In the 1920s, the Birla family began mill production in Gwalior and Delhi. The British loosened restrictions during the two world wars, but it was not until after 1947 that the textile industry received the go-ahead for full-scale expansion.[12]

Initial slow growth, such as into synthetics, vastly expanded after the 1980s economic liberalization. In the early 1980s, synthetics were relatively expensive. Within the decade, these were available to Indians of all social classes at attractive prices.

The second trend was a revival of interest in handloomed textiles. This emerged first in the independence movement, which called on Indians to buy and use Indian products—in particular, *khadi*. But problems abounded.

Elites associated *khadi* with the lower classes, villagers, and members of marginal social groups. Poor people found *khadi* expensive, unavailable, and of worse quality than mill cloth. A huge cultural loss of handloom skills and technology cut into diversity of production and knowledge of, for instance, how to produce the finest and sheerest muslins.

Gandhi did the most to promote *khadi*. He stopped wearing Western dress and experimented with varieties of Indian traditional clothing, before settling finally on a short, wrapped *dhoti* (a men's lower-body garment), which was swiftly dubbed his "loincloth."[13] Gandhi also devised a simple folded *khadi* cap, which replaced both Western, regional, and caste-identifying men's headgear. The Gandhi cap became a symbol of resistance to the Raj.

Soon the revived interest in hand-spun and -loomed cloth led to diversification of color, pattern, and design. This included production of labor-intensive finer fabrics, such as silk. Now, synthetic yarn is also sometimes used in *khadi* textiles.

Following 1947, the government of India subsidized *khadi* producers through institutions such as the Khadi and Village Industries Board and the All-India Handicrafts Board. Marketing is through organizations such as Delhi's Gandhi Ashram Khadi Bhandar, the All-India Handloom Fabrics Marketing Cooperative, and state-run cooperatives. Private entrepreneurs have also developed markets for handloomed textiles, spurred by the late-twentieth-century fashion of ethnic chic. The big firms meet the tastes of the Indian, European, and North American markets. The best of these firms support endangered arts.

Woman handspinning at Khadi Weaving Center,
Pokharan, Rajasthan. Courtesy of the author.

Changing social identities also affected what people wore, and how they wore it. It is no accident that elites discovered "traditional dress" just about the same time that its wearers were shifting to polyester. The Westernized elites were reaching for authenticity. For some, this represented a chance to revive arts that were being lost. Hand embroideries, old fabrics, and jewelry became prizes for the fashion-conscious, sometimes bought directly off rural women's bodies. Others contacted dyers, printers, embroiderers, and other artisans and began production of goods aimed to satisfy this new fashion. Local design vocabularies were often reworked in new ways and forms to appeal to urban consumers. Traditional symbolic associations meant little to urbanites and foreign tourists, other than that this symbolized authenticity.

Ironically, this was the very reason that many former, nonelite wearers bought mill cloth for their next outfits. Traditional prints in many cases marked the wearer as a member of a low-status group. Modern prints such as abstract and floral designs lack these associations. They also are neutral with respect to the cosmological significance attached to certain styles, fabrics, and weaves.

These contradictory interpretations of authenticity came together at a large meeting of NGOs held in a Bhil tribal area of Rajasthan during the late 1980s. *Khadi* prevailed among the visiting social workers. Muted natural shades predominated among the women visitors, who warmed themselves with fine wool shawls. Village women wore polyester fabrics printed with chemical dyes, in bright floral and abstract designs. Most popular was an electric lime green, used for their half-saris draped over the skirt-and-blouse ensembles. Coarse wool or acrylic shawls added warmth, and rubber sandals protected their feet.

COSMOLOGY, SYMBOL, AND STYLE

Sometimes a color or a body adornment is just a fashion statement, sometimes it has important symbolism: a badge of group identity, a woman's marital status, values such as auspiciousness or mourning. Iconography of dress resembles that of art.

Red, green, and yellow are happy colors, associated with fertility and good luck. Brides most often wear red. Pregnant women and new mothers wear saris with red borders and a yellow ground. Young men wear bright turbans. Saffron is associated with religion, now particularly with Hindu fundamentalism, called the saffron wave.

White dress and headgear signal mourning in many areas. Mourning colors can include pale blue and lavender. A man may wear a white turban if his father is deceased.

Blue and green have diverse meanings. Some Brahmans do not wear blue, because the dye process may kill tiny organisms. Members of other groups wear blue as protection against the evil eye. Green has become associated with Islam, though Deccani brides traditionally wear a green wedding sari instead of the bright red seen elsewhere. Green has also long been associated with the Vaishya *varna*.

Women in western India embroider their skirts with symbols of auspiciousness, such as a clay water pot topped with leaf-and-flower, seed, vine, and flower motifs. The edge of the skirt will have a sharp-pointed zigzag border, "thorns," to keep evil at bay. Motifs such as these also appear on saris.

A person's supernatural essence adheres to clothing. Ritual purity demands wearing freshly washed clothes. Loosely woven, porous fabrics such as cotton are more susceptible than tightly woven cloth. Easily polluted are *khadi*, the Brahman's sacred thread, and the coarse thread wristband that sisters tie on their brothers or honorary brothers. When a widow remarries she burns her old clothing. It is imbued with the spirit of her deceased husband.

You are also what you wear. Members of the shepherd Bharwad group of Western India say that if a man doesn't wear their dress, he ceases to be Bharwad.[14] Being Bharwad means dressing Bharwad. Bharwad men wear a distinctive short gathered smock with long, tight sleeves, massive wound turban, gathered pantaloons, and a shawl.

In Bihar, men of the Muria Gonds wear identical clothing: in public, this is a blue shirt.[15] Young men and women who participate in the group's festivals select a particular outfit that all wear as a uniform for the dancing. In the 1980s, rural Rajasthani Muslim men began to wear a light green shirt as a symbol of Islamic identity.

Clothing gifts express social relationships. Prior to independence, rulers awarded subordinates robes of honor. This custom is recalled in the presentation of fine Kashmiri shawls to recipients of government awards. In places where traditional patron-client systems existed, patrons gave clients clothing at times, such as when a patron's child married.

Weddings are occasions for numerous clothing gifts. In Gujarat, the groom's father gives the bride-to-be a large veil cloth, earrings, anklets, and a nose ring.[16] He pledges to give an auspicious number of outfits to the bride, and the jewelry requisite to a married woman. This can also include her wedding outfit.

The bride's family assembles her trousseau. Many outfits must be stitched. Among rural Gujarat families, unmarried girls embroider full long skirts for their trousseau. These are matched to blouses and half-saris. The trousseau is displayed at the bride's going-away ceremony.

Women's jewelry comprises the most valuable portion of her personal adornments.[17] These include bangles, arm ornaments, nose ornaments, earrings, necklaces, rings, anklets, waist chains or belts, toe rings, and forehead ornaments. Those who can afford it give their daughters and daughters-in-law gold. Middle-class married women should have a set of gold bangles, two for each wrist, and a black-beaded necklace with gold ornaments, which is the sign she is married. Toe rings and anklets complete a married woman's basic jewelry ensemble. Many groups have distinctive pieces that they wear.

This includes a rigid ring worn around the neck (worn also by men of some communities), multiple bangles, and wide ivory (or fake ivory) armbands worn above the elbow. Married women wear columns of sparkling glass or practical plastic bangles on their wrists and forearms. The colors often match an outfit. Widows are not supposed to adorn themselves with glass bangles or jewelry. Some discretely wear simple jewelry or a religious medallion.

The finishing touches include kohl around the eyes, nail polish, and a painted-on or stick-on *bindi* in the middle of the forehead. Today's *bindi* comes in many shapes and colors. In this context, it is a beauty spot—not a religious symbol. The final touch for a married lady is for her husband to place a red streak in the parting of her hair. This represents their happy conjugal life.

FIBER, TECHNOLOGY, PATTERN, AND BASIC FORM

Each element of textile production—fiber, spinning technique, weave, texture, color, and design—features in producing fabrics suited to the basic forms of clothing. Designers may work in an indigenous palette or combine this with industrial technologies. Machine textiles compete with handwork, and hand workers sometimes copy machine technology.

India's best-known natural fibers are cotton, silk, and wool. Cotton varieties laid the basis for India's great textile industries. Production of the Chinese silkworm began in eighteenth-century Bengal. Silks include two wild varieties, both from the northeast: *Tasar* silk and the naturally gold-colored *Muga* silk. This is India's most luxurious silk, never to be dyed. Wool ranges in quality from the coarse fiber produced by Thar desert sheep to Kashmir's gossamer wools. India imports Australian merino wool for men's suitings and for use by *khadi* producers, who spin and weave it into adaptations of local designs.

The most complex hand technology produced the Kashmiri shawls of the eighteenth and early nineteenth centuries.[18] This inspired imitations such as the Paisley shawl produced in Scotland in the nineteenth century. Kashmiris developed a hand-embroidered product that today is the standard. Handloom weavers' techniques range from simple plain weave, to more complex twills, tapestry techniques, and methods of adding different yarns (thread) during the weaving process to create contrasting designs.

Historically, Indian weavers had access to brilliant plant-based dyes: reds, vivid yellows, and deep blue, using indigo.[19] A dye based on the insect *Coccus cacca* produced an especially prized red. Indian dyers invented many processes.[20] The most important was the use of mordants, a class of chemical solutions that cause pigments to bond with the fiber. Indian weavers also developed many techniques of resist dyeing. This uses wax, mud, or other substances to keep dye from bonding with the fiber. Specific techniques include ikat, tie-and-dye, batik, and *kalamkari* ("pen work").

In ikat, the yarn is tied up along its length and dyed in different colors. The design appears when the fabric is woven. In tie-and-dye, little bundles of cloth are tied up to prevent the dye from penetrating. This produces patterns of spots or wavy striped patterns. In batik, wax covers areas of the fabric that are not to be dyed. *Kalamkari* designs are made by painting on the design by hand. Painters wield a thick brush with a sponge-like center, which holds either a mordant or a dye.

Hand block printing is one of India's oldest industries. The most intricate patterns are created by a master carver, who produces the blocks. The printer lays on the design, directly stamping the pattern and using resist stamps to produce intricate effects. Printers create tinsel designs by stamping glue on the fabric in a pattern, then rubbing glitter over the fabric. Block-printing centers near Jaipur, Rajasthan, produce cheerful multicolored cottons and silks. Near the Pakistan border, printers make a densely patterned printed indigo blue and dark red dyed cotton fabric that men wear as shoulder wraps.[21]

Embroidery famously includes *zari* work, which uses gold and silver thread. Mughal-inspired designs feature scrolling borders of flowers, vines, and repeated geometric shapes. Lucknow is famous for its *chikan* work. Although master embroiderers know up to seventy-five different detailed stitches, most work today requires minimal technical knowledge.[22] Designs are also made by adding contrasting weight or color weft yarns, "supplementing" the base warp and weft. This technique appears all over India, from Rajasthan's thick big wool shawls spun from wool of desert sheep, to the sheerest cottons.

Indian clothing construction divides into two basic techniques: unstitched clothing, whose forms are produced by wrapping, folding, or tieing around the body; and stitched clothing.

The most common unstitched garment, worn by everyone, is the shawl. Roughly two to three yards in length and about a yard wide, the shawl is wrapped around the body so that one of its long decorative ends hangs over the left shoulder. Shawls often have fancy borders along their length, plus a more elaborate decoration on their endpieces (the design across the width at each end). Fabric ranges from coarse wool to the finest cashmere. Men's unstitched clothing is dominated by the *dhoti*, a man's lower garment wrapped to form loose pant legs, and the *lungi*, a sarong-like garment. Fabrics range from the fine, almost sheer white muslin of a politician or businessman, to the substantial cottons of farmers and workers. There are many ways to wrap a *dhoti*: just below the knee, to long and flowing with extra folds and drapes.

The most distinctive unstitched male dress is the turban. Regional patterns are most evident for special occasions. Rajasthanis wrap bright tie-and-dye

Mr. Khan with children, Barmer, Rajasthan.
Courtesy of the author.

fabric into big, floppy coiled pillows. Rajputs starch theirs and tie it so that a jaunty plume of fabric hangs down the back. Sikh turbans are tightly wrapped, angular, almost geometric.

The sari is the most distinctive unstitched women's garment. Women all over India find this a supremely practical garment, worn in fabrics that range from the everyday to exquisite, expensive special occasion wear. Different ways of wrapping the sari and different fabrics and designs denote regional differences. Although little is known about the history of the sari prior to around the start of the twentieth century, 100 B.C.E. carvings depict a woman wearing a sari-like garment, as do paintings at the fifth century Ajanta cave complex.[23] A typical sari is thirteen to twenty-six feet in length and about four feet in width. A sari contains three distinct zones: the borders, which run along the length of the top and bottom, the interior or field (between the borders), and the *pallu*, the endpiece. The endpiece and borders help to stabilize the fabric so that it hangs correctly on the body.

The *pallu* is the most elaborate section. Simpler versions of its motifs decorate the sari borders. Often, makers include a separate, short matching blouse piece that includes design motifs in the sari. One year, wide borders are in fashion. Another year, narrow borders rule. The *pallu* may be tied to hang quite long, or shorter. There are many different ways to wrap a sari.[24] The most familiar style hails from Bengal, draped around the torso, with the endpiece hanging over the left shoulder, so that it drapes over the back.

Men and some women wear a collarless, loose, long-sleeved shirt with a short front placket opening from the neck. Other stitched clothing includes quilted vests, the short Nehru jacket, and its knee-length version. Grooms often wear silk brocade versions of these coats. Other stitched garments include loose pants and pants that are baggy above the knee and tight below, the model for the West's Jodhpur pants.

Women's stitched clothing includes *salwar kamiz*, skirt-and-blouse outfits, and the *burqa*. *Salwar kamiz* consists of pants (*salwar*) worn with a *kamiz* (a dress-like overgarment) and a wide scarf long enough to drape over the head and shoulders. The *kamiz* reflects fashion and region: it may be above the knee or below the knee, fitted or loose, long- or short-sleeved.

The full ankle-length skirt is pleated and stitched with matching border. It will be worn with a contrasting or matching short bodice with sleeves, which is often covered with a matching short sleeveless tunic. A half-sari wraps over this and drapes over the head. Conservative Muslim women wear the *burqa*—a loose cotton or synthetic overcoat with an attached cape and veil—outside the house.

REGIONAL AND "ETHNIC" DRESS

Each area of India produces distinctive fabrics and designs, many of which maintain a strong appeal. Manufacturers of synthetic saris have found that they must cater to regional tastes. Women's dress much more than men's reflects ethnicity and region. The following account focuses mainly on women's regional dress.

Pale, light colors predominate in Bengal and eastern India. Bengal's sheer cotton muslins set a standard, with their narrow borders and simple endpieces whose designs come from laid-in threads in contrasting colors.[25] Quality ranges from the dappled patterns of sheer white-on-white, called morning dew, to thicker laid-in threads that form angular, contrasting patterns. Bihari saris often use applique techniques for decoration. This is rarely seen elsewhere. Assam's gold *muga* silk, of undyed fiber, is the ultimate in sophisticated understatement. Hill tribal groups use a backstrap loom to produce

Rajput women, Surani. Courtesy of the author.

dense cottons with vivid geometric figures, often on a black or a dark ground.[26]

Far to the north, in Kashmir, women wear *salwar kamiz* and men *kurta pajama* underneath a heavy, voluminous wool caftan-like overgarment that adds warmth. Fine embroidery embellishes neck and sleeves. The most superb work is reserved for the finest wool shawls.

Varanasi is the home of rich silk and gold brocades. Heavy silk *saris* with gold brocade endpieces and borders are woven in spectacular peacock hues. The weaver's crowning glory may be an all-over brocade pattern, or an iridescent sheer tissue, called "woven water."

In Delhi and Punjab, the *salwar kamiz* predominates. *Salwar kamiz* is practical and comfortable for farm women—and has been adopted by college women as their dress of choice. Lucknow's *chikan* industry produces lengths for women's *salwar* suits, kurtas, and saris.

Western India is famous for color combinations of hot pink, bright yellow, and red. The full long skirt, with its accessory blouse and half-sari, is traditional here. Tie-and-dye is popular, such as the auspicious five-color pattern with its five different colored broad stripes, purple, green, orange, red, and yellow. Zari work is highly developed. Fine silk georgette and less-expensive cotton are both embellished with gold embroidery, tape, glittery spangles, and bits of mirror. Jaipur is home to a block-printing industry that produces light cotton and silk saris, *salwar* suit lengths, vests, and quilt covers.

In the far west, women of some groups wear full wool skirts and heavy, dark indigo or red half-saris as protection from the sun. These skirts are embroidered with bright colors in auspicious designs. Gujarat is also home to the double ikat Patola silk saris, created by dying both warp and weft. This fabric is so treasured that it has found a place in ritual.[27]

Perhaps emulating the style of wearing a half-sari, the Gujarati style of wearing a sari passes its ends under the arms (instead of over the chest) and then up over the head to drape the endpiece back-to-front over the right shoulder and chest.

Styles of the Deccan and south India feature rich dark colors, and different ways to tie the sari. In Maharashtra, women wrap the sari so that it has two legs, as with a man's dhoti. Far in the south, saris may be wrapped with the pleats inside and endpiece tied on the shoulder, like a tunic. Tribal women in western Orissa wear a short, thick, knee-length sari. Parsi women prefer pale colors of lace, chiffon, and satin for formal occasions, and white for the wedding sari.

A popular Deccan sari features dark cotton, woven in an extremely fine check, sometimes just one or two threads. This creates a two-toned effect, called sun and shadow. Orissa also produces fine *ikat* textiles.

South India is a major zone of sari production. This includes both traditional south Indian designs as well as fashion saris, produced to meet regional tastes in other parts of the country. Tamil Nadu is home to the nation's oldest handloom cooperative, Co-op Tex, established in 1935. Perhaps the best-known style is the *Kornad* sari, with its wide borders, interior checks, and endpiece stripes. Heavy silk Kanchipuram saris and the gold cloth, a white cotton sari with gold zari work, are for special occasions. Andhra Pradesh's weavers produce bold, intensely colored ikats, while intricate Kalamkari work is more muted.

NOTES

1. K.T. Achaya, *Indian Food: A Historical Companion* (Delhi: Oxford University Press, 1994).

2. Ibid., p. 38.

3. Marvin Harris, *Cannibals and Kings: The Origins of Cultures* (New York: Random House, 1977).

4. K.T. Achaya, op. cit., p. 57.

5. Babur, Emperor of Hindustan, *The Baburnama: Memoirs of Babur, Prince and Emperor*, trans. by Wheeler M. Thackston (New York: Oxford University Press, 1996), p. 343.

6. R.S. Khare, *The Hindu Hearth and Home* (Durham, NC: Carolina Academic Press, 1976).

7. Madhur Jaffrey, *Flavors of India* (Seattle: West 175 Publishing, 1995), pp. 222–223.

8. Ibid., p. 236.

9. Achaya, op. cit., p. 59.

10. Komal Kothari, personal communication.

11. Emma Tarlo, *Clothing Matters: Dress and Identity in India* (Chicago: University of Chicago Press, 1996).

12. Gita Piramal and Margaret Herdeck, *India's Industrialists* (Washington, DC: Three Continents Press, 1985).

13. Tarlo (1996) discusses Gandhi's experiments with dress and adoption of the "loincloth," pp. 62–93.

14. Tarlo, op. cit., p. 262.

15. Alfred Gell, "Newcomers to the World of Goods: Consumption among the Muria Gonds," pp. 110–138 in Arjun Appadurai, ed., *The Social Life of Things: Commodities in Cultural Perspective* (Cambridge: Cambridge University Press, 1986).

16. Tarlo, op. cit., pp. 176–179.

17. Doranne Jacobson, "Women and Jewelry in Rural India," pp. 171–223 in D. Jacobson and Susan Wadley, *Women in India: Two Perspectives* (New Delhi: Manohar, 1995).

18. Monique Lévi-Strauss, *The Cashmere Shawl*, trans. by Sara Harris (New York: Harry N. Abrams, Publishers, 1988).

19. Mattiebelle Gittinger, *Master Dyers to the World: Technique and Trade in Early Indian Dyed Cotton Textiles* (Washington, DC: The Textile Museum, 1982).

20. Kax Wilson, *A History of Textiles* (Boulder, CO: Westview Press, 1979), pp. 96–97.

21. Françoise Cousin, "Light and Shade, Blue and Red: The Azarak of Sind," pp. 103–114 in Jasleen Dhamija and Jyotindra Jain, eds., *Handwoven Fabrics of India* (Ahmedabad, India: Mapin Publishing, 1989).

22. Clare Wilkenson-Weber, *Embroidering Lives: Women's Work and Skill in the Lucknow Embroidery Industry* (Albany: State University of New York Press, 1999).

23. Linda Lynton, *The Sari: Styles, Patterns, History, Techniques* (New York: Harry N. Abrams, Publishers, 1995), pp. 109.

24. Ibid., pp. 14–24.

25. Pupul Jayakar, "Cotton Jamdanis of Tanda and Banaras," pp. 96–102 in Jasleen Dhamija and Jyotindra Jain, eds., *Handwoven Fabrics of India* (Ahmedabad, India: Mapin Publishing, 1989).

26. Jasleen Dhamija, "Eastern India," pp. 133–144 in Jasleen Dhamija and Jyotindra Jain, eds., *Handwoven Fabrics of India* (Ahmedabad, India: Mapin Publishing, 1989).

27. Alfred Bühler, "Indian Resist-Dyed Fabrics," pp. 84–95 in Jasleen Dhamija and Jyotindra Jain, eds., *Handwoven Fabrics of India* (Ahmedabad, India: Mapin Publishing, 1989).

Suggested Readings

Achaya, K.T. *Indian Food: A Historical Companion* (Delhi: Oxford University Press, 1994).

Bharadwaj, Monisha. *The Indian Spice Kitchen* (New York: Dutton, 1997).

Dhamija, Jasleen and Jyotindra Jain (eds.). *Handwoven Fabrics of India* (Ahmedabad, India: Mapin Publishing, 1989).

Khare, R.S. *The Hindu Hearth and Home* (Durham, NC: Carolina Academic Press, 1976).

Lynton, Linda. *The Sari: Styles, Patterns, History, Techniques* (New York: Harry N. Abrams, Publishers, 1995).

Tarlo, Emma. *Clothing Matters: Dress and Identity in India* (Chicago: University of Chicago Press, 1996).

Wilkinson-Weber, Clare M. *Embroidering Lives: Women's Work and Skill in the Lucknow Embroidery Industry* (Albany: State University of New York Press, 1999).

7

Women, Marriage, and Family

IN VILLAGES, the first sound of the day is before dawn: the rasp of the stone grinding wheel as women prepare flour for the day. At night, the last human voice is usually a mother, murmuring to her child. The hard life of the Indian woman is proverbial. Parents say that they give extra affection to a daughter in order to compensate for the hard life that she'll have after she marries and moves into the household of her mother-in-law. Yet India is also one of the few nations of the world that has had a woman as head of state—Mrs. Gandhi, who held several terms as Prime Minister from the 1960s to the early 1980s—and that has many highly educated professional women, heirs to India's modernist and secular traditions. Many of these women work very hard to improve the situation of other women, whose situation for the most part is quite different. For them, poverty, the fact that the necessities of life are produced within family units where women's contribution is essential, and women's exclusion from ownership of significant property contributes to their relative lack of status, compared to men.

This chapter examines women in contemporary India with respect to the family, work, and the more general cultural sphere. Why women in particular, when so many other groups—Dalits, members of Scheduled Castes and Tribes, religious minorities, and others—also live under conditions of social oppression? Women are a focus because their subordination cuts across the vast majority of socioeconomic, ethnic, caste, and religious groups. Female-headed households are poorer than male-headed households. Social customs deprive women of legal rights to land and other resources. Many groups regard women as constitutionally different from men, as sources of ritual pollution and, in the most generalized cosmic sense, of supernatural danger.

Yet India is also a place of great diversity of women's status. Here is one of the world's most vigorous women's rights movements. Women's concerns and activities braid through history, world view, religion, work, landscape, socialization, shelter, dress, food, music, dance, and leisure time.

DEMOGRAPHIC, LEGAL, AND CULTURAL TRENDS

General trends affecting women reflect demography, the legal system, and cultural preferences. Census data document the generally harsher conditions of life faced by women as a group than by men. Despite legal guarantees, women are disadvantaged with respect to inheritance and property rights. Dominant cultural preferences give males priority over females. This is the situation that confronts women as they seek change.

Data for India paint a grim picture of women's situation relative to men (Table 7-1). The national sex ratio of women to men, 927:1,000, shows a deficit. In most countries, sex ratios tend to favor females slightly. Although overall life expectancy (the number of years an infant is expected to live) is roughly the same for males and females, there is high female mortality in all age categories until they pass out of their reproductive years (Table 7-2).

Higher mortality in the earliest years (ages 0–4) is accounted for by selective infanticide, general neglect, and abuse of female children.[1] Women also experience substantial mortality during their reproductive years. This situation results from poor nutrition, inadequate prenatal care, and, in many cases, the absence of appropriate intervention in the case of high risk deliveries.

The total fertility rate of women, however, has declined to approximately 3.3 live births, from 5.5, as recently as 1980. Though infant mortality rates have halved since independence, Indian mothers currently are about eight times as likely to experience the death of a child as mothers in the United States.

The number of girls in primary school has risen, but females lag in higher education. Fewer than 40 percent are enrolled in secondary school. The rate is even lower for postsecondary education (college, technical institutions, university). Education is an important marker relating to status and employment.

This portrait of education reflects women's participation in the workforce. However, it must be noted that the official percentage of women in the workforce (32 percent) is artificially low, since it counts only women in wage labor. The majority of women work in family firms and on family farms, or

Table 7-1
Basic Indicators

	1991
Sex ratio (females/1,000 males)	927
Illiteracy, females aged 15 and above (percent)	62
Illiteracy, males aged 15 and above (percent)	35
Females in primary school (percent of total females in age group)	91
Females in secondary school (percent of total)	38
Females in labor force (percent of total)	32
Total fertility rate (live births per woman)	3.3
Infant mortality rate (per 1,000)	70
Maternal mortality rate (per 100,000)	437
Female life expectancy (years)	58
Male life expectancy (years)	57

Sources: The World Bank, *World Development Report 1997: The State in a Changing World* (New York, Oxford University Press, 1997), Table 7, "Education," p. 226, and Table 6, "Health," p. 224; *Economic and Political Weekly* Research Foundation, "Social Indicators of Development for India—I," *Economic and Political Weekly* (Bombay), May 14, 1994, p. 1228.

Table 7-2
Death Rates, by Age Categories and by Sex, 1988 (deaths per 1,000 population in age group)

	Male	Female
0–4 years	31.8	34.9
5–14 years	2.2	2.5
15–34 years	2.3	3.0
35–49 years	6.4	4.6
50 years and above	36.6	31.1

Source: *Economic and Political Weekly* Research Foundation, "Social Indicators of Development for India—I," Table A, "Estimated Age-Specific Death Rates by Rural/Urban and by Sex, India 1988," p. 1229 in *Economic and Political Weekly* (Bombay) May 14, 1994, pp. 1227–1240.

Table 7-3
Rural Death Rates, by Age Categories and by Sex, 1988

	Rural Male	*Rural Female*
0–4 years	35.1	39.1
5–14 years	2.6	2.8
15–34 years	2.4	3.3
35–49 years	6.8	4.9
50 years and above	37.1	31.6

Source: *Economic and Political Weekly* Research Foundation, "Social Indicators of Development for India—I," Table A, "Estimated Age-Specific Death Rates by Rural/Urban and by Sex, India 1988," p. 1229 in *Economic and Political Weekly* (Bombay), May 14, 1994, pp. 1227–1240.

as uncounted full- or part-time wage laborers for their neighbors. This setting is particularly important for Dalit women, over 70 percent of whom work as agricultural laborers.[2] Women's wages are only about half those paid to men.

The largely agrarian setting of women's lives is also linked to their most pressing legal problem, lack of social empowerment to inherit, buy, or manage land—and land is a farmer's most important resource.[3] Numerous social practices limit women's access to land.

Despite laws calling for the equal division of estates among male and female children, in nearly all cases daughters do not inherit. Daughters' land interests instead get assigned to their brothers. Daughters receive a dowry payment at the time of their marriage. This is typically worth far less than a woman's entitlement would be if she received her share of the land. Most of the dowry transfer goes directly to a bride's in-laws in the form of cash and goods, such as refrigerators, motor scooters, televisions, land, and livestock. The actual amount of the dowry available as a bride's personal asset is well below these amounts. Further, the youthful daughter-in-law may face demands from her in-laws that she turn over even this. The worst-case scenarios in recent years have been those of dowry death, where in-laws killed young married women or drove them to suicide, if their families failed to meet their demands for dowry.

The outcome of the differing expectations on dowry, compared to inheriting land and the family firm, is that women lack ability to muster assets for substantial investment on their own, or to achieve independence outside the extended family. In the case of divorce or early widowhood, the woman may be left with too little for herself and her children. Direct access to assets is just one part of the picture.

In many parts of northern India, societal norms that a woman of good family and reputation seclude herself from unrelated men restrict her physical mobility and interactions, such as in the marketplace or dealing with laborers. Young brides typically must obtain permission from senior family members to leave the family compound. Further, some groups' norms that a daughter-in-law not directly address her husband or senior men of his household restricts her negotiating ability. High illiteracy among rural women over age 15 creates a knowledge gap that handicaps their ability to claim their rights.

Although a daughter-in-law's situation may look bad, that of a relatively young widow may be even worse. Despite her efforts to keep her husband's share of the estate, she often finds herself squeezed out. Her husband's family wants to keep his land in the family. One strategy is for the widow to wed one of her husband's brothers. This does not always work. Personality clashes or lack of suitable candidates can nip this in the bud. And if a widow marries a man from a different family, she loses her rights to her first husband's estate and may also lose custody of any children to his family.

This discussion of legal rights has shaded into the problem area of the cultural practices that shape women's status. Societal norms impose expectations that limit the practical assumption of rights. These are part of a more general set of dominant cultural norms that broadly reflect elite perspectives. These define a moral, good woman as possessing three important characteristics. First, she restricts her personal mobility, unless suitably chaperoned. Second, she effaces her sexuality. Third and most important, she willingly subordinates herself to her family's interests: first her parents, then her husband's family.

Class enters this picture, since working-class and poor women cannot afford to follow these rules strictly. Outsiders may stereotype women of these groups as sexually promiscuous simply because they work outside the home. Sexual harassment and exploitation are facts of life for many poor and working class women. Young women in particular are viewed as fair game for verbal innuendo, even physical groping and intimidation, a practice Indians call "eve-teasing."

Legal norms and cultural issues intertwine in one important area, that of laws relating to marriage. India's family code differs in one important respect from other sections of the civil law in that separate legal codes spell out family law for Hindus, Muslims, Christians, Parsi, Jews, and members of tribal groups. A woman's rights of marriage, divorce, and inheritance depend upon the law under which she wed. The inequities in this system sprang into public prominence in the case of Shah Bano, an elderly divorced woman.

In the case of the Muslim family code, women's and men's rights differ. A Muslim woman must show cause to gain a divorce—while her husband need only pronounce the ritual formula "*Talaq, talaq, talaq*" ("Divorce, divorce, divorce"). The code states further that the ex-husband is required only to support his ex-wife for three months following the divorce, and to give her a sum called *mehr*, which was promised to her at the time of marriage in the event of divorce.

Shah Bano had been married for forty-six years before her husband divorced her. Shah Bano's husband claimed priority for the Muslim law as the reason for not giving her any support. She in turn sought relief under Section 125 of the Criminal Code, which stated that ex-husbands must support ex-wives if they were destitute. This measure attempted to keep these women off public relief. India's Supreme Court ruled in Shah Bano's favor in 1985.

Shah Bano's success was short-lived. Conservative Muslim leaders sprang on the case as an erosion of religious rights. Prime Minister Rajiv Gandhi tried to improve his popularity with conservative Muslim voters by supporting the Muslim Women's (Protection of Rights on Divorce) Bill, which passed in 1986. This reaffirmed the priority of religious law. Shah Bano was back to square one. Liberals who have sought a uniform civil code to cover family law find this a political football, hostage to religious and intergroup political conflicts.

STATUS, WORK, AND GENDER IDEOLOGY

Women's status stems from the convergence of historical and cultural factors linked to the different ways of making a living, plus women's and men's contributions to the family income. In practical terms, this reflects the agrarian nature of society and the use of large animals in agriculture—cattle, water buffalo, and the camel.[4] These are traditionally trained and worked by men, who also carry out the vital activity of plowing the soil. In farming systems such as these, men's labor is seen as more central to agricultural production than that of women. In these systems, as seen, women are systematically excluded from land ownership. The great cereal belt of the Gangetic plain conforms to this pattern.

Regions with other technologies and groups whose economic specializations are based on other important factors diverge from this pattern. One example is found in intensive irrigated rice-producing zones. These start crops in seedbeds, then transplant the young plants, a process that requires heavy labor input. Regions where this technology is important, such as Kerala, grant women a higher status than in the north. Another example is with situations

Village pond—women's crossroads. Courtesy of the author.

where men practice long-distance migration and are absent for most of the year. Here, women's management and work skills become important.

Systems of shifting cultivation are often heavily biased toward women's labor. The difference in women's status and economic contribution is so striking, compared to other production systems, that these are sometimes called "female" farming systems. Systems of this type are extremely rare today. During most of the twentieth century, the government sought to end shifting cultivation, which is associated with extensive use of lands and slash-and-burn techniques. Plantations and the timber industry restricted the amount of land available for this land use, which requires large tracts of forest in order to be sustainable. Economic change, sedentarization, and exposure to dominant values have transformed most of these groups into peasant cultivators. Though women's status has declined markedly in recent decades, their outside reputation as societies in which women hold high status has changed little.[5]

One example are the horticulturalist Garos of Meghalaya, who traditionally transmitted their communally owned lands through the female line. Recruitment of husbands to these matrilineal households occurred through groom capture by agents of the bride.

Historically, the matrilineal (descent through the female) Nayars' primary economic adaptation depended on long-distance migration by men, who sold their services as mercenaries.[6] During the twentieth century, legal reforms initiated by the government promoted the breakup of the Nayar matrilineal joint household and the erosion of Nayar women's traditional rights. As written, the law reflected dominant models of gender that favored men's property rights. Even the rediscovery of long-distance migration, this time in the form of work in the Gulf states, may not be enough to restore the traditional Nayar household.

Equality of earnings among municipal sanitation workers, called sweepers, promoted gender equality.[7] In over half of sweeper households in Varanasi, the wife managed the family budget and gave an allowance to her husband. Men and women shared housework in a manner unthinkable in higher-status households. Women agricultural laborers in Kerala and Tamil Nadu also managed their own earnings in most cases.[8] In fishing communities such as the Mukkavars of India's southernmost tip, while women had no access to fishing technology, they traditionally controlled the family's cash flow and circulation of cash and assets within the community.[9]

These few examples suggest some of the possibilities within which women's status varies. This variation, inevitably, confronts the dominant model, closely associated with the plow agricultural complex: the patriarchal family, arranged marriage, women's seclusion within the household, restrictions on her interaction with unrelated men, the ban on widow remarriage, and the custom of giving dowry along with the bride at the time of marriage.

Related aspects of gender ideology include the concept that women and men have different relationships to the supernatural. In Hinduism, *shakti* is female power. Properly channeled, *shakti* is the source of fertility and creativity. Women are associated with nature and with powerful sources of ritual pollution stemming from menstruation and birth. But *shakti* is formless and dangerous, unless controlled by the masculine principle.

This ideology separates women and men from one another. Masculinity and femininity become defined as distinct, if not opposing, entities. Interestingly, one of the most popular deities of Hinduism's emergence, the great deity Shiva, is sometimes depicted as half-male and half-female.

In this ideology, the control of women's sexuality most properly centers in the family. It reflects, again, familial control over land. A woman's marriage simultaneously activates her sexuality and transfers it to her husband's family. This may be why in north Indian families, one of the last acts of the new bride as she departs to her husband's house is to worship her family's female ancestral goddesses. One of her first acts in her husband's home is to worship his ancestral goddesses. As she passes through the stages of life, she eventually will join them.

How do women view these roles? Rajput women of Udaipur, Rajasthan

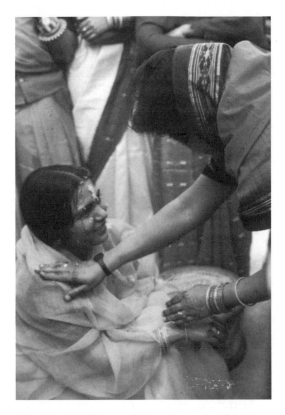

Ritual bath before wedding. Courtesy of the
author.

said that women aspired to become the perfect wives.[10] As a "good wife," a
woman devotes herself to her husband's welfare through her performance of
religious ritual, household duties, and chastity. In extremity, a Rajput wife
must strap on a sword and go to battle. In less dramatic mode, she contra-
dicts, shames, or curses her husband if necessary to force him to do his duty.
Through self-sacrifice, duty, and honor, a woman accrues virtue, which protects the family. She is a domestic warrior for its prosperity and the health
of its members.

The wife who perfectly realizes this role may become a *satimata* (a protective goddess). Although *sati* more commonly is attached to images of wives
dying on their husbands' funeral pyres (an act that is illegal), the Udaipur
women said that a truly virtuous woman could become a living *sati*, one who
personifies goodness and truthfulness, for she had transcended the limitations
of human flesh.

FAMILY AND WORK

Traditionally, a woman's individual role splits between those of daughter and those of daughter-in-law, and between junior and senior woman. A daughter enjoys freedom of movement in her parent's village. Here she need not veil before the men of the village. At her in-laws' village, relationships are more formal and she would cover her face with the end of her sari, half-sari, or long wide scarf that drapes over the head and shoulders, as a sign of respect. Junior women's activities are most circumscribed in the household. As she becomes a mother, then mother-in-law, she becomes a senior woman, one of respect. Senior women enjoy physical mobility and authority over others not granted to young women in their reproductive years.

As previously noted, the caste system restricts the choice of marriage partners, who one should and should not marry. Numerous economic transactions at every stage of marriage arrangements make it clear that marriage is not about individuals, but about families. In the case of young educated professionals, who want to marry for love, it hopefully happens that the special someone matches the families' criteria. Then the arrangements will be made. In other cases, an adult child defers to his or her parents as a matter of demonstrating respect and attachment to family values.

Matchmaking reflects a family's social network. Parents who are good friends with one another may arrange a match for their children. Often the connection is made through relatives or a professional matchmaker. The Sunday editions of newspapers include lengthy matrimonial columns, one for prospective brides, one for prospective grooms. The negotiation involves explicit discussions of where and with whom the couple will live, the bride's career or educational prospects, and career assistance to the groom. Photographs of prospective spouses make the rounds of a family, and everyone contributes to the discussion.

The reality for many young women and men is that the news of a betrothal is when they are told that the wedding is about to take place. In the Thar desert, girls may have been promised at birth or even wed as toddlers. A subsequent ceremony takes place when both bride and groom are old enough to start married life.

Resistance against wedding arrangements includes elopement, refusing proposals, running away, even disappearing on the honeymoon. Couples who elope generally opt for a simple civil ceremony, then hope to persuade family after the fact. If the couple is of different caste or religious status, the bride takes her husband's identity. Her children will belong to his group.

The scandal of an elopement after a match is arranged is more than about the runaways: two families may have exchanged gifts, cash, gold, and material goods, expecting a wedding to take place. It is almost impossible for a bride's family to recover dowry payments, which are illegal. One solution so that everyone doesn't lose face is for the reneging family (as the parties would see this) to offer a substitute bride or groom, such as a sibling.

A bride generally dreads her first days in her in-laws' home. She becomes subject to her mother-in-law's authority and quickly must learn a lifetime's worth of family lore, customs, cooking styles, and food preferences. She may feel caught between her husband and her mother-in-law. And many families expect her to conceive right away, so that soon there will be a new baby to hold and love.

Ideally, the mother-in-law is stern, yet affectionate. She should strive to balance the women's work so that no one feels overly put upon—although of course this happens. Mothers-in-law may fear that growing intimacy between the new couple threatens the unity of the family.

One factor affecting women's relationships in joint families is education. The introduction of an educated bride into a family where the mother-in-law is illiterate creates strains. Another source of tension is when the bride is illiterate—and the groom is not. He may resent his bride because she does not share his interests and values or seems old-fashioned.

In the first few years of marriage, brides and grooms frequently are parted from one another. The bride visits her parents often, then for a longer period as she awaits the birth of her first baby. In her husband's family, decisions about work, the children's schooling, even birth control are made by the family. Sometimes a young husband and wife will take unilateral action, then announce this to the family.

Unresolved family conflicts may force families to split, or a wife to return home to her parents. The women's movement has raised consciousness of domestic violence against women: dowry death, wife beating, and sexual abuse. Divorced or separated women face many problems. Lack of income, problems finding living space, parents' and brothers' lack of sympathy, child care, and limited employment prospects are all barriers.

The family farm is the primary work site for most women. Patterns of rural-urban migration find men, not women, leaving villages for work. In some regions and at all but the seasons of most intensive farm work, such as the harvest, women are the majority of the workforce. Outside a minority of elite households whose women do not work in the fields, all farm women do some agricultural labor. Young girls work with their sisters and sisters-in-law. Brides work under the direction of their mothers-in-law, along with the other women of the household and its visiting daughters. Farming has an endless number of tasks. Women plant (though they do not plow), weed, transplant, chop fodder, harvest, thresh, husk, grind, parboil, and process the crop.

Haymaking. Courtesy of the author.

Women also work in family enterprises, collecting fuel for pottery making or metal work, combing wool, winding yarn, cleaning and packing finished items. Women tend livestock, herd the family's cow or goats, milk the cow or goat, and churn the milk to make butter and buttermilk, then make *ghee* (clarified butter). Women stitch and mend the family's clothes, prepare the daily meals, and tend the children. One important activity is collecting cow dung, which can be shaped into big patties and dried to use as fuel, or mixed into what in English is termed "cow-dung paste." This is used to replaster walls and courtyards. When all this is done, many women still find time to decorate the home with elaborate designs that are thought to bring luck.

Although paid employment is limited in rural areas, women find small income-generating opportunities. Agricultural labor is the biggest employer of women. Work as a common laborer involves headloading bricks and dirt to construction sites, carrying landfill to mining sites, excavating reservoirs, and working on irrigation tanks and channels. Women also work in the stone mines as rock crushers, pounding rocks into gravel. Cutting firewood, making leaf fodder, preparing cow-dung cakes, selling inexpensive plastic bangles and cosmetics, making *ghee,* and lending out small sums of money are a few income-earning activities.

The growth of villages into small towns and market centers has expanded employment opportunities for women. Women from nearby villages may find a daily commute is feasible, where they might be reluctant to travel farther afield. Women participate in the handloom and handicrafts industries, making glass bangles, for instance, or embroidering fabrics. Education brings opportunities for work in government offices, banks, medical centers, and women's organizations.

Most paid work that women do at home requires a low level of skill. Agents for companies pick up and drop off work that they then sell to merchants or intermediate brokers. Few agents are women. As a rule, women lack capital for investment in materials such as cloth and thread for quilt making, tobacco and cigarette papers for cigarette rolling, and flour and spices for cracker baking.

Textile-related production is a steady employer of women in diverse settings from family-owned shops and home-based piece workers, to work in factories that employ large numbers of workers. In Lucknow, for example, Muslim women now dominate *chikan* (white-on-white) embroidery. They produce *kurtas* (loose, long-sleeved tops that enjoyed a vogue in the West in the 1960s), *pajamas* (pants), Nehru caps, and other garments.[11]

Production is organized as a putting-out system. Brokers hand out unfinished pieces and collect finished work from home-based embroiderers. The work has extremely low pay rates and high rates of underemployment and unemployment. *Chikan* workers also embroider garments for the government-sponsored enterprises, which are supposed to promote handloom industries. Low wages to these workers are rationalized by employers on the grounds that they are just part-time—even though for many women, this is their family's sole support.

A different industry, prostitution, employs large numbers of women and girls in major urban centers such as Calcutta and along heavily traveled truck routes. Women who enter prostitution do so because of poverty and abusive conditions at home.[12] In the early 1990s, health workers identified a high rate of HIV-AIDS infection among workers, sparking fears that truck drivers would infect their wives and unborn children. In some cities, such as Lucknow, elite prostitutes have created households, female-owned businesses. Transmitted from mother to daughter, these households' lifestyles overtly contradict patriarchal values.[13] As a general rule, sex workers face severe exploitation.

Educated urban women work in offices, in the ranks of the civil service, as physicians, computer software engineers, bank personnel, teachers, college professors, and lawyers in India's courts. Middle-class women have begun to face the issues of balancing the home and work, along with involvement in charitable and social-work institutions. Many educated women have become active in the women's movement, helping to staff centers for the women, organizing conferences, and working to achieve change.

THE WOMEN'S MOVEMENT

Several key events spurred women's organizations in the 1970s.[14] *Towards Equality*, the 1975 report of the government of India's Commission on the Status of Women (and issued during Mrs. Gandhi's term as Prime Minister), jolted activists with its conclusion that women's status had declined since independence. Middle-class urban women mobilized against dowry deaths, against rapes of women held by the police, and female feticide based on prenatal sex testing. Particular sparks included the Shah Bano case and the burning of Roop Kanwar, a young Rajput widow, on her husband's funeral pyre in 1987. Women's centers, conferences, and periodicals provided a common voice and opportunities for leadership training that were particularly important at this stage to middle-class women.

Poor women brought the movement its greatest impetus in both urban and rural areas. The Self-Employed Women's Association (SEWA) experience is typical. SEWA began as an offshoot of the Textile Labour Association to fight for better wages, fair treatment by contractors, and decent working conditions for the thousands of women who worked in the unorganized sector in Ahmedabad. SEWA organized a social-services division to provide health care, life insurance, day care, and economic cooperative units. Poor women demanded a small-business loan program, citing lack of capital as a major factor limiting their efforts. SEWA's small-business loan program took off and became a model for similar programs—not just in India, but in other nations, too.

Rural women focused on environmental issues. Environmental deterioration meant that women spent more time hauling water from wells as water tables dropped, and more time hunting for firewood, because of deforestation. Declining tree cover sparked conflicts with the government's Forestry Department, which viewed the forests as a resource to be managed by giving out timber contracts to distant corporations, and overlooked local use rights. Under conditions of scarcity, villagers began to fight back.

In the Himalayas, women halted a planned timber operation by putting themselves between the trees and the axe men in 1973. "Hug the trees," they called, and the Chipko movement was born. Though this was a resistance movement that involved villagers against outsiders, Chipko swiftly became identified as a women's movement.[15] Mechanization reduced employment for landless women in Kerala.[16] Women's advocates who organized meetings for poor women in Rajasthani villages found that they denounced the exploitation they as "little people" suffered at the hands of the "big people."

During the 1990s, numerous projects targeted women and women's issues. Programs covered a wide range: literacy, instruction in the national language, sanitation, well-baby and maternity clinics, afforestation, well construction, grassroots organizing, guinea worm eradication, job training, "green" environmental technology, women's banks, credit, marketing cooperatives, and violence against women. Issues of sexuality also emerged, with a tiny lesbian movement joining India's new movement for gay rights.

NGOs provided a vital link between rural women and urban middle-class or elite women. Their access to resources and knowledge of government institutions helped to initiate and sustain projects. Traditions of Gandhian activism remained strong, and inspired local women also to organize for themselves.

Yet, one of the unintended consequences of this institution building has been affirmation of dominant values and erosion of subcultural diversity.[17] Bhil tribal women of Rajasthan were deeply subordinated. Efforts to reduce the impact of the caste hierarchy unwittingly increased the gender hierarchy. Efforts targeted at these impoverished, illiterate women tutored them in middle-class ideology and reaffirmed the dominant values to which these women might aspire but, in the absence of real social transformation, were unlikely to achieve.

NOTES

1. Barbara Miller, *The Endangered Sex: Neglect of Female Children in Rural North India* (Ithaca, NY: Cornell University Press, 1981).

2. S.M. Michael, "Dalit Visions of a Just Society," pp. 25–41 in S.M. Michael, ed., *Untouchable: Dalits in Modern India* (Boulder, CO: Lynne Rienner Publishers, 1999), p. 36.

3. Bina Agarwal, *A Field of One's Own: Gender and Land Rights in South Asia* (Cambridge: Cambridge University Press, 1994); Srimati Basu, *She Comes to Take Her Rights: Indian Women, Property and Propriety* (Albany: State University of New York Press, 1999).

4. Ester Boserup, *Women's Role in Economic Development* (London: Allen & Unwin, 1970); Jack Goody, *Production and Reproduction: A Comparative Study of the Domestic Domain* (Cambridge: Cambridge University Press, 1976).

5. Maxine Weisgrau, *Interpreting Development: Local Histories, Local Strategies* (Lanham, MD: University Press of America, 1997), p. 159.

6. E. Kathleen Gough, "The Nayars and the Definition of Marriage," *Journal of the Royal Anthropological Institute of Great Britain and Ireland* 89:23–33, 1959.

7. Mary Searle-Chatterjee, *Reversible Sex Roles: The Special Case of Benares Sweepers* (Oxford: Pergamon Press, 1981).

8. Joan P. Mencher, "Women's Work and Poverty: Women's Contribution to Household Maintenance in South India," pp. 99–119 in Daisy Dwyer and Judith Bruce, eds., *A Home Divided: Women and Income in the Third World* (Stanford: Stanford University Press, 1988).

9. Kalpana Ram, *Mukkuvar Women: Gender, Hegemony and Capitalist Transformation in a South Indian Fishing Community* (London: Zed Books, 1991).

10. Lindsay Harlan, *Religion and Rajput Women* (Berkeley: University of California Press, 1992).

11. Clare M. Wilkinson-Weber, *Embroidering Lives: Women's Work and Skill in the Lucknow Embroidery Industry* (Albany: State University of New York Press, 1999).

12. A similar thread runs through the stories collected from the Hijras, India's "third sex," collected by Zia Jaffrey, *The Invisibles: A Tale of the Eunuchs of India* (New York: Vintage Books, 1996).

13. Veena Talwar Oldenburg, "Lifestyle as Resistance: The Case of the Courtesans of Lucknow," pp. 23–61 in Douglas Haynes and Gyan Prakash, eds., *Contesting Power: Resistance and Everyday Social Relations in South Asia* (Berkeley: University of California Press, 1991).

14. Radha Kumar, "From Chipko to Sati: The Contemporary Indian Women's Movement," in Amrita Basu, ed., *The Challenge of Local Feminisms: Women's Movements in Global Perspective* (Boulder, CO: Westview Press, 1995), pp. 58–86.

15. Ramachandra Guha, *The Unquiet Woods: Ecological Change and Peasant Resistance in the Himalaya* (Berkeley: University of California Press, 1989), esp. pp. 159–179. An activist perspective is Vandana Shiva, *Ecology and the Politics of Survival. Conflicts over Natural Resources in India* (New Delhi: Sage Publications 1991), pp. 103–124.

16. Mencher, op. cit.

17. Weisgrau, op. cit., pp. 206–208.

SUGGESTED READINGS

Agarwal, Bina. *A Field of One's Own: Gender and Land-Rights in South Asia* (Cambridge: Cambridge University Press, 1994).

Forbes, Geraldine. *Women in Modern India* (Cambridge: Cambridge University Press, 1996).

Harlan, Lindsay. *Religion and Rajput Women* (Berkeley: University of California Press, 1992).

Jaffrey, Zia. *The Invisibles: A Tale of the Eunuchs of India* (New York: Vintage Books, 1996).

Kapadia, Karin. *Siva and Her Sisters: Gender, Caste and Class in Rural South India* (Boulder, CO: Westview Press, 1995).

Lateef, Shahida. *Muslim Women in India: Political and Private Realities 1890s–1980s* (London: Zed Books, 1990).

Minturn, Leigh. *Sita's Daughters: Coming out of Purdah* (New York: Oxford University Press, 1993).

Wilkinson-Weber, Clare M. *Embroidering Lives: Women's Work and Skill in the Lucknow Embroidery Industry* (Albany: State University of New York Press, 1999).

8

Festivals and Leisure Activities

IN UDAIPUR DISTRICT of Rajasthan, Bhils today host and perform an almost unknown forty-day festival. It begins in late summer and culminates at the pan-Indian festival of Dassehra, in the fall.[1] Bhils focus their festival on Gavri, a form of the Hindu goddess Parvati. Gavri comes to villagers at the festival of Raksha Bandhan and makes her wishes known by possessing her followers in trance states. Each year, Bhils in six to seven villages, from among a set of twenty to thirty, sponsor their own Gavri troupe, men whose vow it is to participate in the Gavri dance-drama, to possess and be possessed by the Goddess during this season of the year.

Gavri begins with rituals in the performers' home village. Then the group sets off. For the next forty days, they must not drink liquor, eat meat or green leafy vegetables, or have sex. The troupe is invited to perform Gavri at villages where they have relatives by marriage, and where they have patrons. It's lucky to host a Gavri troupe.

The Gavri festival ends approximately at the festival of Dassehra, in the fall. At this time, members of the troupe return to their village. In a long night, Gavri culminates with worship of the elephant-shaped deity that accompanies the group, dancing, and the presentation of pots of newly sprouted grain to the deity. These then are immersed in a nearby body of water. With this grand night, Gavri ends. Gavri's experiences today are emblematic of issues surrounding festivals and leisure time.

Festivals are periods of intensified social and ritual interaction. These are times when people exit the routines of daily life into festival time. This may be a great public event shared by millions, or a private fast. What people do

Kanana–Sitla Mataji festival. Courtesy of the author.

during festivals, on pilgrimages, and in their leisure time is influenced by their social status and aspirations.

India has hundreds of different festivals that range from domestic events or ones focused on local shrines to great pan-Indian holidays. Every village, city neighborhood, and squatter settlement probably has at least one independent, voluntary committee that plans, raises funds for, and organizes its festivals. These committees compete to put on the best display or hire the most popular musicians.

Sometimes festivals turn political, as in Ladakh. Here, Muslims stopped participating in the Buddhist fall Ladakh New Year's celebrations. This shift was the outcome of political demands and counterdemands by Buddhists and Muslims.[2] The rise of a movement for Assamese identity in the far eastern state of Assam promoted the spring equinox festival as a national day for Assamese.[3] On many occasions, upper castes have resisted lower castes' attempts to parade through upper-caste neighborhoods or past their temples.

The courts, however, have generally sided with the right of citizens to equal access to public space.

Other festivals are almost invisible, yet no less important. Kerala's Kamparamayanam festival, held in temples, includes an eight-night play of shadow puppets. Performers set up their equipment and perform the play each night. All through the dark, the performers play—but no one is there to watch.[4]

Across India, women observe many festivals at home with fasting and prayer. These fasts, undertaken as a matter of private devotion and need, sometimes form important—if almost invisible—activities associated with public festivals.

New festivals have emerged and older ones have vanished. In the 1890s, Indian Nationalist leader Tilak promoted the festival honoring the elephant-headed Hindu deity Ganesh's birthday. The festival involves a procession to the sea, where celebrants immerse Ganesh images in the water. The festival has grown so big that on the day after, Mumbai beaches are awash in half-dissolved images of Ganesh. The waters are tinted with the paints used for decorations, a major pollution hazard, according to city authorities.

This festival has been adopted in a big way throughout Maharashtra and central India. This festival adapts forms from other festivals. The practice of immersion is popular, for it ritually "cools" substances "warmed" by divinity. In eastern Madhya Pradesh, for instance, women planted small pots of seedlings to be taken along with the Ganesh image for its immersion in the water.[5]

Festival forms were adapted to new ends, most famously by Gandhi, who took pilgrimage and fasting, both associated with festivals, and made them into political tools. The best known recent adaptation of festival forms occurred in 1990, when BJP leaders held a "chariot" pilgrimage, which traveled from the rebuilt Somnath Temple in Gujarat to Ayodhya. This event featured a heavily decorated Toyota van as its chariot. Loudspeakers played popular Hindi tunes and the sound tracks from two popular television serials.

FESTIVAL TIME AND STRUCTURE

In festival time, the boundaries of the human social world intertwine with sacred time, space, and beings. The suspension of normal time and relationships during this period is often marked by a key event or ritual that opens the festival or that begins the pilgrimages.

The lunar year's end, for instance, is marked by the great Holi festival. This is the end of the cold season and the start of the hot season, the time of the Goddess. In the weeks leading up to Holi, which takes place in early spring, youths scavenge wood and other materials to build the Holi bonfire.

This is lit on Holi eve and marks the start of the revels. During Holi play, people get to violate normal rules of social respect.

Children mock adults, women tease men, and men engage in bawdy horseplay and joking. Teetotalers swig a marijuana-laced drink and some vegetarians eat meat. Everyone plays Holi by throwing colored powder and squirting colored water on one another. Many Westerners have inadvertently walked out in a favorite or new outfit on Holi—and come home in quite a different-colored outfit.

Holi ends in the late afternoon as people bathe and return to their normal social rules and roles. The only reminders of the annual seasonal excess are the splotches of magenta, purple, and red that deck people's clothes and cattle for days afterward.

Festivals draw attention to group boundaries, intensifying the sense of difference between participants and nonparticipants, and increasing the solidarity of participants. Some festivals emphasize a common identity. Other festivals divide social groups from one another as they become badges of distinct identity.

India's different religions—and sects within them—use different calendars. Historically, different regions of India have used their own dating systems, too. Muslims use a lunar calendar, which starts from the time of the Prophet Muhammad's migration from Mecca to Medina (622 C.E., dated in this system as *Anno Hegirae*, A.H.). Hinduism uses a lunar calendar, popularly known as the *Vikramaditya* calendar, that is fifty-seven or fifty-eight years ahead of the Gregorian calendar (Table 8-1). Secular life uses the Western calendar. New Year's is a great holiday on January 1. But then there is also the Hindu New Year, Buddhist New Year, Muslim New Year, Jewish New Year, and on down the line, celebrated at different times of the year.

Hinduism's *Vikramaditya* calendar dominates the annual round of festivals. Half of the year, from the winter solstice to the summer solstice, is auspicious, "bright." The period from the summer solstice to the winter solstice is inauspicious, "dark." Two other important solar dates are the spring and fall equinox, with the spring equinox important as it serves as the traditional New Year for many. The lunar calendar contains twelve months of thirty days' length each (see Table 8-1). These are lunar days, and the calendar counts thirty days to each month. An extra month is inserted every thirty months in order to keep months synchronized with the season. In addition, there are greater cycles, which govern special festivals such as the Kumbh Mela, which occurs only every twelve years.

The Muslim lunar calendar repeats every thirty-six years. Months move backward relative to the seasons, rotating among all four in a slow time span of somewhat more than a generation. Prominent Muslim festivals such as

Table 8-1
Traditional Hindu Months

Hindi Name/Common Variant	Equivalent
Cait (Chaitra)	March/April
Baisakh	April/May
Jeth (Jyeshth)	May/June
Asarh (Asharh)	June/July
Sawan (Shravan)	July/August
Bhadom (Bhadrapad)	August/September
Kwar (Kunwar or Ashivan)	September/October
Karttik	October/November
Aghan (Margashirsh)	November/December
Pus (Paush)	December/January
Magh	January/February
Phagun (Phalgun)	February/March

Ramadan thus lack the seasonal qualities associated with Hindu festivals (Table 8-2).

Hindu months divide into a dark half or fortnight, *badi*, ending on new moon day and a bright half, *sudi*, ending on the full moon. This is the last day of the month. A lunar date is given in terms of the month, the fortnight, and the day. *Chait sudi* 1, the first day after the new moon of Chait (commonly translated as April/May), is the first day of the Hindu lunar New Year.

Full moon and new moon days have the greatest significance. *Purnima* (*sudi* 15, full moon) is the luckiest day. The fourth (*chaturvedi*), eighth (*ashtami*), and eleventh (*ekadashi*) days are also important. Festivals use these terms, such as Janam Ashtami (Birth Eighth), which commemorates Krishna's birthday (Table 8-3).

Private and public activities intertwine in festivals. Pilgrims consult an expert so that they may leave on the most auspicious day and time. In Rajasthan, *Dev Jhulani Ekadashi* culminates on Bhadom *badi* 11 with a procession to the village pond. Participants include women who carry water pots to mark the termination of their year-long fast to protect their families and the village water supply. Each woman married into the village enters the pond with her brother. He helps her break her fast by giving her a first drink of the water. This is one of the rituals that takes place when the village's chief deity rides out for his annual bath.

Table 8-2
The Islamic Ritual Calendar

Month (Indian Name)	Festival
Muharram	New year begins; festival Muharram, days 1–10
	10 Martyrdom of Imam Hussein (61 A.H.)
Safar	
Rabi-ul-awwal	17 Prophet's birthday
Rabi-ul-akhir	
Jamadi-ul-awwal	
Jamadi-ul-akhir	
Rajjab	1–6 'Urs of Khwaja Muin-a-din Chishti, Ajmer
Shawan	
Ramadan	Ramzan fast (entire month)
Shawal	Id-ul-Fitr—ends Ramadan
Zilkida	
Zilhijja	10 Bakr Id

Popular events at festivals include processions. These, like pilgrimages, traverse sacred space and time. Whereas a pilgrimage aims to reach sacred crossing points, processions mark deities' territories and their connection with worshippers.

Images of deities ride out and then return to their temples, are immersed in water, or even cast into it and abandoned. Sacrifices of goats, chickens, buffaloes, and camels propitiate the gods. Along the route, the palanquin bearing the deity may stop at private homes, so that women can worship and present offerings. Singing, drumming, and dancing accompany processions. Possession states play a role in many festivals, such as when deities "ride" their devotees, as among Paharis of Uttar Pradesh's Himalayan districts. Boundaries of sacred and mundane space blur, or are temporarily erased.

SEASONAL FESTIVALS

India's great festivals cluster in the springtime and in the fall (see Table 8-3). Spring festivals correspond roughly with the conclusion of the winter agricultural season and the beginning of the hot season. The monsoon is an intensive period for farmers. The smaller festivals then emphasize hopes for a good crop. Fall festivals mark the harvest and the beginning of the cold

Table 8-3
Principal Festivals Mentioned in the Text

Month	Festival/Event
Chait (March/April)	*badi* 1–8 Spring Navaratra
	badi 1 Holi
	badi 9 Ramnavni (Ram's birthday)
	sudi 13 Mahavir Jayanti (Mahavir's birthday, Jains)
Baisakh (April/May)	*sudi* 1 Lunar New Year
	Baisakhi Day
	Sikh New Year
	sudi 3 Akshaya Tritya Akti
April 14	Dr. B.R. Ambedkar's birthday
Jeth (May/June)	*badi* 13–15 Savitri Puja
	Buddha's birthday and his enlightenment
Asarh (June/July)	*sudi* 1–10 Rath Yatra (Jagannatha festival, Puri)
	sudi 11 Devshayan Ekadashi
Sawan (July/Aug.)	*badi* 1 swings are set up for Tij festival
	badi 5 Nag Panchmi (snakes venerated)
	badi 15 Hariali
	sudi 3 Tij
	sudi 15 Raksha Bandhan
August 15	India Independence Day
Bhadom (Aug./Sept.)	*badi* 8 Janam Ashtami, Ras Lila
	badi 9 Guga Naumi
	badi 12–*sudi* 4 Paryushan (Jains)
	sudi 4 Ganesh Chaturthi (Ganesh birthday)
	sudi 11 Dev Jhulani Ekadashi
Kwar (Sept./Oct.)	*badi* 1–15 Pitar Pak
	sudi 1–9 Fall Navaratra
	Durga Puja, Ram Lila
	sudi 10 Dassehra
	Ashoka Vijaydashmi (Buddhists)
	sudi 15 Sharad Purnima (Harvest Moon)

Table 8-3 *Continued*

Month	*Festival/Event*
Karttik (Oct./Nov.)	*badi* 13 "Little" Diwali
	badi 15 "Big" Diwali; Lakshmi puja
	sudi 1 Cow-dung wealth veneration
	sudi 11 Devuthni Ekadashi (Vishnu awakes)
	sudi 11–15 Pushkar cattle fair
Aghan (Nov./Dec.)	Ladakh New Year Festival
Pus (Dec./Jan.)	*badi* 10 Parshvanath birthday (Jains)
	Ladakhi calendar: Farmers' New Year
Magh (Jan./Feb.)	*badi* 5 Vasanta Panchami
	sudi 15 Auspicious date for melas, preparations start for Holi
Phagun (Feb./March)	*badi* 14 Mahashivatri
	sudi 15 Holi bonfire

Notes: Badi (or *krsn paksh*) begins the day after the full moon; *purnima* ends 15 days later on *amavashya*, the new moon; *sudi* (or *shukla paksh*) begins the day after the new moon, ends on day 15, the full moon, *purnima*.

season. The cold season, less busy for farmers, is a time for cattle fairs and for weddings. This is when people can get free from work for events such as these.

The hot season is the time of the Goddess: festivals celebrate different aspects of feminine divinity, from the dangerous goddess powers vested in deities such as Shitla Mata ("Smallpox Mother") to the kindly female ancestral deities who protect the family.[6] The monsoon is a time of danger. The god Vishnu goes to sleep until winter arrives. The year is in its "dark" side. Protective rituals become important both for households and for larger social entities. The fall harvest sees territorial festivals such as *Dassehra*, climax of the fall. The cold season features local shrine festivals and observances focused on female river deities.

On Chait *badi* 1 everyone plays Holi. This inaugurates the season of the Goddess. Holi traditionally was enjoyed by members of many different groups. Like many other festivals, Holi is becoming a badge of Hindu identity, seen in the declining shared involvement of non-Hindus in Holi celebrations. In Varanasi, for example, Muslim singing groups that entertained on Holi eve stopped doing so. Hindus became more careful of the directions in which they aimed squirt-gun-like syringes of colors, lest they inadvertently offend a member of the wrong faith.[7] Recently, Dalit organizations have asked their members to boycott Holi.

Chait *badi* 1–9 is the spring Navaratra, the nine-nights' festival. Its mate is the fall Navaratra, which culminates on Dassehra. In the springtime, Shitla Ashtami propitiates the dangerous powers of Shitla Mata with blood sacrifices.

Jains commemorate the birth of the last great founder of Jainism, the Tirthankar Mahavir, on Chait *sudi* 13. On Chait *sudi* 15, newlywed Dhangar shepherds make their first pilgrimage together, to the river goddess shrine of Bhivai in Maharashtra. Varanasi dedicates this period to the Mother Ganges, who is worshipped as a deity. Many city dwellers try to rise early and take an auspicious predawn bath in the river.

Many festivals cluster about the spring equinox. April 13 is Baisakh. Baisakh is an important date for Sikhs, because this is the day that the tenth Sikh Guru instituted the congregation of the faithful. Sikhs celebrate this as their New Year's and Guru Nanak's birthday too. Neo-Buddhists celebrate B.R. Ambedkar's birthday on April 14. Processions and spirited celebrations commemorate the day in Pune, which has a large Dalit population.

South India's Madurai celebrates the marriage of its city goddess Minakshi with Shiva. This festival renews the city's covenant with its protective deity as she marks her sacred territory during the festival events.[8] This twelve day "Wedding of the Goddess" features elaborate processions. These reenact Minakshi's coronation, her conquests, and her wedding.

Minakshi's processions are led by a cannon, which announces the goddess's imminent arrival. She is guarded by police vehicles that clear the way. Bands of priests carrying umbrellas and banners chant as they accompany her. Residents offer coconuts and flowers to the festival chariots, part of which they receive back as the sanctified leavings of the deity from the attendant priests. Vishnu, popular opinion firmly states, is Minakshi's brother. Events make him a day late for the wedding. It is said that he stops at one of his temples— where he spends the night with his Muslim mistress.

Festivals shift to protective rituals in the rainy season. One of the biggest is the chariot procession of Puri's Jagannatha Temple, which is attended by hundreds of thousands of pilgrims. The old wooden images of Jagannatha (a form of Vishnu) his brother, and sister "die" and are replaced by new ones.[9] On the new moon day of Asarh, the new images are revealed for their first viewing. Next, the three images begin their journey on huge wooden chariots pulled by dozens of believers. The deities travel from the temple to a smaller shrine, where they remain for a week, then return.

Ekadashi Devshayan is the date that Vishnu goes to sleep for the duration of the rainy season. Many holy men and women wend their way to Varanasi for their own four-month retreat, until Vishnu awakens. Pious Jains fast by not eating leafy green vegetables. They drink no water after nightfall, lest they inadvertently consume a microscopic organism.

Nag Panchmi ("Snake Fifth") finds villagers leaving milk offerings at shrines to the snake deities. Rainy season floods drive snakes and vermin from their holes into the higher ground of villages. Cattle pastoralists of Maharashtra worship at termite mounds, sacred as the homes of snakes and as the mythical origin site of sheep.

As the season moves toward the beginning of agricultural operations, Hariali ("Plow") is an occasion for farmers to clean, adorn, and worship their plows and other agricultural tools. The cattle get a bath and have their horns painted and their hides dyed with bright orange or red polka dots. They are fed treats. The nights of Nag Panchmi and Hariali are dangerous times when the witches dance naked, with hair loose, in cemeteries and cremation grounds. Villagers do best to stay indoors.

On Raksha bandhan, women honor brothers and ritual brothers by tying a lucky band around their wrists. Merchants display for sale assortments of gold, red, and hot-pink tinsel and plastic bands adorned with auspicious symbols. Men with many sisters and honorary sisters will have several bright bands wrapped around their right wrists.

Hindu god Krishna's birthday is a big festival in Vaishnavite-dominated areas, most particularly in Krishna's sacred land of Braj. In Brindavan, this is the high season for *Ras Lila* troupes to perform. Raslila is a playful dance drama of episodes from Krishna's story. Many pilgrims come at this time to view the plays and visit the sites associated with him.[10]

Neighborhoods sponsor their own Ras Lila troupes. Boys play the deities: Krishna, his beloved Radha, and the women cowherds while adult actors take on other roles. One of the most popular episodes depicts the occasion when Krishna multiplied himself to dance simultaneously with the women cowherds. After an episode, the actors playing Krishna and Radha arrange themselves in a tableau. They—like other performers of sacred roles—temporarily become the deity for a brief moment of worship.

People fast on the night of Krishna's birth: no cereal products are allowed; one can only eat foods cooked in ghee (clarified butter). The focus is on dairy foods, particularly delicious milk sweets.

The night of the seventh to the morning of the eighth is a night wake. People sing the night through, awaiting the first sight of the newborn Krishna at 3:00 or 4:00 A.M. They put on the radio and listen to the broadcast from Brindavan, Krishna's sacred town. On the eighth, images of Krishna are bathed in milk. In Brindavan, the drenching goes on for hours.

Jains celebrate their important festival, Paryushan, two weeks later. The festival celebrates Mahavir Jayanti. Processions, readings from the book that recount his sayings, special fasts, and congregational worship mark the occasion. In Jaipur, members of the two main Jain sects join in a parade through the town.[11]

As the harvest nears, it is time for ancestor remembrance. Food offerings to the crows on Kwar *badi* 1 recognize these birds' symbolic role as ancestral spirits. One day is reserved for veneration of female ancestors. Unpleasant goblins are laid to rest. In Varanasi, this can be done by driving a spike into a tree at the temple of the goblin Pishachamochana.

The fall Navaratra culminates on the tenth, Dassehra. It is one of India's largest festivals. Depending on where one lives in India, Navaratra emphasizes Durga Puja or Ram Lila—and sometimes both.

Durga Puja focuses on goddess worship. In Varanasi, people visit two different temples each day, one associated with a "Durga" and one with a "Gavri"—that is, with a dangerous and with a kindly female deity, respectively. Families honor ancestral goddesses. Durga Puja ends with the victory of the goddess over Mahishasura, the buffalo demon. The temporary images prepared for the festival are ritually cooled by immersion in a river or pond, after which they lose their ritual significance.

Ram Lila is becoming the national drama of India, with its celebration of Ram's exploits in the Ramayana and idealization of *Ram Rajya*, the mythical period of his rule.[12] The climax on Dassehra depicts Ram's victory. In some areas, politicizing of the festival as one of Hindu identity over others has forced authorities to ban public performances, fearing this might spark conflicts. In other areas, Ram Lila has been a celebration of the triumph of good over evil, enjoyed by all members of the community.

Ram Lila has high drama. The climax is Ram's conquest of Ravana, the demon. In one district of Varanasi, the entire crowd of Ram Lila spectators charges Ravana's stronghold right alongside the actors playing Ram and the other heroes.[13] In other areas, the festival's highlight is the burning of Lanka, when a fort constructed specifically for this purpose is set on fire.[14] Dassehra often ends with the torching of huge Ravana effigies.

Buddhists commemorate this date as Ashok Vijaydashmi, when Emperor Ashoka converted to Buddhism. Buddhists decorate their temples and attend worship. In a creative adaptation of Dassehra themes, in Agra, Dalit neo-Buddhists in the 1960s created a huge image of "Untouchability"—and burned it.[15]

It is now time for Diwali preparations. Many enjoy this festival. People clean and freshen their homes with new coats of whitewash and cow-dung paste. Women draw auspicious designs around doorways and at thresholds. Merchants decorate their shops with colored lights and sell fireworks, lamps, and sweets for the occasion. On Karttik *badi* 13, little Diwali, rows of lamps give this holiday its popular name, "Festival of Lights." These are supposed to turn away Death. The new moon, the fifteenth, is big Diwali. This coincides with worship of Lakshmi, goddess of wealth.

Lakshmi *puja* ("worship") winds up the business year and starts the new one. Merchants close up their old books and draw up new ones. Jains celebrate this as a feast day. Families make a shrine that includes family deities, images of Lakshmi, the account books, and tools of the trade. They offer worship at this little shrine.

The cold season opens when Vishnu awakens after his long rainy-season sleep. This is the season for fairs, which usually coincide with a local shrine's festival date, religious gatherings, weddings, outings, and river goddess festivals. In New Delhi, the Buddhist leader, the Dalai Lama, offers his annual teachings, a popular event. In Uttar Pradesh men enjoyed evening events they called "picnics."[16] They cooked meat over a fire, drank, talked, and relaxed in the outdoors, away from village busybodies and village norms.

India's great Pushkar cattle fair takes place from Karttik *sudi* 11 to the full moon. Foreign and domestic tourists come for the camel races, contests to see which camel can hold the largest number of riders, folk music, and other attractions alongside the hundreds of thousands of villagers come to trade in their oxen on a new team, or to purchase a stout draft camel.

Ladakh's Buddhists celebrate the traditional New Year, Losar, in this season. In Jaipur, Jains mark the birthday of the twenty-third Tirthankar with a procession and worship. The full moon of Pus is a popular time for pilgrims to visit the site where the Ganges River flows into the Bay of Bengal.

This is also the season of Christmas and January 1, New Year's. Members of the middle class greet one another with New Year's cards. New Year's eve is celebrated in cities with parties and fireworks. January 26, Republic Day, is a national holiday. Those with television sets tune in to watch New Delhi's parade.

Vasanta Panchami (Spring Fifth) is a sign of the coming spring. During this month, one hears a whirring in the sky, looks up—and sees a small kite dipping and swooping upward. Men and boys fly fighting kites, trying to cut their rivals' kites loose with glass-coated strings.

Magh Purnima is an especially lucky date for a fair. The cold season is also the time for many urban river goddess festivals.[17] Brahmans take a leading role in many of these, organizing neighborhood festival processions and community meals. This is a time when the community's young people return from work and school to enjoy the season and to renew old ties.

Sometime between January and May, villagers in south Kerala schedule their annual Kotai festivals, which honor village deities. These are run by and for middle-ranked caste groups. Neither Brahmans nor Dalits participate. A highlight of these festivals is their bow song performances.

Mahashivatri marks Shiva's marriage to Parvati. Women pour water on Shiva's sacred lingam—sometimes making small images for this purpose— and pray for their husbands' well-being. In one village near Delhi, this festival was most significant for Brahman women; others did not know whether this was a Hindu or a Muslim festival![18]

MUSLIM CALENDRICAL FESTIVALS

Big festivals, Ramzan (Ramadan), Fitr-ul-Id, Muharram, and Bakr Id (the Feast of Sacrifice) cycle according to the Muslim calendar, in which months slowly move among the seasons.[19] Farmers mark agricultural shifts. Ladakhi Muslims have their grain blessed at the mosque before sowing, and do this again at the harvest. Indian ways of celebrating Muslim festivals are best described as similar to the general ways the people in their region organize festivals. South Indian Muslims may have one focus; Muslims in Bengal have something a bit different.[20]

The ritual year begins with Muharram, a festival that commemorates the martyrdom of Hussein venerated by Shi'a muslims, as the third Imam (leader) of Islam after the prophet Mohammad. Thousands pray in the Shi'a Jamma Masjid at Kashmiri Gate in Delhi. Lucknow hosts large parades, which carry a Tazia, a copy of Hussein's tomb. Congregational meetings feature sermons, prayers, and poetry.

In the Thar desert, the Langas gather with other Muslims and make a great procession with the Tazia. A drummer and musician accompany the congregation as it wheels back and forth over the small open space between the village and the sand dunes that loom nearby. The men cry out Hussein's name. Some scourge themselves with knives and chains to feel Hussein's travail. The women mass together and dance slowly, singing loudly. A small fair is nearby where bangles, sandals, and other small goods may be purchased. Another area informally serves as the camel parking lot. In late afternoon, the Tazia will be taken to the dunes and buried.

The Prophet's birthday may be bigger in India than elsewhere. This is a day for fasting, giving alms to the poor, and sharing sweets.

The fast of Ramzan (Ramadan) lasts the entire month. Everyone except the very young or infirm should not eat or drink anything between dawn and sundown. Even the poorest families, such as the embroidery workers of Lucknow, spend extra time preparing tasty dishes to share with neighbors as everyone joins in the nightly fast-breaking.[21] The last day of the fast ends with the sighting of the new moon, at Id-ul-Fitr.

Id dancers, Barnawa, Rajasthan. Courtesy of the author.

This is a major feast. Mosques have special sermons, neighbors greet one another with auspicious greetings. Meat biryani (rice dish), milk-and-vermicelli pudding, and sweets grace tables. Id cards are sent to those who are far away. The end of Ramzan is also the time of departure for pilgrims bound on the pilgrimage to Mecca.

The Feast of Sacrifice or *bakr-id*, as this is familiarly known, commemorates Abraham's sacrifice of his son. This day those who can afford it sacrifice goat—("bakr" means goat) then feast and share the meat with friends and the poor.

Saints' tombs are the focal point of many festivals. Processions, offerings, water rituals, and beliefs about curing and luck surround the many shrine cults focused on saints. As committees prepare for an *'Urs* ("death anniversary"), the shrine will be bathed, and the tomb decked with a freshly embroidered cover. The committee plans readings from the Qu'ran, traditional song sessions, food distributions, and poetry readings. The biggest *'Urs*, with hundreds of thousands of pilgrims and a fair, may be that at the Ajmer shrine of the saint Muin-ud-din Chishti.

South India's shrine of Sahul Hameed Nagore Andawar (ca. 1504–1570) hosts a grand fourteen day *'Urs*. Nagore Andawar, his local title, settled on the Tamil Nadu coast after many travels through west Asia. The festival features flags, which are hoisted to the tops of the shrine's minarets and paraded through the town. Five groups of beggar priests spend forty days at the shrine and assist with the festival events.

Each day a procession comes from the mosque, then wends its way through town to the saint's tomb. On the twelfth day, the procession goes to the seashore, where the individual chosen to embody the saint drinks water. This is supposed to taste first salty, then sweet—a signal of Islam's transcendence of social barriers and differences. On the fourteenth day, the flags come down and the festival ends.

FESTIVALS AND THE TRANSFORMATION OF INDIAN CULTURE

Themes in Indian culture seem to stand out in strongest contrast in festivals: the rise of secularism and national identity, such as in celebrations of Republic Day on January 26 and India's Independence Day, August 15. Conflicts over the role of religion in public life and of the relationships of different groups to one another often break out at festival time. Festivals demonstrate the ways in which Indians are remaking their identities.

The last two decades of the twentieth century saw the increased integration of previously marginal groups into the national culture. Access to mass media and extension of basic education promoted new identities and new claims on public, shared symbolic space. India's underprivileged find festivals an important vehicle for expressing their aspirations.

One big movement is a Sanskritization of festivals, that, their modification to conform to upper-caste and elite norms—particularly among the members of Scheduled Castes and Tribes. This process has been encouraged by some Hindu fundamentalist activists, who see this as a way to counter Buddhism and Christianity, which are attracting converts among those who suffer from or have been excluded from the economic gains of the 1990s.

For these groups, Sanskritization functions as a form of religious revitalization and as a means of identifying with the larger nation. The Bhils, whose Gavri festival opened this chapter, are a Scheduled Tribe comprising some 225,000-plus members. They live in southern Rajasthan and in contiguous states. Bhils are poor—as poor as, if not poorer than, their Dalit and Muslim neighbors.

Diverse social movements during the late nineteenth and early twentieth century claimed for Bhils the right to adopt paraphernalia and customs associated with high-caste groups.[22] These movements largely failed, owing to the higher castes' ability to force the Bhils to keep to their place in life. Following independence, the upper castes' ability to do this has been restricted.[23] Concern with the appeal of Christianity—missionaries are active in the area—has increased Hindu tolerance of the Bhils' adoption of high-caste practices. Also, for urban upper-caste groups—many of whom are imbued with "modern" values—the Bhils' Gavri represents a link to a traditional and authentic Indian heritage that they may feel is lacking in their own lives.

The Gavri festival is carried out on public streets and settings. The festival provides an opportunity for Bhils publicly to demonstrate their Hinduism and orientation to upper-caste values. Audiences include members of the upper castes. The festival is bracketed between major points in the Hindu festival cycle. The dance-drama has points of similarity with Ram Lila (a story from the Ramayana epic). Stories about the origins of the modern Gavri festival talk about how this was banned, then permitted (in tamed guise) by the upper-caste, traditional lord who ruled the Bhils' territory before independence.

The affirmation of a link with Rajputs reminds festival participants of the claimed special relationship between Bhils and Rajputs, the region's traditional rulers. It also reminds Bhils that their Gavri festival is part of the Rajputs' Ram Lila and Navaratri festivals—celebrated all over India—which Rajputs claimed as their special festival in this region. Finally, the Bhil performers' fast asserts ritual parity with the practices of elite Rajputs, Jains, and Brahmans. This whole situation would have been unthinkable 100 years ago.

Today's Gavri patrons include the NGOs, which are trying to promote economic development here. These move in where traditional patrons have lost interest in supporting Gavri. The minority of educated Bhils regard Gavri as a step backward, even if moved in the direction of "correct" Hindu values and interpretations by participants, as urged by members of Hindu fundamentalist groups.

The Udaipur Bhils' Gavri festival occurs in only a small corner of India, yet it resonates with the contradictory pressures faced by culture today. Modernity is more than simply the character in sunglasses, carrying a cassette player, who dances alongside the Gavri troop. New values intervene. For groups such as the Bhils, whose lifestyle and subculture emphasized egalitarianism, modernity means buying into the caste-based hierarchy. Urban Bhils reject the Gavri festival—which at its heart rests on a shared, communal experience—as an undignified and illegitimate rationale for taking leave from middle-class urban jobs.

These contradictions also emerge among many of India's poorest and lower-ranking groups. They historically have been most attracted to the values of egalitarianism, as seen in devotional and other movements, both within Hinduism and outside of it. This converges with values of modernism, yet is played out in symbols that oppose a distinctive Hindu identity against others. These comprise competing and contradictory strands in today's festivals.

PILGRIMAGE

Millions of Indians of all faiths go on pilgrimage every year. Some go to sites along the Ganges, with the duty of bringing ashes and remains of a parent's cremation to this site. Others set out to earn merit, fulfill a vow, or seek a boon from a deity. A pilgrimage may be as simple as an extended trip to a nearby shrine, or as complex as a journey that traverses much of India's sacred space.

The *yatra* is a pilgrimage that lifts the pilgrim from everyday life as she or he travels to a sacred crossing. This period of prolonged contact with the supernatural, as pilgrims halt at shrines and temples and hear teachings by religious teachers, blends seamlessly with tourism. A busload of pilgrims will stop for a little shopping or to see an important historical sight along the way.

The pilgrimage begins with a halt at a temple or shrine, which marks the individual's entry into the status of pilgrim. In Rajasthan, pilgrims might make an official start at Pushkar's holy lake, then travel eastward.[24] Stops might include the Taj Mahal, Varanasi, and Calcutta's Kali Temple en route to Puri and a *darshan* of the ocean. On the return, a group might pause at Ayodhya, Hardwar and Rishikesh, Delhi, Amer Fort near Jaipur, and then Pushkar, where pilgrims close their journey with a final ritual bath.

Though the members of a pilgrim group may come from diverse caste and class backgrounds, pilgrimage etiquette may require the erasing of social distinctions during this time. In south India, pilgrims to the shrine of Ayyappan at Sabari Malai, in Kerala, wore special clothes, addressed one another as "Swami" ("master"), and foreswore (among several vows of austerity) meat, eggs, liquor, and sex.[25] Pilgrims all wore blue or black clothing, performed worship at least three times a day, and temporarily enjoyed the highest social status of all, no matter their social origins in everyday life.

An elaborate ritual of leave-taking divorces pilgrims from everyday life. These rituals denote a person's temporary social death from his or her everyday status. This pilgrimage takes place between mid-December and mid-January. Thousands gather for the walk to the main shrine. At the shrine, after a final purification, pilgrims daub one another with paint—which obliterates the last traces of identity separate from that of pilgrimhood. The pilgrims also visit a Muslim shrine and offer coconuts. Song and dance, a bath, and food shared with the fellow pilgrims mark the intervals between hiking from shrine to shrine in this sacred region.

In Braj, pilgrims retained the services of a religious teacher to guide them among the many sites associated with Krishna.[26] One important activity during this pilgrimage—and, indeed, during all—is making donations to beggars and to the temples that one visits, actions that gain merit for the donor.

SECULAR LEISURE TIME

Middle-class Indians enjoy many activities that are popular in the West: the movies, television viewing, trekking and skiing, going to the beach, visiting an environmental preserve, viewing a historical temple or archaeological site. Sports are popular pastimes of boys and young men. Cricket is a national passion, whether played by schoolboys, who scratch out a playing area, or India's internationally ranked team. In the 2000 Olympics held in Sydney, India garnered one medal, a bronze, in women's weightlifting. Traditional sports, such as martial arts and wrestling, are experiencing increased interest. India's middle classes make their morning power walk, clad in sneakers, baseball cap, and sweatsuits. Video parlors have also gained the attention of youth. Voluntary civic groups such as Lions Clubs and Boy Scout troops are also active.

Following chapters note the popularity of the movies, theater, television, and musical and dance performances. Cities and towns boast amateur theatrical groups, whose performances are always worth looking into and range from Indian plays to Shakespeare and experimental theater. In villages, an evening out may consist of a game of cards, storytelling, or the ever-popular group singing.

Children make mud pies, play house, and try to whack a hoop down the street with a stick. Middle-class children enjoy birthday parties, school fairs, and outings. Grandmothers and grandfathers bask in the sun. Visiting friends is a popular pastime. Urbanites return to their ancestral villages. Married women everywhere enjoy visits with their parents and sisters.

NOTES

1. Maxine Weisgrau, "Gavri," in Peter Claus and M. Mills, eds., *Encyclopedia of South Asian Folklore* (New York: Garland Press, 1997).

2. Smriti Srinivasan, *Mouths of People: The Voice of God: Buddhists and Muslims in a Frontier Community of Ladakh* (Delhi: Oxford University Press, 1998), p. 27.

3. Sanjib Baruah, *India against Itself: Assam and the Politics of Nationalism* (Philadelphia: University of Pennsylvania Press, 1999), p. 88.

4. Stuart Blackburn, *Inside the Drama House: Rama Stories and Shadow Puppets in South India* (Berkeley: University of California Press, 1996).

5. Joyce Burkhalter Flueckiger, *Gender and Genre in the Folklore of Middle India* (Ithaca: Cornell University Press, 1996), pp. 27–29.

6. Lawrence A. Babb, *The Divine Hierarchy: Popular Hinduism in Central India* (New York: Columbia University Press, 1975).

7. Nita Kumar, *The Artisans of Banaras: Popular Culture and Identity, 1880–1986* (Princeton: Princeton University Press, 1980).

8. William P. Harmon, *The Sacred Marriage of a Hindu Goddess* (Bloomington: Indiana University Press, 1989).

9. Frederique Apffel Marglin, *Wives of the God-King: The Rituals of the Devadasis of Puri* (Delhi: Oxford University Press, 1985). Also see N. Patnaik, *Cultural Tradition in Puri: Structure and Organization of a Pilgrim Centre* (Simla: Indian Institute of Advanced Study, 1977).

10. John Stratton Hawley, *At Play with Krishna: Pilgrimage Dramas from Brindavan* (Princeton: Princeton University Press, 1981). David L. Haberman, *Journey through the Twelve Forests: An Encounter with Krishna* (New York: Oxford University Press, 1994).

11. James Laidlaw, *Riches and Renunciation: Religion, Economy and Society among the Jains* (Oxford: Clarendon Press, 1995), pp. 275–286.

12. Darius L. Swann, "Ram Lila," in Farley P. Richmond, Darius L. Swann, and Phillip B. Zarrilli, eds., *Indian Theatre: Traditions of Performance* (Honolulu: University of Hawaii Press, 1990), pp. 215–236.

13. Ibid.

14. For an account of a community's dilemmas in organizing, including Ram Lila in an Orissa village, see F.G. Bailey, *The Witch-Hunt or, the Triumph of Morality* (Ithaca: Cornell University Press, 1994).

15. Owen Lynch, *The Politics of Untouchability* (New York: Columbia University Press, 1969).

16. Richard G. Fox, *From Zamindar to Ballot Box* (Ithaca: Cornell University Press, 1969), p. 100.

17. Anne Feldhaus, *Water and Womanhood: Religious Meanings of Rivers in Maharashtra* (New York: Oxford University Press, 1995).

18. Stanley A. Freed and Ruth Freed, *Festivals in a North Indian Village* (New York: American Museum of Natural History, 1998).

19. Majada Asad, *Indian Muslim Festivals and Customs* (Delhi: Ministry of Information and Broadcasting, Government of India, 1988).

20. Mohsen Saeidi Madani, *Impact of Hindu Culture on Muslims* (New Delhi: MD Publications, 1993).

21. Clare M. Wilkinson-Weber, *Embroidering Lives: Women's Work and Skill in the Lucknow Embroidery Industry* (Albany: State University of New York Press, 1999).

22. Prakash Chandra Jain, *Social Movements among Tribals* (Jaipur, India: Rawat Publications, 1991).

23. Maxine Weisgrau, *Interpreting Development: Local Histories, Local Strategies* (Lanham, MD: University Press of America, 1997).

24. Ann Gold, *Fruitful Journeys: The Ways of Rajasthani Pilgrims* (Berkeley: University of California Press, 1988).

25. E. Valentine Daniel, *Fluid Signs: Being a Person the Tamil Way* (Berkeley: University of California Press, 1984), p. 247.

26. For two accounts, see John Stratton Hawley, *At Play with Krishna: Pilgrimage Dramas from Brindavan* (Princeton: Princeton University Press, 1981) and David L. Haberman, *Journey through the Twelve Forests: An Encounter with Krishna* (New York: Oxford University Press, 1994).

SUGGESTED READINGS

Babb, Lawrence A. *The Divine Hierarchy: Popular Hinduism in Central India* (New York: Columbia University Press, 1975).

Bailey, F.G. *The Witch-Hunt; or, the Triumph of Morality* (Ithaca: Cornell University Press, 1994).

Breckenridge, Carol A., ed. *Consuming Modernity: Public Culture in a South Asian World* (Minneapolis: University of Minnesota Press, 1995).

Daniel, E. Valentine. *Fluid Signs: Being a Person the Tamil Way* (Berkeley: University of California Press, 1984).

Edensor, Tim. *Tourists at the Taj: Performance and Meaning at a Symbolic Site* (London: Routledge, 1998).

Freed, Stanley A. and Ruth Freed. *Festivals in a North Indian Village* (New York: American Museum of Natural History, 1998).

Gold, Ann. *Fruitful Journeys: The Ways of Rajasthani Pilgrims* (Berkeley: University of California Press, 1988).

Harlan, Lindsay. *Religion and Rajput Women* (Berkeley: University of California Press, 1992).

Hawley, John Stratton. *At Play with Krishna: Pilgrimage Dramas from Brindavan* (Princeton: Princeton University Press, 1981).

Mishra, Pankaj. *Butter Chicken in Ludhiana: Travels in Small Town India* (London: Penguin, 1994).

9

Music and Dance

IN THE EARLY EVENING, a group of male performers gather around their makeup boxes and transform themselves into beautiful young women, the king's many wives in tonight's play. This kind of entertainment is called *nautanki*, a form of folk dance-drama. Stock characters include a raja, his many wives, and the clown or fool. He burlesques the dancers and impudently comments on events both on and off stage. The troupe's experiences encapsulate much of the situation of musicians and dancers in India.

The entertainment starts after full dark and lasts almost until dawn. This is the traditional performance time. The audience consists of sunburned farmers and livestock herders. They are in a mood of high anticipation. Hearty repartee between the audience and the performers adds to the mood. During the performance itself members of the audience reach forward with small sums of money and requests for songs. This interaction is characteristic of performance.

India's performing arts combine both music and dance. The range of performance arts, genres, and styles is enormous—yet globalization of mass media, changing tastes, new technology, and new performing arts patrons are profoundly transforming the performing arts. Political and economic changes have transformed social relationships between performing groups and their patrons, sometimes toward conflict. For example, in May 2000, members of upper castes beat thirty Dalits of Themmavur village in Tamil Nadu's Puddokottai District so badly that they had to be hospitalized. Their offense? The Dalits refused to beat the drums for the village's annual Kali Amman festival, stating that this task was socially degrading.

Performance traditions provide space in which to give voice to these regional and local aspirations, set against those of national elites or the nation-state. Music and dance provide a forum in which to protest subordination as well as a means of experiencing a few moments of release from the cares of life. Few studies have examined social protest as a subject matter of music and dance, outside studies of women's music in which women contest their lot.[1]

Among the small group of Rajasthani *nautanki* artists, members worry about competitors such as Hindi films, videos, television, and radio. Some members dream of making it big in "Bollywood" (India's version of Hollywood, located in Mumbai, former Bombay) while others quietly modify or drop traditional song-and-dance repertoires to meet contemporary expectations. The group's all-male composition—men taking the female roles—makes it vulnerable to new entertainments that feature women performers.

This type of performance translates uneasily to tourism, today an important market for folk artists. Tourists can't understand the jokes and are likely to comprehend only pratfalls and swirling movements. Another possibility, patronage by elites, is also distant. Jokes are broad indeed—if not vulgar—the costumes garish, and the men-in-drag aspect is politically incorrect.

Elite patronage can have repercussions: for instance, recognition as a classical form brings pressures such as conforming to upper-caste repertoires, sanitizing subject matter, and subduing regional characteristics in favor of a more syncretic, blended style. The dilemma for the performing arts is stark indeed: survival only through transformation.

Nonelite music and dance are under intense pressure from the mass media, whose aesthetics are dominated by Hindi pop standards. Tourism, with its inexhaustible demand for local color, draws performers to work a circuit ranging from elite hotels to fleabag operations. Regional festivals sponsored by the Indian Tourism Development Corporation, by corporate entities, local governments, and civic groups provide important performance venues. Folk musicians find that these audiences, both domestic and international tourists, are largely ignorant of local aesthetics and are satisfied with stereotyped, shortened displays that meet the call for entertainment that is not too threatening or offensive to middle-class standards.

MAKING TODAY'S TRADITIONS

The seeds of today's performing-arts scene sprouted in the latter half of the nineteenth century, when music and dance became intertwined with issues of national identity. The collapse of Mughal patronage and delegitimation of Muslim courts after the 1857 Rebellion marginalized some performance traditions, while stimulating others.

Some communities of traditional musicians declined. The Mughal emperor's court was disbanded, its performers forced to leave. Lucknow's courtesan community, renowned for its song-and-dance arts, suffered property seizures by the victorious British after 1857. They faced pressure to close down. Some types of performance were banned.[2]

Musician-households replaced courts as centers for training new artists and developing performance traditions.[3] Artists' performance styles became less associated with courts than with their teachers. Today, the teacher-student relationship is the most important aspect of training and of how artists identify themselves.

British indifference or even hostility to Indian music and dance meant little inclination to take over the paramount ruler's traditional patron role of support for elite performing arts.[4] Elite patronage was sustained in the princely states and among Westernizing groups.

Princely states maintained institutions such as Jaipur State's Department of Virtuosos. This at its peak coordinated support to over 700 professionals, including many women artists.[5] The princes sponsored conferences, such as the 1895 meeting at Jaipur, which set terminology for Kathak dance. A second early important meeting, held in 1916 at Baroda, grappled with how to establish a uniform system of musical notation for recording performances.

Westernizing groups saw the arts as a way to express Indian values, values that should be authentic—yet compatible with modernity. The authenticity movement rejected Mughal and British elements as foreign. How to discover pre-Mughal tradition? Temple sculpture and painting, such as at Ajanta, provided clues. So did ancient texts.

Sexuality proved the most problematic. Elites of this era were largely influenced by Victorian values, and these scorned professional women singers and dancers as outside conventional morality. This was a familiar situation in Victorian England, but in India the issues ran deeper than this. Women's reformers recoiled from the pledging of girls to temples, as happened in some regions. In many cases, the highly trained *devadasis* (dancers dedicated to a temple's deity) also were courtesans. This institution was denounced as "temple prostitution," exploitative toward women and a cause of the dance's degeneration into eroticism.

The *devadasi* lifestyle contradicted conventional norms in many ways. *Devadasis* formed women-centered households that passed property and trade secrets along the female line. While *devadasis* received small stipends from the temple or court to which they were attached, a relationship with a patron—often long-standing—could result in substantial income. This included grants of land and other property. Another issue of sexuality and dance stemmed from its sounds, rhythms, dress, and movements. These made it highly improper, especially to nineteenth-century British eyes.

Some hereditary professional artists found themselves or their activities criminalized. In 1947, the Devadasi Bill banned temple dancing in the then-state of Madras. Certain types of courtesan performances were banned.

The Indian model of sexuality and performance seemed incompatible with modernity, so the revivalists muted these elements. First, hereditary performers' communities that were stigmatized as immoral were replaced by other groups whose image was clean. Second, hints of eroticism were deleted.

The first four decades of the twentieth century saw many experiments that ranged from reviving ancient dance to modern dance. One of the most significant figures was Uday Shankar (1900–1977). In the mid-1920s, Shankar collaborated with the famous Russian ballet dancer Anna Pavlova in Europe. He then established his Uday Shankar Ballet Company, which toured Europe and North America. Principal dancer and actress Zohra Segal—whose own career spanned this period to roles in films by the producer-director team of Ismail Merchant and James Ivory, including work in 2001 on their film *The Mystic Masseur*—recounts an extraordinary mix of influences at Shankar's dance school.[6] Shankar combined two innovations, exercises focused on basic body movements and improvisation classes. The school included classes in Kathakali, Bharata Natyam, and Manipuri dance.

In the 1930s Malayalam language poet Vallathol (1878–1958) spearheaded a revival of the south Indian dance Kathakali. He founded the Kerala State School of the Arts, which introduced modern education and helped to sustain this tradition of male ensemble dance-drama. Rukmini Devi (1904–1986) founded the important Kalakshetra dance school, significant in reviving Bharata Natyam. Rukmini Devi focused aesthetics on pure or abstract dance.

The creation of India as a nation-state presented opportunities for artists to participate in constructing a national identity. The result has been a move toward valuing certain forms as exemplars of unbroken, "thousand year old" traditions. India's states also went through this process. In Rajasthan, an innovative multimedia production, "Land of Shifting Sands," provided an image of Rajasthani identity that knit together the new state's diverse elements.[7]

The princely courts' loss of political and economic functions negatively affected elite-oriented performers, those who served noble patrons. Performers outside this orbit faced a different situation, best characterized as mixed.

By the late twentieth century, many performers were the last to play an instrument or to know its repertoire. Some hereditary professional musicians gave up this work and became farmers, though few were as successful as the Charans of Borunda village, Rajasthan, traditionally bards. In some cases, work as a hereditary musician was associated with a low social status, and escaping this meant ceasing to perform. Other performers, whose work was tightly integrated with local institutions, retained traditional patron-client relationships.

Government institutions to support arts training and performance expanded after independence. Important national institutions include All-India Radio and Sangeet Natak Akademi, the national institution for the performing arts. Kathak Kendra, part of the Sangeet Natak Akadeki structure, established Delhi as a center for Kathak dance, alongside the older centers in Lucknow and Jaipur. The states set up performing arts institutions that emphasized regional traditions.

Since independence, private sponsors have built concert halls and supported performances, master classes, and conferences. Urban groups have taken the lead in arts sponsorship. There is a great sense that India's music and dance of all types are national treasures.

Music Basics

Stone carving, paintings, and ancient texts reflect music's role in aesthetic expression. Hindus designate the goddess Saraswati as music's patron saint. Although orthodox Muslims frown on the religious use of music, Indian exuberance has won out in producing distinct Indo-Islamic musical subcultures. Many blends are evident in theory, instruments, and performance style.

The music chronicled in the first or second century drama treatise Natya Shastra lacked the *raga* concept, a melodic structure that is now basic to Indian musical theory. The *raga* traditionally was introduced by poet Khusrao (1253–1325). Ancient music also used a different system of parent scales than is heard today.[8] The drone, a single repetitive note or short note sequence that accompanies the music, appeared in the seventeenth century. The *qawwali* form of group singing was brought by Sufi leader Khwaja Mu'in ud-din Chishti (1143–1234). Amir Khusrao also popularized the sitar, a long-necked plucked string instrument, and the *tabla*, an instrument made up of two small one-headed drums set next to one another and played together.

In 1562, the ruler of Gwalior dispatched his star performer, Tansen, to the court of Emperor Akbar.[9] Tansen was extraordinarily influential. A famous story brings together the Emperor, Tansen, and Tansen's guru, a Vaishnavite singer and poet. Other stories emphasize Tansen's closeness with

Muslim figures such as religious teacher Shaikh Salim Chisti (d. 1572). Tansen is buried at Gwalior and his tomb is a shrine.

Khyal, a classical song form, rose to prominence in the eighteenth century. In south India, Tyagaraja (1767–1817) developed the region's classical three part composition, called *kriti.* Balaswami Dikshitar (1786–1858) experimented with the violin and introduced it to Karnatak music. The most notable other European instrument to make an impact was the harmonium, a small, hand-pumped organ. The harmonium is controversial, for it replaces traditional stringed instruments.

Today's instruments include all these, plus many more. Categories, like those in the West, are percussion instruments, such as bells, gongs, cymbals, and drums; wind instruments; and stringed instruments.

The *tabla* is the most important percussion instrument in north Indian classical music. Folk musicians favor the small barrel-shaped, two-headed drum called a *dholak.* South Indian music uses the *mrdanga,* a large barrel-shaped, two-headed drum. In mythology, this was first played by the elephant-headed Hindu deity Ganesha. Other percussion instruments include tambourine, wooden castanets, and small brass cymbals. One unusual instrument is the *ghatam,* a clay pot that is played in Karnatak music.

Drums accompany many different events. The pulsing rhythm helps create trance states. The drum announces a man's or a woman's death. Drummers delineate the different strokes or beats, plus the repetitions of beat patterns. In Hindustani music, this is called *bol.* One rhythm pattern, called *tihai,* consists of the repetition of a pattern three times in succession, for instance: "*taka dha, taka dha, taka dha!*"

Wind instruments include the flute, associated with Krishna. There are many reed instruments, such as the oboe-like *nagaswara* of Karnatak music and north India's *shenai.* Westerners will associate this with the snake charmer's art. Sometimes two instruments are played simultaneously by the artist: one is a drone, the other produces the melody.

The sitar is the most familiar stringed instrument. This plucked lute-like instrument produces its shimmering tone with sympathetic strings. The *sarod* is a second important north Indian plucked lute-type instrument. The long-necked *tambura* is played as a drone, its principal string tuned to *Sa,* the note that begins the Indian scale. South India's most important classical instrument is the *vina,* which has resonating gourds at each end of its long neck.

Bowed instruments include the *sarangi,* which recently shifted from a folk to classical instrument, although it still has strong folk roots. One common instrument has just one string that is played, such as the Rajasthani epic

Langa boys practice Sarangi, Jodhpur. Courtesy of the author.

performer's *ravanhatto*, with its principal horsehair string, steel drone string, and sympathetic strings.

The most unusual stringed instrument may be far south India's *vil*, the Tamil bow, which is lashed to a large clay pot. The vil is hung with bells and played with a pair of sticks. The instrument is known as a demon drum, because of its ghostly sound.[10]

Five key elements are important in making music: the *raga*; the set of tones and microtones used within the *raga*; the beat; the drone; and the interplay between improvisation and composed segments within a particular work.

The *raga* establishes the main musical choices of a composition. The *raga* is the sketch of an aesthetic sentiment. It is the musical expression of a key idea for the performer to embellish, to invert, and to rework.[11] Classical music is organized in terms of *ragas*. These are classified in many ways, most importantly according to the time of day and the season of the year. Although Hindustani and Karnatak *ragas* overlap, terminology, classification, and emphases differ.

Folk musicians use the concept of *raga* too, but they often subordinate this to melodic tunes. Nevertheless, the statement of a *raga* will guide the whole conception of the composition, its ascending tones and descending tones, plus microtonal intervals. These basic tones are *Sa, Re, Ga, Ma, Pa, Dha,* and *Ni.* Other terms denote microtonal intervals. These too must be defined. *Sa* is the most important: its pitch defines the rest.

The third formal theory element is the beat. Drummers know many different rhythmic patterns with complex beats using different parts of the drum head, struck by different parts of the hand or sticks. The fourth component of performance is the drone. Whereas classical musicians often use the *Vina* as a drone, in everyday settings the harmonium is popular.

Fifth, classical compositions alternate composed and improvised subsections. Different types of works subdivide differently. Improvisation allows the performer to demonstrate his or her virtuosity. Vocalists use vocables such as "aah, na, ta" for improvisation.

In concert, the soloist introduces each piece by naming its *raga* and *tal.* This announcement will be followed by a rustle of anticipation in the audience. A typical classical composition includes a slow, low start. This is played without percussion or drone. These join in at specified points after the artist's initial exploration of the *raga.* Tempo and intensity increase, and the music rises from the middle to the high register. As the percussionist and soloist explore the *raga*'s themes and build to a climax, the musician on the drone sits serenely, repeating a pattern of one or two simple notes.

CLASSICAL AND NONCLASSICAL FORMS

Hindustani classical vocal music divides into the main forms of *dhrupad, dhamar, khyal, thumri, dadra,* and *ghazal.*[12] *Khyal* is the most important today. *Bara* ("big") *khyal* is sung at a slow to medium tempo, while *chhota* ("little") *khyal* has a rapid tempo. *Thumri* and *ghazal*—sung in Urdu—are deemed light classical forms. They, too, have become popular in recent years.

Karnatak classical genres include *varnam, kriti,* and *ragam-tanam-pallavi. Kriti* is the most important. Its subject matter ranges across romance, heroism, and devotion. *Ragam-tanam-pallavi* highlights improvisation as the artists gradually join with the soloist, adding rhythm and musically commenting on the soloist's work.

In contrast to classical forms, which often feature soloists, nonclassical music is rooted in group traditions. The most popular nonclassical vocal music consists of group songs. Some groups are informal, while others are formal. Religious songs are popular, such as Hindu *bhajans* and *kirtans;* Sikh *asa divar, shabad,* and *kirtan;* and Muslim *milad, majlis,* and *qawwali,* sung at a saint's death anniversary. Dalits have crafted new Buddhist songs using local traditions, Hindi films, and even pop sources. Contemporary religious figures continue this tradition of creating songs. There are also many old favorites, such as songs by Guru Nanak, Amir Khusrao, Kabir, and Mira Bai.

Group membership reaches across caste and religious categories. A good voice, musical talent, and enthusiasm are what count. The eclecticism of music appears in Varanasi *qawwali* traditions. Though this form is best-known for its connection to Muslim traditions, members of Hindu subcastes often participated in sessions, at least until recently.[13] Song themes also included tales from the great Indian epic, the *Mahabharata*. One Varanasi festival featured three distinct forms: Muslim *qawwali* on the first day, *biraha* on the second, and "orchestra" on the third.[14]

Biraha is performed by groups of men. Songs recount diverse topics. One list made in the 1980s included subjects such as the Apollo 11 moon mission, train wrecks, dowry deaths, and Mrs. Gandhi's assassination.[15] Orchestra, a new form, uses Western instruments such as bongo drum, organ, banjo, guitar, cymbals, and drums. This may be an outgrowth of the "English band," a uniformed brass band that accompanies processions with folk music, marches, ragas, and film songs.

Women's lives are brightened by song sessions. These often commemorate family events. New brides contribute new songs to the family repertoire.[16] Songs reflect on women's condition: the sadness of a new bride at leaving her mother's home; the hard work that she must do for her mother-in-law; her longing for her husband, who is far away. An earthy sense of humor often characterizes these songs. These also include segments in which the group extemporizes lines—teasing a visitor, for instance.[17]

In the countryside, music carries for miles on a quiet evening or night. *Khari biraha* is a rural field "holler" tradition sustained by cowherds in Uttar Pradesh. This consists of a short poem—just a few lines, but one that is vocally embellished, gliding, and vibrato-laden. It is a more complex and stylized vocal form than, say, the Western equivalent of yodeling.

HEREDITARY PERFORMERS AND PATRONS

Traditional relationships between performers and patrons still exist in some areas, though less now than prior to the 1950s and 1960s reforms. Often, these performances are desired by patrons because of their ritual significance. A good example of the current situation for hereditary performers and their patrons is the case of the Manganiyars and Langas, Muslim hereditary folk musicians of Rajasthan.[18]

In this region, each subcaste had a special relationship with genealogist and musician groups. Services included performing at patrons' birth, wedding, and memorial services, and verifying the family tree when families sought marriage partners for their children. Manganiyars serve Hindu patrons whose subcaste status ranges from high to low: Rajputs, Suthars (carpenters), Meghwals (leather workers), Kumars (potters), and Bhils (Rajasthan's largest tribal group). Langas serve Muslim Sindhi Sipai patrons as both musicians and genealogists. Manganiyars sing and perform on a variety of instruments, including the *kamaycha*, a bowed instrument; the flute; *shehnai*, an oboe-like instrument; *dholak*, a small two-headed drum; and wooden castanets. Langa instruments include the *sarangi*, a bowed stringed instrument, and a type of double clarinet.

The repertoire is broad: songs that accompany specific activities, such as weddings; songs of abuse; playful songs; and serious songs that explore themes of life, loss, and love. Performances divide into ordinary events and *kacheri* sessions, which highlight aesthetic virtuosity. Rukhma Devi, one of the few professionally active Manganiyar women who sings before mixed-sex audiences, performs a special genre, the Rani Bhatiyani songs.[19] Their purpose is to stimulate trance states at religious gatherings.

The postindependence closing of the India-Pakistan border cut off the musicians' access to patrons, family members, and the makers of their instruments. Land reform did little to replace lost income, for the two groups received little. Patrons' tastes in entertainment changed and they became less likely than before to host *kacheri* sessions or to develop the deep knowledge that underwrites this aesthetic experience. Today, there are never enough patrons, although the tourism circuit helps out. Some Manganiyars work as construction workers, since not all are musically inclined or talented. Nevertheless, many are indebted to village moneylenders.

The Manganiyars also curtailed women's public performances. This action claimed higher status for the group. It also, members say, safeguarded Manganiyar women against sexual advances by patron men. This is a tradeoff that entails the erosion of women's genres. Some women's songs are now performed by men or boys. It is unlikely now that a woman performer will develop her skills to virtuoso levels.

In the 1980s and 1990s, groups such as the Langas and Manganiyars helped Rajasthan to gain a reputation as a reservoir of traditional performing arts. Carefully prepared for their encounter with Western culture, these artists appeared in folk festivals in such widely scattered venues in Europe and the United States. The lively compositions made this music accessible to outsiders who neither understood the language nor knew anything about Indian music. The most successful gained well-deserved reputations as virtuoso folk arts heritage performers.

CLASSICAL DANCE IN THE TWENTIETH CENTURY

Classical dance such as Bharata Natyam, the closely related dance of Andhra Pradesh, eastern India's Odissi, Kathakali, Kathak, and Manipuri achieved it contemporary form in the twentieth century. Very little is known about the historical development of nonclassical dance. As some dances have been recognized as classical forms, their history, aesthetics, and biographies of significant artists are studied. Still, the time depth for this is quite shallow, within the past 100–150 years.

Dance shares many elements of vocabulary with music. Expressive gestures, glances and movements combine with a strong rhythm that is beaten out by the feet. The dancer wears rows of bells on his or her ankles to emphasize footwork. The vocabulary of gesture and expression allows the dancer to sketch a setting, a character, a movement, or an idea.

Kathak, north India's classical form, highlights the rhythm and the tempo. At points in the performance, the dancer chants *bol*, the syllables that denote the beat. Precise footwork alternates with graceful, swift turns, gestures, and glances. Kathak dance is performed by both women and men and by soloists as well as by troupes, which perform dance-dramas. These include contemporary themes. The overall trend in the classical traditions, however, has been toward abstract or pure dance, which minimizes mime and acting.

Dancers work to establish flexibility and strength. One of the most intensive training regimes is associated with the male Kathakali dance of Kerala. Dazzling leaps, spins, and jumps derive from this area's martial arts heritage. Kathakali is visually exciting. The characters wear flamboyant full-skirted costumes, elaborate headpieces, horns, fangs, and long fingernails. Stylized facial makeups—green, black, orange, and red in particular—denote the character. These include the green makeup worn by heroes, the black and red beards of evil characters, and the black faces and fangs of female demons. Makeup extends to the whites of the dancers' eyes, which they redden by placing a tiny crushed seed between the eyeball and lid.

The best-loved dance-dramas are episodes from the Hindu epics, myths, and traditional stories. Contemporary choreographers have experimented with new themes and brought Kathakali to new audiences. *People's Victory*, performed in 1987, showcased the Marxist themes of the struggle between the World Conscience (played by a green-faced character) and Imperialism (a red-bearded character). Another effort was the controversial *Kathakali King Lear* (1989–1990), a collaboration with Western artists.

Classical dancers like to remind their audiences that one can see the very poses, facial expressions, and hand gestures of ancient temples come to life. Others include emphasizing their dance's relationship with a Hindu temple or festival. Kathak dancers, for instance, highlight the dance's connection with the *Ras lila* festival, which celebrates Krishna—not the dance's association with north Indian courts and their Indo-Islamic culture.[20]

The most striking change in dance relates to personnel. Members of hereditary, low-ranking artist groups have given up this work. Members of high-ranking, middle-class, and elite groups have enthusiastically taken up the dance. In part, this reflects the ambiguous status of traditional women performers, stigmatized by the reputation of immorality. A case that illustrates the consequences of this attitude occurred in Puri, where hereditary *devadasis*, dancers dedicated to a temple's deity, worked in the Jagannatha temple and performed Odissi dance. Revivalists relied on the male hereditary dancers, who traditionally danced outside the temples, to reconstruct the dance. The *devadasis* complained that, further, they were turned down when they attempted to secure government aid to found their own dance school.[21]

The case of Bharata Natyam, now celebrated as the national dance of India, demonstrates both this change and pressures for Sanskritization.[22] Bharata Natyam formerly was a solo or pairs dance performed by the women members of the *Isai Vellala* subcaste of Tamil Nadu and Karnataka.

Isai Vellala dancers on the verge of puberty were dedicated to a Hindu temple and married to its presiding deity.[23] The young artist's dance debut was an important professional milestone. *Devadasis'* work included performing early morning protective rituals, singing, and dancing before the image of the deity. *Devadasis* also served the royal courts. They entertained at girls' puberty ceremonies and at wedding processions, where they symbolized good luck: as a deity's wives, they could never be widowed.

T. Balasaraswati (1918–1984), the last well-known performer descended from *devadasis*, saw many changes during her lifetime. The emphasis on descriptive dance, a vivid element in T. Balasaraswati's performance, lost favor under the influence of nonhereditary revivalists such as Rukmini Devi. She focused aesthetics on pure or abstract dance. Rukmini Devi and many other revivalists were from outside Bharata Natyam's traditional region— Rukmini Devi herself was from Bengal—and they brought the dance into a national orbit. Today Bharata Natyam is studied throughout India.

Most of those studying the dance today are upper-caste young women. Bharata Natyam ranks for them as a genteel accomplishment that enhances their marriage prospects. Training shifted from the system of apprenticeship under a *guru*, a teacher, to one of classes and paid teachers. Most students study just long enough to debut with a full evening's dance recital. This has become a major social event for the young dancer, second only to her wedding.

Most recently, the process of Sanskritization has moved toward the addition of sacred elements. In the first decades of the twentieth century, dancers began the concert by standing in place on a bare stage. Today's stage is often decorated with the icon of a deity. The dancer enters, and usually drops flowers and makes a graceful gesture of respect to the deity. Dance has recently been revived in temples with the institution of dance festivals at Khajuraho, Konarak, and Tamil Nadul's Chidambaram, dedicated to *Shiva Nataraja.*

South India's dance-drama Kathakali took a different path, most likely because this is traditionally performed by men who are high-caste Nayars and Nambudri Brahmans. Formerly, Kathakali was danced only in temples owned by upper-caste groups. Others were not permitted to enter. The movement to secular settings eased this issue. Recently, there has been a reopening of temple performance sites.

Two classical dance forms, Manipuri and Chhau, stand out because of their folk roots. In northeastern India, Manipuri dance features unique women's costumes—slick barrel-shaped skirts, topped by a gathered short overskirt. Dancers move in a smooth, gliding fashion in intertwined patterns of male and female dancers.

Manipuri's roots lie among the Maiti tribe and its Sun Festival dance. While basic movements are similar, they are simplified. Costumes are less intricate, and women dancers often replace the barrel-shaped skirt with a tightly wrapped sarong.

Chhau (mask) dance emerged in the region where Bihar, Orissa, and West Bengal converged. This region contains Hindu and animist groups. The Hindu rulers of Seraikella, a princely state in this region, developed the mask dance as a classical form. This features highly stylized, round, plain-featured masks, emphasis on graceful movements, and more pure dance sequences than in other forms of the mask dance.[24] Training of specialists in this dance takes place at the Government Chhau Dance center in Seraikella, as well as other institutes. Dance themes stem from Hindu mythology. In fact, the rulers used this dance to help popularize Hindu ideas among the region's non-Hindus.

The mask dance as practiced in villages differs in terms of its movements and emphasis. At Purulia, a West Bengal village, the name for the dance, *chhau yuddha*, means "mask war." Hand positions and motions mimic holding a spear and shield. The mask war is danced by landless laborers, small landholders, and service providers at the spring festival.

NONCLASSICAL DANCE

In general, as the above discussion suggests, classical and nonclassical dance forms overlap. Nonclassical forms often use a simple vocabulary of stylized movements. They are sustained by nonspecialists rather than by professionals, and are learned in neighborhood or family settings, rather than through lengthy professional training. In northern India, norms of upper to middle-caste-based society favor the separation of women and men dancers, who dance in separate groups or as separate halves of a circle. Female roles are played by male dancers. These conventions separate these groups from the members of Scheduled Tribes and Castes (women and men may join hands in the dance) and also from elite classical dancers, whose ensemble performances now include male and female dancers.

Thus, for example, in the region where Chhau is danced by Hindus, members of the Santal tribe—traditionally animists in their religion—have an entirely different dance for their spring festival. Women and men alternate, hands linked, in a ring. The local Hindus regard this hand-holding between the sexes as indecent. In this way, Santals and non-Santals distinguish themselves from one another.

There is interaction between the classical and nonclassical dance forms. The mass media provide images of classical dancing. Classically trained dancers often help to organize or act as judges for competitions of local dances at festivals. This process entails many changes: the relationships of the dancers to one another, the event, even aesthetic features of the dance.

Examples of overlap include that of Kathak movements and basic posture with nonelite north Indian dance, such as in the graceful slow twirls of full-skirted Rajasthani and Gujarati women and men, and in round dances in which the participants periodically stop their circling, and spin in place. Similar, too, are the basic dances of pariah groups such as the Kalbelias (gypsies) and the Hijras, eunuchs who live as women and traditionally dance in front of houses where a birth has occurred or where a wedding is in progress.

Some of the most distinctive folk dances include masks and other props.[25] In Orissa, huge puppets are made to dance. Some are carried by teams of men, and others are so large that they are wheeled on carts. A festival of Orissa, held in the first month of spring, features large hollow bulls, which dance a "bullfight." Elsewhere, sixteen- to twenty-foot-tall puppets dance scenes from the Indian epic, the Ramayana. A staple theme of puppetry in Rajasthan is the dancing girls and acrobats who deftly twirl and leap about as they portray the adventures of kings, their queens, and their courts. Here, fairs also draw interactive performance artists, who use makeup and large puppet props to portray diverse characters, to the amusement of their audiences.

Pairs of crossed bamboo rods clicked together and moved apart feature in a dance of the eastern state of Mizoram. The dancers move across these rhythmically, their feet flashing in and out of the moving grid. Stilts feature in a children's dance of Madhya Pradesh's Gonds region.

Kalbeliya dancer. Courtesy of the author.

Dancers create their own syncopation and sound effects with ankle bells, chants, and cymbals. *Bhangra*, the most popular men's dance in Punjab, is an athletic circle dance characterized by jumps, flying kicks, and acrobatics. A ring of dancers circles one man or a pair in the center of the ring. The center men call out a verse, while the others rhythmically interject a simple repeated refrain, such as "*Uh-Uh!*"

In nearby Rajasthan, women of the Kamar tribe perform *Tera tali*, a sitting dance. The dancers rhythmically strike tiny cymbals tied on their bodies. They display their virtuosity by clutching swords between their teeth and balancing a stack of decorated pots on their heads. Gradually, the dancers increase the sinuous movements of their torsos and the speed at which they ring their cymbals.

Group dances are associated with festivals and fairs. In Rajasthan, the smallpox goddess is honored with a dance at her festival. Groups of male dancers, clad in long, full-skirted men's robes, circle to the deep beat of a kettledrum. They stop, spin slowly, then click long poles against those of the man next to them, first one side, then the other. The dance will go on all day and all night to honor the *Devi*.

In recent years, dances have reached beyond their social roots to mass tourism, concert stages, secular festivals, and community events. Schoolchildren learn simple versions of dances as part of their region's cultural heritage. Performers reference themselves as classical or folk dancers while others position themselves in the pop mainstream, whose influence is surely largest in recent years.

The music industry also has undergone transformation. Satellite TV, cable, the VCR, and Internet access provided a new technical basis that has supported growth and diversification. Privatization of the radio industry and appearance of FM stations also expanded music's popular reach. Two associated trends include the appearance of music and video stores and the introduction of multinational entertainment companies into the Indian market. In many respects, for the middle-class music consumer, the industry resembles its counterparts in the west.

Changes have also been occurring in the market share of various genres. Although the music industry is still heavily dominated by the genre of Hindi film music, non-film music has significantly expanded its markets. This includes the genres of international music (primarily Western classical and popular music), classical Indian music (both north and south Indian traditions), devotional music, regional music (non-Hindi language music and musical traditions), and the new genre of Indipop.

Indipop eclectically fuses many different traditions, ranging from reggae and rock-and-roll, to classical Indian ragas and regional folk music. Its key elements seem to be a strong beat and catchy tune, along with lyrics that appeal to its core audience of urbanized teens and young adults, which importantly includes expatriate Indian youth living in Europe and North America. A youthful club subculture and international audience linked through the Internet are also new ways in which this genre has expanded since its beginning in the past decade, and also created a challenge to the established "*filmi* music" industry of Bollywood.

NOTES

1. This reflects a scholarly division of labor into studies of "classical" and "non-classical" ("folk") forms. The former by definition are not regarded as vehicles for social protest. Studies of folk performing arts have regarded protest as a tangential element.

2. Veena Talwar Oldenburg, "Lifestyle as Resistance: The Case of the Courtesans of Lucknow," pp. 23–61 in Douglas Haynes and Gyan Prakash, eds., *Contesting*

Power: Resistance and Everyday Social Relations in South Asia (Berkeley: University of California Press, 1991).

3. Daniel M. Neuman, *The Life of Music in North India: The Organization of an Artistic Tradition* (Detroit: Wayne State University Press, 1990).

4. Gerry Farrell, *Indian Music and the West* (Oxford: Clarendon, 1997).

5. Joan L. Erdman, *Patrons and Performers in Rajasthan: The Subtle Tradition* (New Delhi: Chanakya Publications, 1995).

6. Joan L. Erdman with Zohra Segal, *Stages: The Art and Adventures of Zohra Segal* (New Delhi: Kali for Women, 1997). Also see Joan L. Erdman, "Towards Authenticity: Uday Shankar's First Company of Hindu Dancers and Musicians," in David Waterhouse, ed., *Dance of India* (Mumbai: Popular Prakashan, 1998), pp. 69–100.

7. Joan L. Erdman, "Becoming Rajasthani: Pluralism and the Production of *Dharti Dhoran Ri,*" in Karine Schomer, Joan L. Erdman, Deryck O. Lodrick, and Lloyd I. Rudolph, eds., *The Idea of Rajasthan: Explorations in Regional Identity, Volume I: Constructions* (Columbia, MO: South Asia Publications–American Institute of Indian Studies, 1994), pp. 45–79.

8. N.A. Jairazbhoy, *The Rags of North Indian Music: Their Structure and Evolution* (Middletown, CT: Wesleyan University Press, 1971).

9. Bonnie C. Wade, *Imaging Sound: An Ethnomusicological Study of Music, Art, and Culture in Mughal India* (Chicago: University of Chicago Press, 1998), pp. 108–117.

10. Stuart Blackburn, *Singing of Birth and Death: Texts in Performance* (Philadelphia: University of Pennsylvania Press, 1988), p. 13.

11. N.A. Jairazbhoy, *The Rags of North Indian Music: Their Structure and Evolution* (Middletown, CT: Wesleyan University Press, 1971).

12. Bonnie C. Wade, *Music in India: The Classical Tradition* (New Delhi: Manohar, 1987).

13. Edward O. Henry, *Chant the Names of God: Musical Culture in Bhojpuri-Speaking India* (San Diego: San Diego State University Press, 1988).

14. Nita Kumar, *The Artisans of Banaras: Popular Culture and Identity, 1880–1986* (Princeton: Princeton University Press, 1980.

15. Henry, op. cit.

16. Janice S. Hyde, "Women's Village Networks: Marriage Distance and Marriage Related Folk Songs," in N.K. Singhi and Rajendra Joshi, eds., *Folk, Faith and Feudalism: Rajasthan Studies* (Jaipur: Rawat Publications, 1995).

17. Gloria Goodwin Raheja and Ann Grodzins Gold, *Listen to the Heron's Words: Reimagining Gender and Kinship in North India* (Berkeley: University of California Press, 1994).

18. Komal Kothari, "Musicians for the People: The Manganiyars of Western Rajasthan," in Karine Schomer, Joan L. Erdman, Deryck O. Lodrick, and Lloyd I. Rudolph, eds., *The Idea of Rajasthan: Explorations in Regional Identity, Volume I: Constructions* (Columbia, MO: South Asia Publications–American Institute of Indian Studies, 1994), pp. 205–237.

19. Shirley Trembath, "The Rani Bhatiyani Songs: New or Recycled Material?" in N.K. Singhi and Rajendra Joshi, eds., *Religion, Ritual and Royalty* (Jaipur: Rawat Publications, 1999), pp. 214–226.

20. Sunil Kothari, *Kathak: Indian Classical Dance Art* (New Delhi: Abhinav Publications, 1989).

21. Frédérique Apffel Marglin, *Wives of the God-King: The Rituals of the Devadasis of Puri* (Delhi: Oxford University Press, 1985).

22. Anne-Marie Gaston, *Bharata Natyam: From Temple to Theatre* (New Delhi: Manohar Publishers, 1996).

23. This custom, of prepubertal marriage, was well known in South India. It was considered bad luck for a young woman's family if she menstruated before her marriage ceremony was held. In the case of the Isai Vellalas, this ceremony signified her status as a "wife" of the god. Any children she bore were considered legitimate.

24. Andrew Tsubaki and Farley P. Richmond, "Chau," in Farley P. Richmond, Darius L. Swann, and P.B. Zarrilli, eds., *Indian Theatre: Traditions of Performance* (Honolulu: University of Hawaii Press, 1990), pp. 359–383.

25. Kapila Vatsyanan, *Traditions of Indian Folk Dance* (New Delhi: Indian Book Company, 1976).

SUGGESTED READINGS

Blackburn, Stuart H. *Inside the Drama House: Rama Stories and Shadow Puppets in South India* (Berkeley: University of California Press, 1996).

Chakravarty, Sumita S. *National Identity in Indian Popular Cinema, 1947–1987* (Austin: University of Texas Press, 1996).

Erdman, Joan L. and Zohra Segal. *Stages: The Art and Adventures of Zohra Segal* (New Delhi: Kali for Women, 1997).

Farrell, Gerry. *Indian Music and the West* (Oxford: Clarendon, 1997).

Flueckiger, Joyce Burkhalter. *Gender and Genre in the Folklore of Middle India* (Ithaca: Cornell University Press, 1996).

Kumar, Nita. *The Artisans of Banaras: Popular Culture and Identity, 1880–1986* (Princeton: Princeton University Press, 1980).

Neuman, Daniel M. *The Life of Music in North India: The Organization of an Artistic Tradition* (Detroit: Wayne State University Press, 1990).

Richmond, Farley P., Darius L. Swann, and P.B. Zarrilli, eds. *Indian Theatre: Traditions of Performance* (Honolulu: University of Hawaii Press, 1990).

Smith, John D. *The Epic of Pabuji: A Study, Transcription, and Translation* (Cambridge: Cambridge University Press, 1991).

Vatsyanan, Kapila. *Traditions of Indian Folk Dance* (New Delhi: Indian Book Company, 1976).

Wade, Bonnie C. *Imaging Sound: An Ethnomusicological Study of Music, Art, and Culture in Mughal India* (Chicago: University of Chicago Press, 1998).

Zarrilli, Phillip B. *Kathakali Dance-Drama: Where Gods and Demons Come to Play* (London: Routledge, 2000).

10

Social Customs and Lifestyles

A GLIMPSE of an Indian community—perhaps a village at dawn—finds the women are already grinding the flour for the day, and men and children trudging back from the fields, ready to wash up before drinking a hot sweet cup of tea. After milking, the cows assemble in the dusty space where the street widens, ready to head out for the day's grazing under the supervision of a few youths.

Men, women, children—and even the cows—represent the community, multiple ties between households, and connections between this particular community and others. This intimate, face-to-face setting frames the rules and roles of social life. Childhood socialization, family, shared work, neighborliness, and interdependence create strong bonds, the bedrock of social life.

This chapter looks at social life and customs. The focus is on important social institutions that provide frameworks for action—and also sometimes, today, serve as focal points for dissent. There has been much change in the past two decades. In recent years, social life and customs have become politicized with the rise of identity consciousness. Lifestyle is not simply a matter of choice, for it reflects how both individuals and communities position themselves in the changing nation-state.

COMMUNITY

Surani, a Rajasthan village, is a good model of an Indian community. Most everyone's life there is spent among kin, neighbors, and friends. Their most important relationships and core identity are here. Even when a man must migrate for work for long periods of time, he always considers this to be his home. It is where family lives and for almost all, this is the location of a family's most important basis of material support. Surani's soil has supernatural and natural qualities that affect everyone who is born and lives here—an unbreakable tie.

Long-standing, shared histories of interaction are recalled in folklore, the commemoration of important events, and informal social codes. Even the villagers' cows reflect social connections. Some cows have been given to a family as part of marriage settlements, others may be on loan from one family to another that needs milk. Yet other cows may have been given to the priestly family that maintains the temple, in fulfillment of a vow.

Other communities are urban neighborhoods and squatter settlements. Recent government housing schemes have supported construction of new housing, initiating community development. In the countryside, some villages are growing and beginning to look like small towns. This may strain older ties of community as new personnel, vocations, and concerns enter the mix of social life.

Origin myths provide clues to a community's self-identity. A god said, "Live here." Other stories are mundane. The king said a man could be a landlord if he developed the land and attracted settlers. The names of villages tell stories, too: "Ram's Well," "Salty Unpleasant Place," "Little Gold Hill." This can reflect local irony, if Gold Hill is really a swamp. Alternatively, "Big Sand Dune" could be a pretty good place that has been given this bad name to keep the Evil Eye from noticing.

Some incident, some fateful event sets in motion a settlement at a particular spot. This is usually framed in terms of a larger set of social relationships. The story of Surani village's founding is a good example.

Surani's important founding families, members of the Purohit Brahman subcaste, said that their ancestor, Somaji ("-ji" is an honorific), came here with his family, supporters, and livestock about 300 years ago. This was in return for a good deed that Somaji did for the Maharajah of Jodhpur. While it is unlikely to include all the details, a seventeenth-century document records Somaji Purohit as Surani's landlord. About half of Surani's family lines said they descended from an ancestor who accompanied Somaji on his trek from his old village. And finally, Surani—unlike adjacent villages that had noble Rajput landlords—was classified as a "religious gift" village in this document.

Just as the Maharajah gave Surani to Somaji Purohit, Somaji in turn invited his relatives and dependents to come along. In other words, one did not simply move as one liked. Local networks constrained physical movement. In later years, people moved to Surani for many reasons. The landlords invited them, or the landlords were powerful enough to protect them from problems in their old villages. Several men commented that ancestors fled here because of conflicts in their old villages. Sometimes a man married into a Surani family that lacked sons. Sometimes a man moved here because people liked him, and there was a spot that he could fill in the fabric of community life.

Two influxes of newcomers occurred in the twentieth century. The first was after the great famine of 1899–1901. At this time only "one out of ten" remained alive, people said. The second influx came during the land reforms after independence.

Members of this second group include the blacksmith family, which migrated here recently because of the promise of farmland and good, steady work. They belong to the traditionally nomadic Gaduliya Lohar group, whose boat-shaped ox carts are a distinctive presence on Rajasthan's byways. In the middle of the crop season Surani's Lohar men, who follow their group's tradition of working as blacksmiths, will be busy sharpening and fixing farm tools. Children born to this family will now share Surani's supernatural substance and revere its earth spirits.

In the old days the Purohit Brahmans owned most of the land. Having Brahmans on top meant that a Brahman-oriented ideology affected aspects of local life. Meat should only be cooked outside the village settlement proper, not inside, because the Brahmans were vegetarian. Nearby villages whose landlords were Rajputs did not face such a ban: Rajputs traditionally eat meat. Men could not ride their camels through the village, because then they could see over the high mud walls that surrounded homes—and violate women's privacy. A community defines its practices through consensus. There is a shared sense of what is right and due its members, and what is wrong. Every village is just a little bit different—in its view—from all others. In fact, these definitions reflect a community's sense of itself compared to others.

"BIG" AND "LITTLE" PEOPLE

The second important aspect of the social life is the community's subdivision into those who are more powerful and those who are less powerful. This has an enormous impact on interaction and on social customs, for these are defined by those who are "big" and those who are "little" or, to use an Indian idiom, those who are "cooked" and those who are "raw."

Land reform was supposed to reduce this inequality, but its impact has been uneven. Former landlords managed to hold onto their position, or others have used their skills, entrepreneurship, and good luck to rise to the position of most important and powerful member of the community. At an individual level, these families act as patrons to other members of the community. They employ others, lease them land, and are often called on for help. Patrons are the "big" people in the community. Their voices are the first to be heard, and they are usually the ones to have the final say.

At the group level, because of the small scale of community life and patterns of kinship, patron families within a village often belong to one or two subcastes. The biggest one, with the largest number of members and most important families, is what anthropologists call the community's "dominant caste." A dominant caste need not be at the top of the ritual hierarchy: it needs—most importantly—to be richer than everyone else, to conform to community standards of patronage, and—if of low-caste status—to adjust its standards to those of the higher castes in the community.[1]

The desirable patron relationship is paternalistic, modeled on the ideal parent-child relationship. The patron is stern but just, generous to subordinates, and protective. The ideal client is loyal. The underside of patrons is that they exploit and abuse clients. In some parts of India, patrons reportedly set up their own goon squads that enforce compliance. Clients have an underside, too. They lie, cheat, and run off at the worst possible time.

Prior to independence, the patrons' and dominant castes' positions in the community often were supported by a special type of economic institution, the *jajmani* system. This drew its ideology from the caste system. Each subcaste specialized in a particular kind of work. The translations of subcaste names meant occupational groups: "sweeper," "leather worker," "water carrier," "farmer," "warrior," "priest," and so on. In the caste ideology, work was hereditary. Ritual purity considerations excluded the wrong people from doing certain work, and fear of loss of ritual purity kept others from moving into certain occupations. In practice, of course, most work—open to all—focused on the hard physical labor of agriculture.

Put together, all the different subcastes in a community performed all the needed tasks to sustain it. In south India, for instance, it was very common that landlords were Brahmans, the tenants were members of middle-ranking subcastes, and the landless laborers were Dalits.[2] Brahmans (or other landlord groups) managed the land; farming castes farmed it, with the help of laborers; service castes produced necessary tools and household furnishings; Dalits did farm labor and ritually polluting work. This setup favored dominant subcastes' ability to sustain their position in several important ways. Of course, only a big village might have all needed groups. A small place—such as Surani—had to turn to its neighbors.

Instead of working for cash and bargaining for wages, as in a market economic system, tradition governed the amount given. Lower-ranking subcastes received smaller amounts for their work than higher-ranking subcastes. Everyone in a community performed his or her work throughout the year. Then, at the harvest, each family received its share of the grain heap. Ideally, everyone's share was enough for his or her family. In practice, these payments could be reduced on various pretexts and people at the bottom of the status hierarchy were worst off.

This system worked to keep everyone in his or her place. Unhappy clients had few alternatives. Just about the only one would be to leave one's community and seek a new patron. This worked only if other patrons needed workers and supporters.

A complication is that debt tied clients to patrons. In fact, in Gujarat, a system of bonded labor (debt servitude) prevented individuals from switching employers or resigning from their jobs. After independence, the courts ruled that bonded labor systems were illegal, a form of slavery.[3]

This situation has changed in many respects since independence. The *jajmani* system crumbled after land reform. Wages have replaced most traditional payments. Contractual relationships replaced hereditary ones. Changes in the economy promoted new patrons. For example, government aid to rural areas in the 1950s and 1960s established new patronage networks of those connected with program management. In some areas, this was captured by local elites. New groups such as NGOs also found themselves in the position of patrons, even when they attempted to promote democratic and egalitarian institutions.[4]

Today's customary services tend to focus on fulfilling ritual needs, such as duties in conjunction with festivals. Work relationships, even when based on wages, may be overlaid with ideas of reciprocity and morality. Concepts of ritual pollution also continue to be associated with certain activities, generally those considered the most highly polluting or demeaning.

SUBCASTES

In everyday life, the behavioral units of caste and kinship look somewhat different than in the idealized model of the four *varnas*. Three important characteristics emerge when viewing the caste system from a local perspective. First, as noted previously, non-Hindu groups get absorbed into the local hierarchy. Non-Hindus are often organized into very similar types of kin groups, which also tend to marry only within themselves. Second, local customs define the range of appropriate behavior for top-, middle-, and bottom-ranking groups. Third, these local customs and ideas provide a context within which people try out new ideas, dispute with one another, and make changes.

The most important unit of hierarchy in everyday life is the subcaste or endogamous (in-marrying) kin group, which may be Hindu or may belong to other religious groups. Membership in a subcaste defines an individual's perceived basic nature, how she or he is supposed to interact socially with others, and the subset of potential marriage partners.[5] Each subcaste regards itself as having a separate history, mythological origin, and relationship to all others. There is a consensus about the subcaste's special customs such as food habits, women's traditional dress, occupation, and deities. Most important, the set of families whose children are potential marriage partners defines the group membership.

In meeting a new person for the first time, villagers will ask—if not evident from a person's name and the place she or he is from—"What is your subcaste?" In this way, new acquaintances establish the basic parameters of social etiquette. Even if they personally disagree with the norms of caste, at home they may conform in order to maintain social harmony.

A change in occupation, social habits, and lifestyle sometimes has been associated with the splitting of an old subcaste into two new ones. Over time, members of the two groups go separate ways. Amalgamation is another possibility where there are convergence and a strong sense of shared commonality in terms of status markers and historical tradition.

All the members of a subcaste are unlikely to be in the same place at the same time. Meetings to discuss matters of concern usually occur at weddings or death feasts, when a large number of members are most likely to be present. A number of subcastes, more urban-oriented, have established formal organizations, newsletters, and even websites to keep everyone up on the news.

Subcastes monitor members' behavior. A man who marries a woman from outside the subcaste will probably have to perform ritual, pay a fine, and throw a feast for the group to erase the ritual pollution. In this way, group members accept the marriage as legitimate. The most important thing is that couples' children now will be considered acceptable marriage partners for other members' children. A subcaste also may announce a decision to change some aspect of their behavior, though their ability to enforce the change may be limited. Members of other subcastes may disagree. For example, who will do the polluting work of removing dead animals if the subcaste that does this work stops doing it?

One basic status divide is between vegetarian and nonvegetarian. Another is between subcastes that prohibit widows from remarrying and those that permit it. The type of work that a subcaste does also matters. The subcaste rises or falls in the ranking system—not the individual—and there can be quite a bit of jockeying for position.

Food consumption is a visible status marker. Upwardly mobile groups often adopt the food customs of higher-ranking groups. The shift with the biggest ramifications is from meat eating to vegetarian. Often this begins when the women decide to become vegetarian. They tell the men that if they want meat, they must cook it for themselves on a separate hearth outside the house. In other cases, the members of a subcaste collectively decide to become vegetarians.

Vegetarianism clearly signals that a lower-ranking group has status aspirations. It is also a safe bet. Higher-ranking vegetarian groups will not force nonvegetarians to slaughter and eat animals. However, in the nineteenth century, tribal Bhils in Rajasthan who joined a temperance (antialcohol) movement were rounded up and forced to drink liquor! A group that decides to become vegetarian may have to change its deity if the goddess or god traditionally worshipped receives blood sacrifices. Members may have to "discover" a new deity, deemphasize the old one, shift to its vegetarian incarnation, or find some way to mediate the contradiction between the deity's tastes and those of its followers.

Ideas of hierarchy are part of social etiquette. In Surani, if a member of a higher-ranking subcaste visited a member of a significantly lower-ranking subcaste, it was possible that the host might not offer the arriving guest water. Hosts always want to offer a drink of water to a guest, who may have traveled far over hot, dusty dunes. What would cause an eager host not to show this important symbol of hospitality? The higher-ranking person may be sensitive about caste etiquette or fear ritual pollution. It is up to the higher-ranking person to indicate a preference.

In some situations, a guest might consider such an offer "uppity" or even confrontational, an assertion that the host was of equal or of higher subcaste status. In some parts of India, members of higher castes have threatened, beaten up, or even murdered lower-caste people for getting "above their place." The power to enforce distinctions in behavior is greatest in small, isolated areas and places where people are dependent upon only one patron. In small villages, one's preferences are probably already known to the host and people also probably have a consensus on which broken rules to ignore and which to note.

KINSHIP

Subcastes subdivide into two different kinds of family units: households and *gotras*, a group whose members regard themselves as closely related—too close for marriage. Households are easy to identify in everyday life. A household consists of those individuals related by birth, adoption, or marriage who contribute to a common budget and eat from the same hearth. In most of India, the ideal household is based on descent through the male line.

Paternal grandparents, their adult sons and wives, and their grandchildren should live together under one roof and eat from the same hearth. The most senior man heads the family. He speaks for it in village affairs and directs the work of the family's men. His wife is the most senior woman. She manages the food budget and the women's work.

Gotras are less easy to observe. In many villages, most of the men of a subcaste in a community may all descend—or believe that they descend—through the male line from a distant male ancestor. *Soma* Purohits of Surani, for example, trace their ancestry to Somaji Purohit. Most of the households who live in the Purohit section of Surani are headed by men who are one another's brothers and cousins, linked through the male line.

In north India, Hindus follow the four-*gotra* rule, meaning that marriages are not permitted between members of the father's, father's mother's, mother's father's, and mother's mother's *gotras*. This helps to ensure that a household (and community) has ties to many different other communities. Over 300 different villages were represented in the matrimonial ties of Kishan Garhi, a small north Indian village near Delhi.[6] Furthermore, potential spouses—even if otherwise eligible—had to come from outside Kishan Garhi.

In other parts of India, the rules may emphasize different ties. In Rajasthan and parts of western Uttar Pradesh, two siblings from one family will marry two siblings from another—two sisters, say, marry two brothers. People here say that this improves cooperation within the family because two sisters are more likely to get along with one another than women who are strangers! Also, women feel more secure in this situation. In the desert, men often must migrate with the livestock or move for work. Women who are close kin, sisters, or "cousin-sisters," from the same village, will be more likely to cooperate in guarding the village's property than women who are strangers.

Very different rules are followed in south India. Here, the four-*gotra* rule is not followed. Instead, many subcastes assert a cultural preference for cousin marriage: a man marries his mother's brother's daughter in some groups, his father's sister's daughter, in others. This family connection can be sustained over time. Marriages within a village also help to sustain clusters of inter-married families.[7]

The highest-status form of marriage involves the ideology that the family that receives the bride is superior to the family that gives the bride. In this sense, women marry "up." Traditional forms of social etiquette influence how the two families interact. An alternative—and low-status—form of marriage emphasizes the equality between the two families. This occurs in marriage by exchange. In this, a brother-sister pair from one family marries a sister-brother pair from another. In both the high-status and the low-status forms of marriage, the "sisters" and "brothers" may not be actual siblings, but cousins who are treated as such.

Groups that trace descent through women are also found in India. The Nayars, a wealthy Kerala group, sustained large households focused on sisters. Brothers, who traditionally were absent, had their closest ties with their sisters' homes. Children were born to these households through an institution of visiting husbands, some of whom were quite temporary and others of whom had long-term relationships with a woman in the household. Many of India's tribes also had inheritance through the female line. Most of these groups face strong pressure, through legal reforms and social pressure, to shift to inheritance through males.

Individual households have their own flavor. Household deities may have placed a prohibition on members' wearing certain types of clothing and jewelry or eating certain types of food. Households have reputations: one is "modern," and another is "conservative."

The dynamics of the domestic cycle as families add members over time create differences between older and younger members. The current generation has seen a split between the educational attainments of older and younger brothers. Older brothers were more likely to be pressed into full-time farm work by their teen years. Families with several adult men may have plentiful labor and income, making it possible for the youngest brother to seek a college degree. He is likely to have little interest in doing farm labor—and he may be infected with urban ideas about love marriages and personal freedom.

Still, having a family member who lives in the city is useful. This is a base others can use to find a better-paying job than is available in the village and to send children to school. The urban relative leaves the village and goes back to the city with a big bag of wheat or rice, village food specialties—and sometimes even a milk cow or goat!

Just as a family appears to be strongest, it is the most vulnerable to division. Member priorities diverge. A son with a grievance triggers the accounting of the family's assets and its partition. This is not an easy time. Every villager is familiar with a lawsuit that eats up a family farm.

Sometimes only one son takes his share and departs, while everyone else stays together. Sometimes all the brothers form separate households. Some groups prefer that the grandparents keep one share and live with the youngest son. In others, grandparents rotate among their sons' households.

New brides join the family, and daughters marry and depart to their husbands' households. Marriage decisions are where the *gotra* comes into play, for different *gotras* that form marriage ties among themselves constitute the effective unit of the subcaste, its "marriage circle."[8] These are the families among which almost all potential marriage partners will be found. In the case of a very small subcaste, the marriage circle may be the same as the subcaste; in the case of a larger subcaste, this will be a set of families that overlaps with other marriage circles of the subcaste.

Women shuttle back and forth between their parents' and husbands' villages, particularly in the first few years of marriage. Labor and resources are shared between households and villages through norms of helping out. A family employs a needy but worthy boy who is well known to the in-laws' family, shares or leases land to one another in hard times, and sends a troubled member to visit for a "cooling off" period. Informal networks of friendship also connect to these kin-based networks through idioms of ritual kinship, which can link members of separate subcastes, too. Networks of friendship and kinship through women link communities to one another. They provide paths for the flow of many things between communities, not simply material assets and personnel, but also ideas and customs.

NOTES

1. M.N. Srinivas, "The Dominant Caste in Rampura," *American Anthropologist* 61: 1–16, 1959.

2. E. Kathleen Gough, "Caste in a Tanjore Village," pp. 11–60 in E.R. Leach, ed., *Aspects of Caste in South India, Ceylon and North-West Pakistan* (Cambridge: Cambridge University Press, 1971).

3. Jan Breman, *Patronage and Exploitation: Changing Agrarian Relations in South Gujarat, India* (Berkeley: University of California Press, 1974).

4. Maxine K. Weisgrau, *Interpreting Development: Local Histories, Local Strategies* (Lanham, MD: University Press of America, 1997), pp. 70–79.

5. Pauline Kolenda, *Caste in Contemporary India: Beyond Organic Solidarity* (Prospect Heights, IL: Waveland Press, 1978).

6. McKim Marriott, "Little Communities in an Indigenous Civilization," pp. 171–222 in M. Marriott, ed., *Village India: Studies in the Little Community* (Chicago: University of Chicago Press, 1955), p. 175.

7. Alan R. Beals, *Village Life in South India: Cultural Design and Environmental Variation* (Chicago: Aldine Publishing Company, 1974), pp. 114–116.

8. Morton Klass, "Community Structure in West Bengal," *American Anthropologist* 74 (3): 601–610, 1972.

SUGGESTED READINGS

Agarwal, Arun. *Greener Pastures: Politics, Markets, and Community among a Migrant Pastoral People* (Durham: Duke University Press, 1999).

Beals, Alan R. *Village Life in South India: Cultural Design and Environmental Variation* (Chicago: Aldine Publishing Company, 1974).

Berreman, Gerald D. *Hindus of the Himalayas: Ethnography and Change,* 2nd ed. (Delhi: Oxford University Press, 1963).

Beteille, Andre. *Caste, Class and Power: Changing Patterns of Social Stratification in a Tanjore Village* (Berkeley: University of California, 1965).

Klass, Morton. *From Field to Factory: Community Structure and Industrialization in West Bengal* (Lanham, MD: University Press of America, 1996).

Srinivas, M.N. *The Remembered Village* (Berkeley: University of California Press, 1976).

Wadley, Susan S. *Struggling with Destiny in Karimpur, 1925–1984* (Berkeley: University of California Press, 1994).

Glossary

ahimsa [ahiṃsā]	अहिंसा	principle of nonviolence
ayurveda [āyurvaida]	आयुर्वेद	traditional Hindu medical system
bhajan [bhajan]	भजन	devotional song, hymn
bhakti [bhakti]	भक्ति	devotional
brahman [brāhmaṇ]	ब्राह्मण	one of the four varnas
braj bhasha [braj bhāshā]	ब्रज भाषा	form of Hindi used in the Braj region associated with Hindu god Krishna
bindi [biṃdī]	बिंदी	dot, point
burqa [burkā]	बुरका	long, loose overcoat with hood
chaitya [caitya]	चैत्य	Buddhist shrine
chamar [camār]	चमार	cobbler, leatherworker
chipko [cipko]	चिपको	environmentalist movement, from Hindi chipana, "to hug," lit. tree-huggers' movement, from key tactic
dalit [dalit]	दलित	downtrodden, a term adopted by members of this group

darshan [darshan]	दर्शन	mutual sight of deity and worshipper
devadasi [devadāsī]	देवदासी	temple dancer
devi [devī]	देवी	goddess
dharma [dharma]	धर्म	duty
gotra [gotra]	गोत्र	local kin group whose members trace descent through the male line to an ancestral figure
kaccha [kaccā]	कच्चा	raw, uncooked, impermanent
kalamkari [kalamkārī]	कलमकारी	pen work
kamaycha [kāmāicā]	कामायचा	stringed instrument
khadi [khādī]	खादी	handspun and woven fabric
kirtan [kīrtan]	कीर्तन	religious song; hymn
kriti [kritī]	कृती	South Indian classical music genre
kshatriya [kshatriya]	क्षत्रिय	one of the four varnas in the Hindu caste system
kurta [kurtā]	कुरता	longsleeved, collarless man's shirt
linga [limga]	लिंग	stone that symbolizes Hindu god Shiva
lota [lotā]	लोटा	small brass pot used for drinking and carrying water
mahatma [mahātmā]	महात्मा	great soul
mandala [mamdala]	मंडल	magical circle or set of concentric circles
masala chai [masālā cāī]	मसाला चाई	spiced tea
mela [melā]	मेला	fair, meeting

mubarak [mubārak]	मुबारक	blessings
pakka [pakkā]	पक्का	cooked, ripe, permanent, complete
pan [pān]	पान	a digestive of tobacco, sugar, and betel nut folded inside a leaf
puja [pujā]	पुजा	worship
qawwali [kawwālī]	.कव्वाली	religious song, hymn
raga [rāga]	राग	the basic framework of a musical composition, its musical setting and mood
rajput [rājpūt]	राजपूत	caste group whose members were often rulers
rasa [rasā]	रसा	sentiment, mood
sadhu [sādhu]	साधू	Hindu holy man, hermit
salwar [salwār]	सलवार	long pants which are tight below the knees
sangeet [saṃgīt]	संगीत	music and dance
sarangi [saraṃgī]	सरंगी	stringed musical instrument
sarod [sarod]	सरोद	stringed musical instrument
satimata [satī mātā]	सतीमाता	deity who in life was a virtuous wife
satyagraha [satyāgraha]	सत्याग्रह	nonviolent resistance
shakti [shaktī]	शक्ती	feminine supernatural power
shenai [shahnāī]	शहनाई	Indian wind instrument similar to a clarinet
shudra [shūdrā]	शूदरा	one of the four varnas in the Hindu caste system
soma [somā]	सोमा	in ancient texts, an intoxicating substance

stupa [stūpa]	स्तूप	Buddhist shrine that contains the relics of a holy person
swadeshi [swādeshī]	स्वादेशी	native; indigenous
tabla [tablā]	तबला	a pair of small drums that are played together
tantra [taṃtra]	तंत्र	mystical practices
tazia [tāziyā]	ताज़िया	replica of tomb carried by Muslim processions at Muharram
tirthankar [tĩrthaṃkar]	तीर्थंकर	one of the 24 Jain founders who gained salvation and taught others
vaishya [vaishya]	वैश्य	one of the four varnas in the caste system
varna [varṇa]	वर्ण	a basic subdivision of humanity in the caste system
vina [vĩṇā]	वीणा	stringed nstrument with two sounding bowls, one at each end
yatra [yātrā]	यात्रा	pilgrimage, journey

Selected Proper and Place Names

Baisakh	[baisākh]	बैसाख
Dassehra	[dashāharā]	दशाहरा
Diwali	[divālī]	दिवाली
Gavri	[gaurī]	गैरी
Holi	[holī]	होली
Khalsa	[khālsā]	खालसा
Kumbh Mela	[kumbh melā]	कुंभ मेला
Muharram	[muharram]	मुहर्रम
Navaratra	[navarātra]	नवरात्र
Ram	[rām]	राम
Ramzan	[rāmzān]	राम्ज़ान
Ras Lila	[ras līlā]	रस लीला
Vikram Samvat	[vikram samvat]	विक्रम संवत

Index

About the Author

CAROL E. HENDERSON is Research Associate and Visiting Part-Time Lecturer in the Department of Sociology and Anthropology at Rutgers University, Newark, New Jersey.